THE WEL

Essays on Neoliberalism
and Devolution

THE WELSH WAY:
Essays on Neoliberalism and Devolution

Edited by Daniel Evans, Kieron Smith & Huw Williams

With a foreword by Michael Sheen

Parthian, Cardigan SA43 1ED
www.parthianbooks.com
ISBN: 9781914595028
© The Contributors 2021
Cover Design: The Focus Group
Typeset by Elaine Sharples
Printed by 4edge Limited
Published with the financial support of the Welsh Books Council
A cataloguing record for this book is available from the British Library.

To the memory of Ceri Evans, Ed Rooksby,
Neil Davidson, Mel Corry & Dawn Foster.
Socialists of great integrity.

Contents

Foreword

by Michael Sheen

'Someone once said that it is easier to imagine the end of the world than to imagine the end of capitalism. We can now revise that and witness the attempt to imagine capitalism by way of imagining the end of the world.'

Fredric Jameson

In his 2009 book, *Capitalist Realism: Is There No Alternative*, Mark Fisher wrote about the 'pervasive atmosphere' of neoliberal ideology and its effects on every aspect of our lives. His concept of 'capitalist realism' describes 'the widespread sense that not only is capitalism the only viable political and economic system, but also that it is now impossible even to imagine a coherent alternative to it.'

The shapeshifting, parasitic nature of what is commonly referred to as neoliberalism is well described in this book's introduction. Its ideology and implementation can be heavy-handed to the point of naked brutality, if deemed necessary, but also hidden and insidious much of the time, too.

Resisting its open shows of strength – whether as an individual, a movement or a society – is something that many have attempted, are indeed currently in the throes of attempting, and have paid, and are paying, a high price for it.

Financially, physically, spiritually.

Revealing its more hidden aspect, while less obviously confrontational can, nevertheless, take great courage and soul-sapping resilience. As Baudelaire said, 'The greatest trick the Devil ever pulled was convincing the world he didn't exist.'

While the ideology, and those who are its agents, may prefer to go unnamed as such these days, the manifestations of its cold logic are all too apparent – huge and ever-increasing inequality, cold and indifferent exploitation, the sacrifice of entire communities, the removal of decent human values from the heart of our discourse and policy, the needless waste of human potential and lives.

In *Why Wales Never Was*, Simon Brooks said, 'The pace and nature of industrial development did indeed play a role in the Welsh failure, but so too did discourse, and the parameters of discourse limit the possibilities of what can and cannot be said.'

This book is filled with essays that are attempting to expand the parameters of discourse around what can and cannot be said about the current state of Wales and its direction of travel.

Forums for this kind of discourse are few and far between and that, of course, is part of the problem. How certain underlying realities are able to remain unseen and nameless. Thank God for those that do exist and let us continue to do all we can to protect and support them and endeavour to create more.

Another reason for the obfuscation involves certain narratives about who we are, how we do things, how our long-held values and beliefs, cherished for generations, have shaped us and kept us different and special, and hc difficult they are to even question, let alone let go of.

But question them we must.

As Raymond Williams taught us – it is vital that we 'pu questions to those simple, confident, unitary identities which really belong to an earlier historical period.' We can no longer afford to make a 'proud and dignified with-drawal to Fortress Wales: the old times, the old culture;', as he put it.

Writing in 1975, in his piece on 'Welsh Culture', Williams said, 'Real independence is a time of new and active creation: people sure enough of themselves to discard their baggage; knowing the past as past, as a shaping history, but with a new confident sense of the present and the future, where the decisive meanings and values will be made.'

This book, I think, represents an expression of that con-fidence that Williams is talking about, an attempt to discard that baggage, to build a bridge towards that place where our decisive meanings and values can be made.

Here be monsters, and before they can be defeated they must first be named. They can no longer move freely in the shadows or walk our streets in disguise. They must be seen for what they truly are and for what they are doing to our country.

Only then can we begin to imagine a coherent alterna-tive to it, and take our first meaningful steps toward making it a reality.

Michael Sheen, 1 August 2021.

Introduction: The Welsh Way

Dan Evans, Kieron Smith, Huw Williams

Wales, a nation with a proud history of working-class politics, popular protest and dissent, has long been imagined both east and west of Offa's Dyke as a kind of sanctuary, its political identity safely inoculated from the worst excesses of whatever successive Westminster governments could throw at it. Wales is the land of the Rebecca Riots, the first flying of the red flag, the birthplace of the NHS. While British politics lurched irreversibly to the right under Thatcher, and buckled under the demands of neoliberalism under Blair, the Welsh continued – and continue – to vote, indefatigably, Labour.

During the referendum campaign in 1997, devolution was sold by its proponents as a means of setting in stone Wales' distinctive sense of political identity. Without needing to commit to outright independence, devolution was pitched as a way of protecting Welsh communities from the seemingly endless succession of callous Tory governments, while simultaneously benefiting from the fruits of its relationship with the British state. The best of both worlds.

Every devolved government that has sat in the Senedd since 1999 has been led by the Labour Party. And in May 2021, with Tory polling skyrocketing across the UK in the wake of Brexit and the Covid-19 pandemic, the party under Mark Drakeford once again returned a comfortable victory, securing for itself another five years of power, amongst assertions from the British commentariat of Welsh Labour's bona fide socialism. It is worth reminding ourselves that this win equates to continuing influence over almost all aspects of social and political life in Wales: education, health and social services, economic development, the environment, culture, the Welsh language, and more.

Labour's persistent success can partly be attributed to the way it has woven the idea of Wales' political distinctiveness into its own mythology of Welshness. This was perhaps most famously expressed in a 2002 speech given by the then First Minister, Rhodri Morgan. There, Morgan championed Wales' socialist tradition, claiming that the Labour Government in the new Welsh Assembly would put 'clear red water' between the Labour Party in Wales and the right-wing Blair government in Westminster. In this resonant phrase, Wales is figured almost as an island, with the 'redness' of the Labour party diffused almost elementally within Welshness itself, dissolved within the very substance of the water separating it, clearly and righteously, from the murky territory of Tory England. The way we do things on this side of the 'water', Morgan proudly asserted, was the 'Welsh Way'.

This idea of Labour's unique, practically God-given status within the Welsh political mindset persists powerfully today. Take an address made by the current First Minister, Mark Drakeford, to the IPPR's (Institute for Public Policy Research) 'economic justice' event, held in Cardiff in July 2019. It is worth quoting Drakeford at length:

Austerity and Brexit simply but sharply intensify the failings of the 40-year-long neoliberal project here in the United Kingdom, a neoliberal project which has had the deliberate and intentional pursuit of inequality at its heart. Not, as its proponents will often tell you, some unfortunate or regrettable by-product of the necessary actions they have taken: the neoliberal agenda requires inequality. It requires it to be, in their lexicon, the spur to economic activity amongst the majority of the UK citizenry. Now, at the heart of the Welsh Government lies exactly the opposite ambition. Our ambition is to create a more equal Wales. And that ambition is not simply the Welsh Government's ambition, but crucially it is the ambition of the National Assembly for Wales, because a more equal Wales is the unifying goal of that most radical piece of legislation, the Well-being of Future Generations Act.[1]

Wales, for Drakeford, despite its unquestioned place within the British union, stands apart from the neoliberal consensus that has come to define UK politics over the last forty years. It stands as a social democratic sanctum – indeed one in which a 'radical' commitment to equality is hegemonic and accepted by all parties – exemplified by the Future Generations Act and Wales' historic recognition of the climate crisis.

All this was inspired by Wales' socialist past. Later in the speech, Drakeford goes on to say that 'here in Wales we continue to draw on our great history of collective action to solve common problems'. Labour's present 'radicalism' was part of a recapturing of that sense of civic, municipal socialism that was alive, well and practiced widely in Wales' communities particularly within the lifetimes of people who are still with us today [i.e., between 1945 to now] ... it is socialism that teaches us to have optimism that the arc of history does in the end bend to justice, but the courage to know that it does not do so without a struggle, that nothing has ever been won for progressive causes or working people without the determination to take the action that wins those rewards ... and that struggle, to return to the Future Generations Act, is not just a struggle simply for today but is a struggle to create the conditions that lead to better tomorrows....

Rousing stuff. The speech had it all: radicalism, a sense of a Wales that is distinct (and always defined against England as a yardstick) in its pursuit of equality, motivated by hagiographic notions of Wales' radical, socialist past, but also influential and central to the UK labour movement (at that time led by the socialist Jeremy Corbyn).

Drakeford's speech received warm applause. This was unsurprising. This narrative of Welsh social democratic distinctiveness, of progressiveness, communal struggle and success, is an article of faith which has been widely accepted by the Welsh political class (consisting not just of politicians, but academics, journalists and commentators), as well as the labour movement across the UK as a whole – and which was apparently affirmed once more by the 2021 Senedd election, which contrasted starkly with the travails of Labour in the English council elections.

Drakeford's speech reiterated and updated a taken-for-granted set of beliefs about the successes of devolution and Wales' divergence from its right-wing, Tory-voting neighbour.

The problem, of course, is that none of this is, or indeed ever has been, remotely true. Despite Welsh Labour's relentless self-mythologising over the past twenty years, Wales is, in practice, a deeply neoliberal country. Devolution has so far achieved little except to shore up Labour's dominance in this struggling, disenfranchised, poverty-ridden enclave of the British Isles. It has, moreover, provided us with a most telling case study of the irresistible potency of neoliberalism: a country apparently unique in its 100-year electoral dominance by a social democratic party has succumbed almost completely to its virulence.

The Welsh Way

For all Drakeford's talk of the successes of devolution, inequality in Wales since 1997 has climbed steadily to unforgivable levels. The existing wounds of poverty and disengagement, far from being healed, have worsened. Child poverty has reached epidemic levels: the worst in the UK, with more than one in three children now living in poverty.[2] Educational attainment remains stubbornly low, particularly in deprived communities: less than one third of pupils eligible for free school meals attain 5 A–C grades at GCSE.[3] The recruitment of new teachers remains well below target.[4] At roughly the time of Drakeford's speech, homelessness in Wales was the highest since records began, with over 30,000 households applying for homelessness assistance in the year to March 2020.[5] The city of Cardiff, where the speech was held, is the epicentre of the homelessness crisis, with rough-sleeper numbers skyrocketing: people are sleeping and dying in doorways of empty student blocks and luxury flats. Prison population rates are among the highest in Europe, and expected to rise considerably in the coming years.[6] Unemployment remains stubbornly high.[7] House prices are rising, with the private rented sector lining the pockets of an ever-increasing number of private landlords.[8] All this is not to mention the devastatingly disproportionate impact of the coronavirus pandemic on poorer communities in Wales.[9]

This is a society devastated by the worst ravages of capitalism. And yet not a single delegate at Drakeford's IPPR speech felt it appropriate to raise any of these issues as a counterpoint to Welsh Labour's narrative of kindness and success. A basic question for any journalist or delegate might have been to ask why he thought issues like child poverty were rising; by any objective measure Labour's 'radical' strategy wasn't working – things were getting worse – why did he think this was the case? If the UK is an innately neoliberal project as Drakeford claims, why are he and his party so committed to it, and so hostile to the idea of seceding from it? If the Welsh Government is radical, why had there been such a concerted effort to distance itself from the Corbyn project? If the devolution of welfare could help, why had Drakeford resisted calls for this to be devolved, despite pressure from anti-poverty campaigners and groups like the Bevan Foundation?

It is not polemical or partisan to ask these questions, but a basic democratic necessity. If a politician makes a claim, this should be checked against how it measures up to reality. In any country with a functioning democracy and a meaningful public sphere, this speech would have been low-hanging fruit for journalists and commentators. Even in Tory England, one would expect a modicum of dissent or pushback. The Welsh Way, however, is to avoid confrontation – to not ask questions or challenge, in a nepotistic culture enabled by an anaemic public sphere. In Wales, it does not pay to point out that the emperor is not wearing any clothes.

Murky Brown Water

In contrast to the dominant image of Wales as a progressive, socialist country safely distanced from Tory policy by Welsh Labour's 'clear red water', this book offers a dose of the truth. We argue that Wales is, in many respects, a troublingly reactionary country. This book demonstrates that the notion of 'clear red water' amounted to, and is nothing more than, a rhetorical device designed to obscure reality and secure the ascendancy of the Labour Party in Wales. As one commentator described it in 2003, the reality, even back then, was much closer to 'murky brown water'.[10]

Unlike most other books on Welsh policy, this one is not dominated by tenured Welsh academics gushing over the successes of devolved government. It is written in the main by those on the margins of academia and the mainstream commentariat: PhD students, early career academics, ex-academics, and activists. Importantly, it is written from an engaged epistemological standpoint: by those actually conducting empirical research, working, living, or engaging in activism in the fields they write about. This has enabled our contributors to challenge the lazy claims made in Welsh Government policy documents, regurgitated by the media and the political class, and to see things as they really are, from the ground up. The combined experience of precarity, outsiderdom, and a lack of careerism and partisanship means that our contributors are not hamstrung by the myopic groupthink brought about by absorption into the backslapping culture that characterises much of Welsh academia and the political sphere. This book, and the story it tells, comes from a new generation of scholars and activists writing from outside the consensus, rather than from safely inside it.

Our leftist analysis of devolution's self-proclaimed 'achievements' points to the acceptance and promotion of the marketisation of higher education (Healy); the introduction of school league tables and punitive testing and inspection regimes (Evans); the repeated rejection of calls for a national care service and acceptance of for-profit care homes (Burdett); the deliberate exclusion of working-class parents from the 'most generous childcare package' (Ashton); the unequal, intersectional pressures on minority, protected characteristics groups (Jones, Jones); the enthusiastic pursuit of the nuclear/military industrial complex (Idris); the embrace of the prison-industrial complex (Manning); the promotion of marketised housing policies and the integration of landlords and other vested property interests into the fabric of government (Evans); the marketisation of parts of the NHS (for example tendering out renal services in North Wales) and the closure of community hospitals; the increasing authoritarianism of Welsh police forces (Harrison); the wholesale acceptance of Tory immigration policy (Clarke); the acceptance of austerity budgets, and more.

This book argues that radical rhetoric at the macro level – set out in strategy documents, speeches, and social media, and recirculated by an attenuated news media – is useless when it is not accompanied by the political will to take the necessary steps to actually *implement* policy to achieve real socialist goals. As this book firmly demonstrates, Welsh Labour have lacked the political will or the competence to turn their rhetoric into reality. This hollowness is reflected in its antipathy towards Welsh independence and the 50% of their voters who support it but is perhaps epitomized best by the Future Generations Act: a piece of potentially useful legislation handed to a powerless Labour insider and rendered completely useless (Williams). While politicians clink glasses at the success of 'radical' policies such as plastic bag charges (which have in fact enabled supermarkets to make vast profits from plastic bags), proposed changes to residential speed limits, and penalties for parking on pavements, children go hungry and people live on the streets.

The logic of neoliberalism and its pernicious practices of targets, datafication and economism have poisoned and diluted policy ideals the world over. At best, Welsh Labour has remained the passive observer of this tendency; at worst, it has actively implemented straightforwardly neoliberal economic policies and Blairite social strategies, with devastating results. We argue that the 'Welsh Way' is not political distinctiveness built on a proud socialist past, but a toxic mix of incompetence, bland passivity and corporate complicity.

Neoliberalism

Neoliberalism is the dominant model of contemporary capitalism. Among its most definable features are the mass privatisation of public services and land; increasing financialisation and a move away from productive capitalism; and the restructuring, deregulation and 'internationalization' of the national state apparatus to serve global capital rather than local economies.

The foundations of neoliberalism are rooted in an extreme interpretation of philosophical liberalism. Classical liberalism held that human freedom is best achieved and expressed politically through laissez-faire, liberal economics, which promotes democratic representation and an unfettered capitalist market. However, from the late 1970s onwards, inspired by economists at the Chicago School of Economics (in particular Friedrich Hayek, Milton Friedman and George Stigler), western economies began to take this idea to the extreme. The Chicago School had called for a world order in which all human relations and activities take place within an unregulated free market, totally unrestricted by any factors that may interfere with it, such as democratic states, public institutions or labour movements. Yet, in reality, despite its libertarian mantra of individual (i.e., economic) freedom, neoliberalism was bolstered by states around the world by a concerted strengthening of repressive state apparatuses: policing, the criminal justice system, prisons, and defence.[11] Hence Gamble's characterisation of neoliberalism as the combination of the 'free economy and the strong state'.[12]

Aided by US imperialism and international institutions such as the IMF – though often delivered on the back of crises like war[13] – from the 1970s onwards, neoliberalism has moved from a niche passion of right-wing intellectuals to a hegemonic global system. It has profoundly transformed the 'common sense' of society, becoming in other words so dominant and all-encompassing that it has become taken for granted and pre-reflexive not just as a way of ordering the economy, but as part of the very fabric of culture, society, and lived experience.[14]

To facilitate its economic policy elements – which must be implemented by actors within governments and their attendant state apparatuses – neoliberalism has driven, and is reciprocally driven by, its own 'logic' or way of working, sometimes termed 'new public management' or 'proceduralism'.[15] This is characterised by an increase in the use of figures and targets, and an impetus to quantify, bureaucratise and 'data-ise' workplaces. This is particularly noticeable in public sector workplaces like education and healthcare, where data and the inexorable drive towards new forms of efficiency and growth have almost completely replaced the values upon which those institutions were built. Thus, even in those remaining areas of life which have not (yet) been privatised, and which therefore ostensibly lie outside market forces, the logic of neoliberalism has insidiously infected worker's lives through these disciplinary tools.

Above all, neoliberalism is a socio-political project designed to 're-establish the conditions for capital accumulation and the restoration of class power' of elites through the suppression of organised labour and collective action.[16] It has been wildly successful in this regard: following the brief period between 1945 and the mid-70s, when capitalism and the rate of profit was somewhat tamed by the post-war Keynesian settlement, wealth inequalities have increased to the point where we have essentially returned to a form of feudalism. Wealth and power are increasingly concentrated in the hands of fewer and fewer people – the '1%' – whilst the bulk of the world's population has become immiserated.[17] The cumulative impact of the saturation of everyday life with an essentially economic logic is that neoliberalism has now completely transformed the social relations of contemporary society. It inflects and infects all areas of personal, social, cultural and political life. It has profoundly changed the way we think about ourselves, and how we view and relate to one another as citizens and as human beings. It is, to quote one commentator, 'in here, in our heads and in our souls'.[18]

Neoliberalism and Wales

Although neoliberalism is by its very nature a global tendency, it embeds and manifests in different places in different ways, adapting to and even camouflaging itself within the distinct political culture and historical traditions of nations and territories. Thus, while there are clear commonalities among forms of neoliberalism across the world (such as privatisation and securitisation), as Stuart Hall argued, neoliberal restructuring is facilitated by its chameleon-like quality: 'It works on the ground of already constituted social practices and lived ideologies. It wins space there by constantly drawing on these elements which have secured over time a traditional resonance and left their traces in popular inventories.'[19] This is inflected by the history and political culture of each specific country.

Neoliberalism is arguably at its most transparent and brutal in the US, where it is buttressed by historical appeals to a libertarian tradition. In Australia and New Zealand, neoliberalism was ushered in by labour governments ostensibly committed to social democracy.[20] In Latin America, unfortunate satellites of the US are assaulted with predatory, more openly oppressive and highly racialized forms of neoliberalism, often administered by formerly leftist movements.[21] In countries like Turkey[22] and Iran[23] neoliberalism co-opts and co-exists alongside conservative culture and religion. In the UK, as Brett Christophers argues, rentierism is disproportionately central to neoliberalism,[24] which is in turn a function of Britain's unique historical development, specifically the lack of a bourgeois revolution.[25]

There are two related historical and political streams that have converged to influence the direction of neoliberalism in contemporary Wales. One is Wales' uneven and

13

combined development under conditions of political and economic absorption into England. Wales' status as an appendage to British imperialism resulted in a perilously narrow industrial economy based on the extraction and refining of natural resources, with most profits leaving the country. Whether this development was strictly 'colonial' is largely beside the point; the fact is that Wales' subordination and integration into Britain meant that Wales did not develop a diverse modern economy, but remained narrow (i.e., based on a few large industries), with its internal infrastructure painfully underdeveloped and geared almost entirely towards English capital and trade. Politically, the experience of absorption and the resultant lack of native political or public institutions meant that the transition to capitalism created a warped class structure. Wales was not only a vast bed of natural resources but also a reservoir of cheap labour; as such, it did not develop a national bourgeoisie as did Scotland (for example) – instead, capitalistic activity was dominated in the main by capital originating outside Wales and profit which in turn flowed back out of the country. This state of affairs continues to underpin a profound internal unevenness in terms of economic development and identity.

Second is the (related) hegemonic dominance of the Labour party in Wales, which remains without comparison in world politics.[26] In a country possessed of an outsized proletariat, the lack of a national bourgeoisie led in turn to a very weak national movement which emerged far later than small national movements on the continent.[27] The Welsh economy and its attendant political institutions were only belatedly and partially 'national' (i.e. developed for the sake of the Welsh nation by a national bourgeoisie), and set up to service the empire and international capital. Later, during the post-industrial period, the experience of the welfare state and its subsequent dismantlement led Wales to become further stitched into the British state. The post-war welfare state represented a remarkable (and never to be replicated) hegemonic project of class collaboration which accrued significant material concessions to peripheral regions and subaltern classes through schemes like mass council house building and the (relatively brief) nationalisation of key industries. In the decades that followed, as crisis and deindustrialisation engulfed the Keynesian project, Westminster administrations became increasingly desperate to 'prop up' Wales, and moved public sector work like the Royal Mint and DVLA into once heavily industrialised areas. This acculturation and integration was mediated by the Labour party, who thereby consolidated their power in Wales. As a result, and as the May 2021 Senedd elections demonstrated, politics in large parts of Wales has been reduced to an unreflexive cultural habit.

However, as this book argues, Labour's dominance in Wales has emphatically not equated to Welsh socialism. While the ascendence of Thatcherism and the crushing of the organised labour movement radically altered Wales' relationship with the British state, further entrenching the support for Labourism, Thatcherism also involved what Gramsci called a more insidious war of manoeuvre, involving the rapid privatisation and sale of public services, the accelerated transition to a service economy, the agglomeration of manufacturing on the South Wales coastal belt, the culture of seeking FDI (which was begun under the Wilson government), and the powerful cultural-economic phenomenon of right to buy and the promotion of a new hegemonic petite-bourgeois ideology. These all transformed and had been present in Wales for many years before devolution arrived in 1999, despite the assumption that Wales was a socialist society somehow preserved in aspic behind Offa's Dyke.

Thus, regardless of devolution and Welsh government policy, Wales had been a 'neoliberal' state in the sense that it had been part of the UK, and hence totally transformed by this mode of capitalism from the late 1970s onwards. Devolution under Labour was therefore layered on top of this deeply entrenched settlement. We cannot explore events that have unfolded since 1997, nor can we also study modern Wales as an entity, divorced from the British state or international capital and other global forces. When we say *Welsh* neoliberalism, we refer not only to the policies of the Welsh Government and the Labour party, but the complex ways in which the Welsh devolved state interacts with British, European and global neoliberalism, just as local capital interacts with national and international capital.

That said, the politicians in the Senedd have a lot to answer for. Indeed, much of this book provides evidence of the hypothesis that devolution was nothing more than what Evans describes as passive revolution,[28] one that sought to entrench Labour's power and stymie genuine change. The result has been the continued collapse of Welsh society under the pressures of late capitalism.

Welsh Neoliberalism

In the early years of devolution, the new Welsh Assembly adopted a measure of redistributive and 'state-centric' policies, largely absorbing 'Keynesian counter-cyclical resources from the UK government'.[29] The 'filling in' of the state at the Welsh scale – using the apparatuses of the devolved government to aid 'universalism' – reflected the deep-seated tradition of welfarism and the role of the state in Wales.[30] Yet the early policy divergence pursued by the first devolved administration, however timid, was facilitated by a mini economic bubble which emerged during Blairism. The apex of actually existing Welsh distinctiveness was the One Wales coalition (2007–2011), where Labour were dragged to the left by Plaid Cymru in numerous areas of policy. However, following the end of this coalition and the ascendency of Carwyn Jones in 2009, coupled with the coming to power in Westminster in 2010 of the Tory-Lib Dem coalition government, any traces of Wales' supposed 'clear red water' began to evaporate.

Indeed, something approaching a counter-revolution began. While of course the radical rhetoric remained in place, as did a general approval of the public sector and logics of the welfare state – particularly unionisation – the 'pro-business' Jones began enthusiastically to pursue a strategy of attracting foreign direct investment, whereas his predecessor had been loudly suspicious of the 'all eggs in one basket' approach of the WDA. To this end, CBI advisers were placed into the upper echelons of the Welsh Government and the focus of the Welsh Government and state apparatus shifted significantly. Jones' tenure precipitated a step change in culture and policy direction, and many early timid forays were undone: school league tables and testing were reintroduced, as was a punitive inspection regime; the curriculum was refocused on the needs of business and promoted entrepreneurialism; universities were privatised and fees charged; nuclear power was back on the agenda.

Under Jones' tenure in particular, Wales became a cosy place for international capital (although Morgan himself had begun implementing austerity measures). This has continued unabated throughout Drakeford's tenure. As Parry's chapter in this book makes clear, the pursuit of FDI remains a pillar of Welsh Government economic policy, and regardless of the personnel in charge, huge amounts of public money have been and are being handed to footloose foreign capital with no strings or clauses: Amazon, Kancoat, Virgin Atlantic, Aston Martin, TVR.

Take the recent Ineos debacle. In 2019, Welsh Government was under pressure to act on Ford's decision to abandon its Bridgend plant, which was about to leave thousands of skilled employees out of work. Ignoring calls to repurpose the site, it instead embarked on one of its 'social partnership' investment schemes. It made an agreement with Ineos, a vast multinational petrochemical company who had recently announced it was to start manufacturing a gas-guzzling, eye-wateringly expensive 4-wheel drive vehicle. Economy Minister Ken Skates made an agreement with Sir Jim Radcliffe – CEO of Ineos and one of the richest people in Britain – to spend a rumoured £10 million of public money preparing a new site for the company to build the vehicle in Bridgend. Consider the facts for a moment: Welsh Government – whose two greatest 'progressive' achievements in twenty years of devolution were the introduction of mandatory plastic bag charges and signing a Well-being of Future Generations Act committing future Welsh governments to action on climate change – made a multi-million pound agreement with one of the world's largest *petrochemical* companies, indeed one of the world's 20 largest producers of non-recyclable plastics and a major voice in the UK fracking lobby – to build 4-wheel drive vehicles for the wealthy. Not only this, but Ineos was also a well-known tax avoider and union buster, having relocated to Switzerland to avoid tax in 2010 and aggressively going to war with Unite during disputes at their Grangemouth oil refinery in 2013.[31] Mercifully, Ineos decided at the last minute to pull out of the deal, instead choosing a site in Germany for their new plant. Welsh Government had, however, already spent £4 million on preparing the site. No refunds, said Radcliffe.

What these and many other embarrassingly inept and misguided groundhog-day situations make clear is that the Welsh Way is to play the *subordinate* partner in its relations with international capital. Indeed, Wales' history of dependency means that this is an ultra-subordinate relationship in a comparative sense. The state here has become merely a facilitator between the people and those who provide employment, i.e., private businesses. Indeed, the evidence of the subordinate role of the state is in fact crystalized in the concept of the 'social partnership', which is a misnomer. The state is subordinate to international capital and business, and the unions are subordinate to the state. This is overwhelmingly the function of Welsh 'intervention' in the devolved economy; the notion of the state itself providing employment through nationalisation is now completely alien.

Granted, the Welsh Government has had to fight its battles with one hand behind its back, lacking at present the macroeconomic levers that would allow it to adopt wholesale economic changes, and (until recently) forbidden by EU rules on state aid. However, we do not have a local political elite that is fighting back or resisting this system, nor displaying any ideological commitment to a more autonomous Wales with access to such levers. The Welsh Way is to tinker around edges with schemes like 'cash equivalent services', removing charges for prescriptions and hospital car parking.[32] While these are of course to be welcomed, they are limited subsidies – headline-catching schemes which would be unnecessary under universalism. On the whole, the Welsh Government's approach to public services is not universalism but means-testing in areas such as tuition fees, childcare, social care and free school meals. For instance, it is estimated that 70,000 children below the poverty line in Wales are ineligible for free school meals.[33] This tinkering extends to things like plastic bag charges, 20 mph speed limits, banning pavement parking, and so on. These are small gestures within a system that continues to immiserate people.

By any objective measure, the Welsh Government has wholeheartedly embraced a system of capitalist accumulation which prioritises growth, which disregards the environment, and in which human flourishing is marginalised. The Labour-led Welsh Government refuses to push for the levers it needs, content instead to exist in a purgatory of helplessness. Labour claims it is unable to do 'x' because it doesn't have the political-economic levers, yet the party is unwilling to agitate for more powers as this would be 'nationalistic'. This resistance to any bold steps towards greater autonomy can itself be understood as a symptom of neoliberalism, in its lack of underlying political conviction (Williams).

However, despite claims that Welsh Government is powerless in the face of grand global forces, this new statelet has significant agency. The Senedd, its state apparatuses and devolved institutions, have their own culture and logic. They must be held to account.

Together, the contributions in this book allow us to scrutinise the nuanced, interconnected histories of neoliberalism and Welsh devolution. They enable us to consider at once the local and the global: to examine the patterns that have emerged in Wales since devolution whilst simultaneously looking outward to the global trends and tendencies that have given shape to them. These essays encourage us to move beyond the stagnant Labourist view of the Welsh past and present, towards a tentative political-economic theory of *Welsh* neoliberalism, both in its outward appearance as well as its underlying logic, rooted in a Marxist understanding of Wales' distinct historical development and political culture. Ultimately, these essays encourage us to imagine, and demand, another Welsh future. Contrary to Mark Drakeford's timid mantra following the May 2021 election – 'stable and

progressive' – this book argues for a new Welsh Way, one
that is truly radical and transformational.

---

[1] https://www.ippr.org/media-item/watch-mark-drakeford-speech

[2] https://www.bbc.co.uk/news/uk-wales-57157436

[3] https://www.bbc.co.uk/news/uk-wales-51629420

[4] https://www.bbc.co.uk/news/uk-wales-57328488

[5] https://www.homelessnessimpact.org/post/what-the-latest-statistics-tell-us-about-homelessness-trends-in-wales

[6] https://assets.publishing.service.gov.uk/government/uploads/system/uploads/attachment_data/file/938571/Prison_Population_Projections_2020_to_2026.pdf

[7] https://www.bbc.co.uk/news/uk-wales-56803837#:~:text=Unemployment%20in%20Wales%20rose%20by, of%204.9%25%20for%20the%20UK

[8] https://undod.cymru/en/2020/07/03/tai-housing/

[9] https://www.walesonline.co.uk/news/wales-news/coronavirus-mapped-poverty-deprivation-deaths-20623243

[10] https://www.angelfire.com/alt/ceri_evans/other_material/murky_brown_water.htm

[11] Ian Bruff and Cemal Burak Tansel, eds., *Authoritarian Neoliberalism: Philosophies, Practices, Contestations* (London: Routledge, 2019).

[12] Andrew Gamble, *The Free Economy and the Strong State: The Politics of Thatcherism* (London: Macmillan, 1988).

[13] David Harvey, 'Neoliberalism as Creative Destruction', *The Annals of the American Academy of Political and Social Science* 610 (2007), 22–44. Naomi Klein, *The Shock Doctrine: The Rise of Disaster Capitalism* (London: Penguin, 2008).

[14] Stuart Hall and Alan O'Shea, 'Common-sense Neoliberalism', *Soundings: A journal of politics and culture* 55 (2013), 8–24.

[15] David Graeber, *The Utopia of Rules: On Technology, Stupidity, and the Secret Joys of Bureaucracy* (London: Melville House, 2015).

[16] Harvey, 'Neoliberalism as Creative Destruction'.

[17] Grace Blakeley, *Stolen: How to Save the World from Financialisation* (London: Repeater, 2019).

[18] Stephen J. Ball, 'Neoliberal Education? Confronting the slouching beast', *Policy Futures in Education* 14:8 (2016).

[19] Stuart Hall, 'The Great Moving Right Show', *Marxism Today* (January 1979), 20.

[20] Guy Redden, Sean Phelan and Claire Baker, 'Different Routes Up the Same Mountain? Neoliberalism in Australia and New Zealand', in Simon Davies and Marc Lenormand, eds., *Neoliberalism in Context: Governance, Subjectivity and Knowledge* (London: Palgrave, 2019), pp. 61–83.

[21] Carlos Eduardo Martins, *Dependency, Neoliberalism and Globalisation in Latin America* (Leiden: Brill, 2019).

[22] Cihan Tuğal, 'Turkey at the Crossroads?', *New Left Review* 127 (2021).

[23] Kevan Harris, *A Social Revolution: Politics and the Welfare State in Iran* (Berkeley: University of California Press, 2017).

[24] Brett Christophers, *Rentier Capitalism: Who Owns the Economy and Who Pays for It?* (London: Verso, 2020).

[25] Tom Nairn, *The Breakup of Britain: Crisis and Neo-Nationalism* (London: Verso, 1981).

[26] Paul Chaney, 'How does single party dominance influence civil society organisations' engagement strategies? Exploratory analysis of participative mainstreaming in a "regional" European policy', *Public Policy and Administration* 31:2 (2015), 122–146. Ian McAllister, 'The Labour Party in Wales: The Dynamics of One-Partyism', *Llafur* 3:2 (1981).

[27] Simon Brooks, *Why Wales Never Was: The Failure of Welsh Nationalism* (Cardiff: UWP, 2017).

[28] Dan Evans, *Devolution's Passive Revolution* (IWA, 2015) https://www.iwa.wales/agenda/2015/10/devolutions-passive-revolution/

[29] Philip Cooke and Nick Clifton, 'Visionary, precautionary and constrained "varieties of devolution" in the economic governance of the devolved UK territories', *Regional Studies* 39:4 (2005), 437–451.

[30] Rhys Jones, Mark Goodwin, Martin Jones, Kevin Pett, '"Filling in" the state: economic governance and the evolution of devolution in Wales', *Environment and Planning C: Government and Policy* 23:3 (2005), 337–360.

[31] https://www.theguardian.com/commentisfree/2013/nov/09/ineos-unite-union-grangemouth-oil-refinery

[32] https://gov.wales/sites/default/files/publications/2020-01/child-poverty-strategy-2019-progress-report-annex.pdf

[33] https://cpag.org.uk/news-blogs/news-listings/two-five-uk-children-under-poverty-line-are-not-eligible-free-school-meals

BELIEFS, FOUNDATIONS & STRUCTURES

A Progressive Veneer:
Neoliberal Feminism in Wales

Mabli Siriol Jones

On International Women's Day 2018, First Minister Carwyn Jones declared his ambition to make the Welsh Government a 'Feminist Government'. Commenting on the ambition, he said there was *'no point politicians being able to see a difference ... members of the public need to see that something positive is being done to their lives'*.[1] The reality since devolution, however, is that the various commitments and policy initiatives towards gender equality have had minimal material impact on most women's lives. This is because politics and policymaking in Wales are captured by the neoliberal consensus, and feminism as practised by the political class is no exception. The feminism that has been dominant in Welsh public life, as in the UK and other western states, is a neoliberal feminism, aiming for the advancement of individual women within the existing neoliberal framework, rather than a genuinely emancipatory project committed to dismantling that framework and securing justice for all.

Progressive Neoliberalism and Neoliberal Feminism

Nancy Fraser argues that the hegemonic political worldview in western states over recent decades has been *progressive neoliberalism*.[2] This is defined as a political consensus combining a neoliberal politics of distribution (financialisation, deregulation and privatisation) with a progressive politics of recognition (increased social status for oppressed groups, such as women, LGBT people and people of colour). Fraser argues that in order for neoliberalism to become truly hegemonic in states shaped by the post-war economic consensus and the social movements of the 1960s, it needed the gloss of progressive recognition politics. This combination allowed neoliberalism to triumph, and it has dominated since. It is only recently, following the financial crisis, that this consensus has begun to shatter, with the rise of outsider populist politics on the right and left. As Fraser identifies, feminism has played a large part in this project of progressive neoliberalism. This is due in part to the unwitting perversion of some of its central tenets, and in part to the championing of a certain kind of feminism by privileged women based on their personal advancement relative to men of their own class. Feminism has become, in Fraser's words, the '*handmaiden*' of neoliberalism, which '*turns a sow's ear into a silk purse by elaborating a narrative of female empowerment*'.[3]

Neoliberal feminism is characterised by a reformist approach to existing social structures, seeking the advancement of individual women within those structures rather than fundamental change for all. It is therefore preoccupied with representation, having women in visible leadership positions within high status workplaces, such as politics, the media and boardrooms. Its agent is the individual and her *empowerment*, rather than the collective. It locates oppression primarily in the interpersonal, rather than the structural. It operates by 'raising awareness' and attempting to change attitudes and behaviours, rather than the material conditions and social relations that give rise to them. It is process-oriented and imagines that inequality can be tackled by changing institutions' procedures, rather than questioning the power imbalances inherent in those institutions themselves. Its theory of change rests on the assumption that promoting more women into positions of power will lead to improvements in everyone else's lives − a 'trickle-down feminism' mirroring the trickle-down economics of neoliberalism. Crucially, it does not have an analysis of *power* itself − a word that is usually absent from its lexicon, which prefers the language of 'equality', 'diversity' and 'inclusion'. It situates the achievement of feminist aims in the actions of a benevolent state that will (someday, if we get the right people into power) address the needs and concerns of women. Above all, in Fraser's terms, it prioritises recognition over redistribution: changing attitudes and women's social status rather than the allocation of wealth, power and resources.[4]

Neoliberal feminism speaks to the concerns of a class of women for whom being a feminist becomes another lifestyle label, rather than a political praxis; a way to prove one's progressive credentials while securing one's own advancement. These are predominantly wealthy, white, middle-class, able-bodied, cisgender and heterosexual women; women who benefit from existing social structures, despite the disadvantages they encounter due to their gender. They therefore tend to privilege gendered oppression above other forms, as that is the only, or primary, oppression they experience. This is nothing new. The history of mainstream feminism is one of exclusions, and the use of feminism to secure the class position of certain women relative to their male counterparts. Neoliberalism has been able to use feminism because these schisms already existed. Women at the top have long been content to secure their own position at the expense, and by using the labour, of working-class women, often drawn from communities of colour and the Global South. As a result, the primary political purpose of neoliberal feminism, unwittingly or not, is to reinforce neoliberalism as the dominant mode of ordering society by giving it a progressive veneer.

The truth is there will never be equality for women (or any oppressed group) under neoliberalism, as it is a system based on the exploitation of women's unpaid labour and tearing apart the social fabric within which women's material conditions can be improved, and where the comfort and wealth of some comes at the expense of many others. Yet as Fraser notes, the neoliberal consensus is fracturing everywhere. Feminism must ask itself what its role will be in what takes its place.

Neoliberal Feminism in Wales

Wales has been radically reshaped and deeply scarred by neoliberalism and its processes of deindustrialisation, austerity and privatisation. As Gabriel Winant has noted, it is those who bear the brunt of neoliberalism who also have to manage its consequences, particularly women in working-class communities, deindustrialised areas and communities of colour.[5] As neoliberalism destroys the notion of the collective and cuts back on social provision, women experience increasing poverty and precarity and have to pick up the pieces through unpaid care and the feminised workforces of the caring professions. This is illustrated by the fact that 86% of the reductions in public spending through cuts to welfare and tax changes under austerity came from women.[6] One in four people in Wales lives in poverty[7] and for single parents (90% of whom are women) the figure is 44%.[8] Women are more likely to be in insecure employment, and 41% work part time.[9] They make up the bulk of the workforce in the caring professions, as 80% of workers in health and social work[10] and 66% of the education workforce.[11] They are therefore on the frontlines of managing the vicious circle of increased need and reduced capacity in public services due to cuts, privatisation and the inequality and human misery generated by neoliberalism. In a country with an ageing population and high levels of disability and long-term illness, they also provide the bulk of unpaid care, doing 60% more unpaid care work than men and making up 59% of those providing family care.[12] The Covid-19 pandemic and recession have exacerbated all these issues and underlying structural trends – economic, social, demographic – mean they will only intensify in future. Yet 20 years of devolved policy on gender equality has prioritised recognition over redistribution and attempted, with little success, to manage the impact of neoliberalism on women's lives.

Due to the focus on recognition over redistribution, the framework for 'equalities' policy under neoliberal governance is to treat it as an area apart, with little influence on major policy areas. The Welsh Government is typical in this regard. The approach is incrementalist, managerialist and focused on processes, with the neoliberal tendency to generate new forms of bureaucracy with little real value. The language used reflects the managerialist approach: people have 'protected characteristics', they are 'stakeholders' or 'service users'. Policy interventions tend towards creating new procedures, training programmes and awareness-raising campaigns, as was evident in the response by Senedd politicians to the Me Too revelations of sexual harassment in politics. The actions taken concentrated on awareness-raising, strengthening complaints procedures and 'Dignity and Respect' policies, without a deeper reckoning or acknowledgement that these would be inadequate in a workplace with vast and inherent power imbalances and limited labour rights.

The rhetoric on gender equality does not match the reality, as demonstrated by the government's *Advancing Gender Equality in Wales Plan*[13] on how it will fulfil the feminist government ambition. While accepting the need for far-reaching change, the plan is short on detail, light on action, heavy with managerialist language and focused on instituting new processes rather than substantive policy change. Meanwhile, the government's flagship gender equality legislation has also fallen short. The Violence Against Women, Domestic Abuse and Sexual

Violence Act was heralded as 'world-leading' when it was introduced in 2015, but its interventions focus on training and procedures and implementation has been painfully slow.[14] Funding of the sector is piecemeal and short-term, provision is patchy and services are stretched. Austerity has made women both more vulnerable to abuse and less able to access support – what's needed above all is significant investment in the sector. This failure has a human cost: in 2019–20, 574 people were turned away from domestic abuse services and 251 were on waiting lists for rape crisis support.[15]

A common thread through the missed opportunities to materially advance gender equality is a lack of class analysis and aversion to redistribution. The Welsh Government's Childcare Offer, which funds 30 hours of childcare to working parents of 3 and 4-year-olds, is a key example. Parents who aren't in work are excluded, with the result that the offer benefits some of Wales' wealthiest families while giving nothing to the poorest. Anti-poverty organisations, opposition politicians and the Children's Commissioner[16] called for the offer to be extended to all parents,[17] but the government refused to change direction. The episode demonstrated how deeply wedded the government is to neoliberal doctrine, including the aversion to universalism, increasing conditionality in welfare and public services and the belief in work as the route out of poverty and a good in itself.[18] This thinking has also been evident in its opposition to the devolution of welfare administration, despite the fact this would allow it to offset some of the harmful elements of Universal Credit, such as allowing payments to more than one member of the household, rather than the current primary earner policy that leaves women financially dependent on their spouses and more vulnerable to abuse. Likewise, the government's refusal to move away from the current model of for-profit social care provision towards a universal and free publicly owned service shows a lack of understanding of the material benefit this would have to women who, as well as providing the majority of unpaid care, make up 83% of workers[19] in a sector where low pay, precarity and exploitation are widespread.

This lack of class analysis is also behind much of mainstream feminism's approach to sex work, with an inability to understand sex work *as work* and the material realities that lead people to sell sex. This includes support from gender equality organisations and politicians for the 'Nordic model' that criminalises the purchase of sex, rather than decriminalisation and labour rights for sex workers. The Nordic model makes sex workers less safe[20] and rests on a fundamental misunderstanding of what drives a lot of sex work – which is sex workers' need to make money. This has led to bizarre alliances, including the Welsh Government backing the introduction of equivalent legislation in the UK to a Trump administration law that shut down sex work websites and drove workers underground into more dangerous practices.[21]

Contrasted with the lack of a focus on redistribution is the fixation on representation in discussions of gender equality since devolution. Much has been made of the fact that the Senedd was one of the first parliaments in the world to achieve 50/50 representation in 2003. A Cardiff University study is often cited for the claim that this made for better policy development, noting women were more likely to raise gender equality issues.[22] Yet as the examples given above show, it is not clear that this has led to improved outcomes for most women. The drive for 50/50 representation has continued however, with the Expert Panel on Assembly Electoral Reform recommending in 2017 that the Senedd introduce a legal quota to ensure 50% of representatives would be women and 50% men.[23] This was welcomed despite the perverse implication that Wales would therefore be introducing a *ceiling* on women's representation and ensuring protected seats for men. It is a fallacy to assume that women are naturally kinder, more level-headed and ethical actors in positions of leadership. It is a particularly bizarre claim in a country whose social safety net was unpicked most radically by its first female prime minister, and whose second created the hostile environment. To argue otherwise is to accept that women are somehow not full political actors in the same way as men – people who can advance a range of political projects, and their own interests, in positions of power. Any discussion of women and power that neglects an analysis of power itself – or treats it as a neutral sphere, a tool that is wielded *better* somehow by women – is inherently superficial and flawed. History shows that women are just as capable as men of upholding oppressive systems where they benefit from those systems themselves.

It is, of course, essential that women participate fully in decision-making structures, and it is obvious that is not currently happening. This is not adequately addressed, however, by the suppositions of a feminism that focuses on representation to the detriment of other issues, and talks more about the sexism female politicians face than the structural barriers that shut others out. Quotas do not solve a problem at its root, they just put in place mechanisms at the end of a system to change its output. They therefore mainly benefit women who are already near the top of these systems, and the issues these women are more likely to care about or understand will reflect their own experiences and class position. These mechanisms will not necessarily lead to improvements in most people's lives, as they leave unaddressed the question of who will be put in power and what they will do with it. They do not address deeper questions of how power is distributed and wielded, or advocate for real democratisation of institutions that disenfranchise the majority.

Wales' 'progressive consensus' has often been lauded, but it is precisely on those issues where that consensus appears to be most well-established that political commitment is at its most shallow. Politics is the field of contestation, and consensus achieved without contestation tends to be around quite hollow ideals, as they are those that do not represent a threat to the established order. Political consensus around 'gender equality' amounts to a general idea that equality (ill-defined and broadly conceived) is a good thing, and few policies go beyond increased representation. Demands for redistributive policies are dismissed and 'gender equality' and 'feminism' become floating signifiers, empty of the commitments that would make them transformative.

This shallow consensus has meant that Welsh politics and mainstream feminism has been inadequately prepared to answer the challenge from the growth of anti-feminist politics. This has been evident in the fifth Senedd with the election of more than one representative who has endorsed the ideas and language of the alt-right; the backlash to the Me Too movement and the use of anti-feminism in the Plaid Cymru leadership election with the claim that Leanne Wood was too focused on the 'niche issues' of the oppressed. Reactionary politics feeds off the wounds and resentments generated by neoliberalism, telling those for whom progressive neoliberalism has failed to secure improvements in their lives that it is its politics of recognition, not redistribution, that is to blame. The answer from neoliberal feminism tends to be dismissal or ridicule, as it struggles to articulate a more robust defence of its programme that has, after all, neglected redistributive policies that would have a material benefit to men as well as women. Wales has many characteristics that make it fertile ground for reactionary political currents: a small and exclusive political class, low levels of political engagement and a weak media and public sphere. The response to anti-feminism, which is often at the vanguard of reactionary political projects, does not bode well for the response to other reactionary projects in future, including the growing anti-devolution movement. The Welsh political class appears ill-equipped to meet these challenges, or even understand them.

Towards an Alternative Feminism

We live in a moment of deepening and cross-cutting crises, lived every day in the experiences of those in our society who cannot insulate themselves through wealth. Neoliberal feminism cannot help when you are unable to feed your children without the aid of a food bank, shafted from one underpaid job to another and navigating the cruel and arcane processes of decimated public services. Where are these women in the narratives and concerns of neoliberal feminism? Its women tend to be those who have risen to the top, or the girls who need encouragement that with hard work they can get there too. When working-class or marginalised women appear, it is usually as an afterthought or in a paternalistic frame that presents middle-class liberal feminists as their saviours. They are never agents in their own right, nor comrades in struggle. They are women to be 'empowered' by their benevolent feminist leaders, not people who find ways to survive, resist and even triumph within a system engineered against them. Neoliberal feminism will never lead to emancipation because it precludes the only way we get there – through struggle, together.

We urgently need to rebuild feminist politics on a different foundation. This should be based on a fundamental rejection of neoliberalism and reclaiming the collective good. This feminism must centre an analysis of power: how it works, who has it and what they do with it. Rather than 'equality', 'inclusion' and 'diversity', we need to talk about dismantling and sharing power, and wielding it for our own ends. We must work, in the words of bell hooks, *'from margin to center'*,[24] starting from the needs of the most marginalised. The woman imprisoned for protecting herself from her abuser; the woman made destitute by our immigration system; the woman turning to sex work due to the inadequacy of Universal Credit. This is a feminism that would talk less about promoting individual women within institutions and more about transforming those institutions to serve the rest of us. This is not a feminism that can be generated or led by politicians or NGOs; it must be built from the ground up, as part of a project to democratise society.

While rejecting progressive neoliberalism, we must also reject a certain brand of leftism that dismisses 'identity politics' and says the rights of women and marginalised people are 'distractions' from the only true struggle, class struggle. This dismisses decades of Marxist thought on gender, race and imperialism, as well as the needs of working-class people who experience multiple forms of oppression. As Fraser reminds us, justice requires both recognition and redistribution. This means a real commitment to intersectionality and situating feminism within a broader movement for social, economic and climate justice. It is feminism as a project for the redistribution of wealth and power, and socialism that puts feminism, anti-racism and anti-imperialism at its heart, understanding that there is no liberation for some, without liberation for all.

Despite the ravages of neoliberalism, a long tradition of communitarianism and radical activism still exists in Wales. A truly feminist government would use this to reject the neoliberal consensus and reorientate the economy and society around care – the antithesis of neoliberal economics. The confrontation between capital and the stubborn human need for care has been brought to the fore by the Covid-19 pandemic and will only increase with current trends. The caring professions were on the front-lines of Covid-19, with the pandemic exposing both the damage of decades of neoliberal reforms to these services, and that they are the true creators of value in our society. Reproductive labour of all kinds has been undervalued precisely because it is done for free by women and is one of capitalism's foundational sites of exploitation. Yet care is resistant to automation and our need for it will only grow. This need should be met by high-quality universal services, not unpaid labour and for-profit provision. Rejecting neoliberalism and centring a politics of care can help us weave together the commitments and solidarities we need to build an alternative.

The neoliberal order is fragmenting and what takes its place is undecided. As Fraser argues, this can lead to ever more reactionary politics, or a progressive project for recognition *and* redistribution. Neoliberal feminism has shown itself incapable of delivering justice. Drawing on a rich countercurrent of feminist scholarship and activism, we must turn to something else – a political project working for the liberation of all women from violence and exploitation within a wider movement for a radically different society, one based on the realisation of care, dignity and joy for all. We need a different kind of feminism that will demand, and win, much more.

---

[1] Hannah Al-Othman, 'This Politician Wants To Make Wales The Most Feminist Country In Europe', *Buzzfeed* (21 May 2018) https://www.buzzfeed.com/hannahalothman/this-politician-wants-to-make-wales-the-most-feminist

[2] Nancy Fraser, *The old is dying and the new cannot be born: from progressive neoliberalism to Trump and beyond*, (London: Verso, 2017).

[3] Nancy Fraser, 'How feminism became capitalism's handmaiden – and how to reclaim it', *The Guardian* (14 October 2013) https://www.theguardian.com/commentisfree/2013/oct/14/feminism-capitalist-handmaiden-neoliberal

[4] Nancy Fraser, 'From redistribution to recognition? Dilemmas of Justice in a Post-Socialist Age', *New Left Review*, I/212 (1995).

[5] 'The Social Question with Gabriel Winant', *The Dig* [podcast] (3 January 2021) https://www.thedigradio.com/podcast/the-social-question-with-gabriel-winant/

[6] Richard Cracknell and Richard Keen, 'Estimating the gender impact of tax and benefits changes', *House of Commons Library* (18 December 2017).

[7] Department for Work and Pensions, *Households below average income report* (26 March 2020) https://statswales.gov.wales/Catalogue/Community-Safety-and-Social-Inclusion/Poverty/householdbelowaverageincome-by-year

[8] Chwarae Teg, *State of the Nation 2020* [research report] (28 January 2020) https://chwaraeteg.com/research/state-of-the-nation/

[9] Ibid.

[10] Welsh Government, *Annual population survey July 2018–June 2019* (18 September 2019).

[11] Chwarae Teg, *State of the Nation 2020*.

[12] Women's Equality Network Wales and Oxfam Cymru, *Feminist scorecard 2020: tracking Welsh Government's action to advance women's rights and gender equality* [research report] (21 April 2020) https://wenwales.org.uk/wp-content/uploads/2020/04/Feminist-Scorecard-Report-2020-Eng.pdf

[13] Welsh Government, *Advancing Gender Equality in Wales Plan* (10 March 2020).

[14] A 2019 Audit Wales report found that years after the Act was passed, survivors are still being let down by a complex and inconsistent system. Audit Wales, *Progress in implementing the Violence Against Women, Domestic Abuse and Sexual Violence Act* (21 November 2019) https://www.audit.wales/publication/progress-implementing-violence-against-women-domestic-abuse-and-sexual-violence-act

[15] Welsh Women's Aid, *Time to act on sustainability: State of the sector 2020*, (27 November 2020) https://www.welshwomensaid.org.uk/2020/11/time-to-act-on-sustainability-welsh-womens-aid-state-of-the-sector-2020/

[16] Children's Commissioner Wales, *Policy position: childcare*

https://www.childcomwales.org.uk/our-work/policy-positions/childcare/

[17] Disappointingly, gender equality charity Chwarae Teg supported the Government's approach of focusing on working parents rather than calling for a universal offer. They have since called for the offer to be extended to all families in their manifesto for the 2021 election. See evidence by Chwarae Teg to the Senedd Children, Young People and Education Committee (24 May 2018) https://cofnod.senedd.cymru/Committee/4799 and Chwarae Teg, *Manifesto for a Gender Equal Wales* (11 November 2020).

[18] This is despite the Government's own analysis showing that two thirds of children in Wales who live in poverty live in a household where at least one parent is working. Welsh Government, *Child Poverty Progress Report 2019* (10 December 2019).

[19] Chwarae Teg, *Manifesto for a Gender Equal Wales* (11 November 2020).

[20] Sarah Boseley, 'Criminalisation of sex work normalises violence, review finds', *The Guardian* (11 December 2018) https://www.theguardian.com/society/2018/dec/11/criminalisation-of-sex-work-normalises-violence-review-finds

[21] Senedd, Business Statement and Announcement (3 July 2018) https://record.senedd.wales/Plenary/4996#C105792

[22] Paul Chaney, 'Devolved Governance and the Substantive Representation of Women: The Second Term of the National Assembly for Wales, 2003–2007', *Parliamentary Affairs*, 61.2 (2008).

[23] Expert Panel on Assembly Electoral Reform, *A Parliament that works for Wales* (12 December 2017).

[24] bell hooks, *Feminist theory from margin to center*, 2nd edn (London: Pluto Press, 2000).

Neoliberalism: Perpetuating Welsh Underdevelopment?

Sam Parry

Wales is in a peculiar and in some ways unenviable position with regards to macroeconomic policy. On one hand, it is the role of the Welsh Government to develop, build and grow the Welsh economy. In the words of the ex-First Minister for Wales, Rhodri Morgan, 'the most important task for any government is to create the conditions in which the economy can prosper'.[1] On the other hand, important levers in the fields of economic and monetary policy, financial markets, import and export control and trade competition laws are reserved to the Westminster Government.[2] Whilst analysing the economic policies of Wales, we must consider the endogenous forces within Wales whilst simultaneously understanding the exogenous forces and pressures exerted on Wales from outside. This chapter will critically assess these contending forces, arguing that the 'logic' of neoliberalism – and of capitalism more generally – holds that there will be forces that both pull and push on Wales; 'unskilled' and low-wage work will be pushed from the centre to areas of the periphery like Wales, while external forces pull important decision-making, Research and Development (R&D) and value-added employment to areas of the centre such as London and the south-east of England.[3] Wales' role within the international division of labour would continue to be one of a peripheral region, it is courted for its relatively educated, low-paid workers and its large reserve army of labour but is not seen as a region for 'high value-added' work. Furthermore, although neoliberalism was incubated outside of Wales, and despite their progressive, social-democratic rhetoric, Welsh policymakers have bought into neoliberal thinking, and have thus perpetuated the effects of neoliberal orthodoxy on the Welsh economy and people.

Defining Neoliberalism

At its most basic level, neoliberalism is an ideological project of a resurgent right wing whose principles can be found in the works of Friedrich Von Hayek and the Chicago School. The fundamental role of neoliberalism is to embed market principles and market 'rationality' into everyday government decisions. This process is undertaken in two different, yet complimentary ways called 'roll-back' and 'roll-out' neoliberalism.[4] Roll-back neoliberalism refers to 'the active destruction or discreditation of Keynesian-welfarist and social-collectivist institutions',[5] the clearest example of which is the privatisation of state-owned industries. Roll-out neoliberalism on the other hand refers to the consolidation of neoliberal state forms which includes public-private initiatives such as the Mutual Investment Model in Wales and punitive policy programs that seek to discipline, criminalise, and control poor and marginalised social groups. The use of ASBOs in

England and Wales and the continued overrepresentation of marginalised groups in our prison system exemplify this process.

Neoliberal ideas manifested themselves on both sides of the Atlantic, and were embodied in the politics of Margaret Thatcher, Ronald Reagan and most inhumanely under Augusto Pinochet's Military Junta in Chile. Neoliberalism was able to embed itself and spread globally via the support of global institutions such as the International Monetary Fund, the World Bank, and the World Trade Organisation which was a global form of roll-out neoliberalism. A concurrent major factor in the solidification and precipitation of the spread of neoliberalism was the collapse of the Soviet Union and the Eastern bloc. This challenged the validity of alternative economic systems whilst simultaneously curbing workers' bargaining power in the West. The inculcation of neoliberal orthodoxy in the West is best illustrated by the rise of the supposed 'Third Way' exemplified by Bill Clinton, Tony Blair, and Gerhard Schroder. These politicians pushed centre-left parties in 'market-friendly' directions, thus further closing the ideological space on the left.[6] Nancy Fraser characterised these leaders as being part of an ideology called 'progressive neoliberalism' which on one hand embraced 'diversity, multiculturalism and women's rights'[7] while simultaneously reigning over a period of financial deregulation, and the inclusion of private businesses within public services. This process is best exemplified in England by the introduction of Private Finance Initiatives in areas such as the London Underground, the NHS, and within schools.

It is important to note that neoliberalism is not a rehashing of classical economic liberalism which is usually attributed to Adam Smith and the publication of his book *An Inquiry into the Nature and Causes of the Wealth of Nations* in 1776. Liberalism's fundamental principles are personal liberty (rather than collective bargaining), private property (private ownership of the means of production), and limited government interference in economic affairs.[8] Liberalism holds that self-interest is an innate part of human nature and within the economic realm, producers produce, and labourers labour to fulfil their desires (the purchasing of goods). Through individual self-interest and freedom of production as well as consumption, the best interests of society are fulfilled, guided by the invisible hand that co-ordinates the 'free' market. Their argument is that governments cannot improve on this 'natural' position and thus its role is reduced to the protection of property rights and the enforcement of laws conducive to the workings of a 'free' market.

Under neoliberalism, however, the market is a heavily administered entity. The neoliberal market is constructed 'by law and political institutions and requires political intervention and orchestration. Far from flourishing when left alone, the economy must be directed, buttressed and protected by policy as well as by the dissemination of social norms designed to facilitate competition, free trade and rational economic action on the part of every member and institution of society'.[9] This is the contradiction at the heart of neoliberalism: the need for intervention in the name of non-intervention.[10] Under neoliberalism, the 'free' market can only be the 'natural' arbiter of decision-making within a repressive state apparatus. The hand of the market is not invisible; it is a clenched fist, wielding the power of the state. Andrew Gamble analysed this contradiction, stating that under neoliberalism, 'if the economy is to remain free the state has to become strong'.[11]

Numerous modern theorists like Mark Fisher[12] have argued that neoliberalism extends over all parts of life and that the state will be used to expand its reach. Yet, this view does not differ in any meaningful way from Marx's view that capital penetrates and transforms every aspect of our lives. Capitalism is not only an economic system, but also a 'definite form of ... life' where every value is calculated by its cold rationale:

> The way in which men produce their means of subsistence depends first of all on the nature of the actual means of subsistence they find in existence and have to reproduce. This mode of production must not be considered simply as being the production of the physical existence of the individuals. Rather it is a definite form of activity of these individuals, a definite form of expressing their life, a definite mode of life on their part. As individuals express their life, so they are. What they are, therefore, coincides with their production, both with what they produce and with how they produce. The nature of individuals thus depends on the material conditions determining their production.[13]

The Economic Structure of Wales

It is outside the scope of this chapter to give a full historic account of the economic structure of Wales.[14] I will instead concentrate on the Thatcher and post-Thatcher eras. The Welsh economy in these periods is defined by its reliance on investment from firms outside of Wales for employment. This economic process is called Foreign Direct Investment (FDI). FDI is here defined as 'investment abroad by an individual or firm with the objective of obtaining ownership and influence over income-generating assets'.[15]

The reliance of the Welsh economy on FDI is not a new phenomenon in all economic sectors. In the manufacturing industry, for example, 'only a tenth of large manufacturing plants in Wales were Welsh-owned, and branch plants accounted for 70 per cent of all manufacturing employment' in 1973.[16] Although the absolute numbers of those employed in manufacturing in Wales has declined, it is still Wales' second largest area of employment[17] and the industry is still heavily reliant on foreign firms. In 1996, foreign-owned firms accounted for 39%[18] of total manufacturing employment, and this number has remained steady with 40% of total employment in the field being foreign owned in 2005.[19]

In areas such as the service, tourism, and retail sectors, however, there has been a sharp increase in the role of foreign-owned firms. In 1998, there were only 8 foreign-owned hotels and restaurants in Wales, which employed 162 people. By 2005, there were 209 such institutions, employing 6,032 people.[20] By 2013, an absolute majority

48

of the profit made by the tourism industry in Wales left the country.[21] During the same timeframe, the number of foreign-owned wholesale and retail sites increased from 486 to 7,373 with employment increasing from 1,128 to 24,693. Perhaps most worryingly, in 2005 there were 67 foreign-owned, private companies in the health and social care sector, employing 2,802 people, thus showing the creeping privatisation and neoliberalisation of the Welsh healthcare system.[22] The neoliberalisation of the Welsh healthcare system showed that the 'clear red water' between England and Wales – if it ever existed – was evaporating.

Today, the capturing of inward investment is still a stated policy goal of the Welsh Government. In 2015, their *Wales in the World* report stated that 'as our heavy industries declined, we looked outwards to bring investors into Wales. They were attracted by an excellent and productive workforce, good communications, a *competitive cost base* and access to the massive European marketplace. Today, hundreds of foreign companies invest in Wales and employ many thousands of workers' (italics added).[23] Similarly, the Welsh Government's Economic Action Plan of 2017 states 'our exports and levels of Foreign Direct Investment (FDI) continue to impress. ... Our export performance and levels of FDI demonstrate how much confidence the world has in the quality of Welsh business, products and services and how much they value our people and places as an ideal destination for business investment'.[24] Inward investment is therefore a clear policy goal for the Welsh Government and there are no signs that this is likely to change soon.

Foreign Direct Investment: Deepening Dependency?

The preceding pages have shown that chasing inward investment is a stated policy goal of the Welsh Government. The question remains as to why chasing FDI could lead to a dependent economic structure. Constantina Kottaridi segregated FDI into two main groups: investments that are asset-exploiting, and others that are asset-augmenting.[25] The types of investments that are asset-augmenting are those primarily in the fields of R&D whereby the firm's assets are augmented by new technologies they develop in their firm abroad. Under asset-exploiting investments, a firm wishes to use pre-existing firm assets while exploiting the labour market access already existing in a location.[26] These types of investment are less likely to be embedded within local communities and therefore the wider economy is less likely to benefit from spill-over effects.

In Wales, perhaps unsurprisingly, it is asset-exploiting investment that is prevalent, with poor linkages between foreign firms and the wider Welsh economy. This is due to Wales' economic structure, which includes a large reserve army of labour, lower wages, and a relatively well-educated workforce.[27] In fact, 'low wage costs in Wales and hence low unit costs is a principal attraction' for those looking to invest.[28] To highlight the fact that poor linkages exist between foreign firms and the wider Welsh economy, Max Munday showed that within the foreign manufacturing sector, only 17% of non-wage spending actually occurred within the region the company was based, and that 'the foreign-owned manufacturing sector generally purchases less within Wales than the domestic sector'.[29] Outside the very direct outcome of work, there seems to be very little associated positive benefits to FDI in these sectors. Even the benefit of work must be tempered when it is remembered that this work is usually of a low-wage and is susceptible to be moved.

The FDI opportunities that firms seek out in places like Wales are therefore by their very nature unstable. These firms are highly mobile, flexible and are not embedded within their communities.[30] Their 'rootlessness' is their most defining characteristic, whereby 'once they have squeezed as much profit as possible out of a region, they have the ability to move to new regions at a moment's notice'.[31] This situation has been exacerbated since the fall of the Eastern Bloc with Wales ending up 'in competition' with these countries for jobs and investment as well as the other countries of the UK. This is a trend that is likely to continue, exemplified by the European Union's attempts to pry open the Ukrainian and Belarussian markets for foreign investors.

The issue remains as to why some areas attract certain types of inward investment whilst other areas attract investment of a different type. Firms in similar areas of expertise tend to cluster and agglomerate for a myriad of reasons such as a decrease in the cost of production, attraction of suppliers, attraction of highly skilled workers and a large local market. When a highly developed 'core' already exists, it continues to attract and accrue resources from the periphery as workers, opportunities and capital are sucked in, which in turn deepens inequalities between geographical regions.[32] These 'two areas cannot be considered in isolation from each other because they are linked through numerous different channels, such as trade, investment, government transfers and migration'.[33] The 'logic' of the market dictates that there will always be peripheral regions (north-east England and Wales) and core regions (south-east England) due to the uneven spread of capitalism and the international division of labour. In other words, peripheral regions 'are not formed autonomously, having, as it were, their own independent existence. Neither are they created incidentally, as a kind of accidental, haphazard by-product of growth elsewhere. Rather, they are part and parcel of the growth process in the core, and essential to it'.[34] Unequal development between regions and nations is the very essence of capitalism, and is, as Mandel suggests, 'on the same level as the exploitation of labour by capital'.[35]

These are the external factors that have pressed on the Welsh Development Agency, the Welsh Office and, after 1999, the Welsh Assembly (and Parliament) with regards to inward investment, yet this does not fully explain why these institutions followed the path of inward investment to such an extent.

The Welsh Development Agency as a quasi-autonomous non-governmental agency (quango) during this period did possess agency, an internal logic, and defined parameters within which it could work. It was not predetermined that the Agency would continually follow FDI as a policy aim in its 30-year existence, nor was it predetermined that the Welsh Government would continue with this policy after it gained the powers of the Agency in 2006.

The continuation of chasing FDI is instructive of how neoliberalism has become a hegemonic idea within Wales. FDI embodies the rationale of neoliberalism in important ways; firstly, as a form of roll-out neoliberalism, it holds that private companies, rather than the state should be the main source of employment, further eroding the linkages between the people and their government. Secondly, FDI shows how the cold rationale of the market has become dominant; what society may deem valuable such as local ties, social value, and linkages with the wider community do not factor into the decision-making process for those foreign companies looking to extract wealth nor for those governments looking to attract them. FDI leads to a race to the bottom in the name of competition whereby regions and nations – especially those that are post-industrial – are encouraged to chase inward investment.[36] This competition between peripheral regions leads governments to attempt to 'win' foreign investment by offering grants and by making their workforce seem like an attractive proposition (usually by alluding to lower wages in the case of Wales). The Welsh Government highlight this neoliberal thinking in their 2020 paper *A Framework for Regional Investment in Wales* in which they talk of the need to create a 'mobile', 'adaptable' and 'competitive' workforce.[37] This is, ironically, very similar to the divide and rule tactics the European Union use whilst creating trade agreements with African, Caribbean and Pacific States.[38] This form of governance has led to a situation whereby impoverished regions attempt to outbid (or undersell) one another, whereby the need for 'investment' trumps other concerns. Phelps and Tewdwr-Jones highlighted this case and argued that Welsh agencies were so successful in attracting inward investment due to 'their ability to establish streamlined institutional frameworks for dealing with inward investors, the most notable features of which have been site assembly *and overcoming planning and environmental obstacles*' (italics added).[39]

Concluding Thoughts

Exogenous forces – such as the election of Margaret Thatcher, and the rolling out of neoliberal capitalism via global institutions – were instrumental in beginning the neoliberal process in Wales. However, governments do have autonomy, even though they are shaped and influenced by external pressures. Welsh governments since 1999 have not tried to revert the neoliberalisation of Wales despite their rhetorical assertions of being radical and socialist in nature. In fact, their economic policy shows astounding continuity with the Thatcher-era. 'Neoliberalism by default' may best describe their policies due to a lack of ideological consistency *against* the spread of neoliberal, capitalist orthodoxy, and their subsequent rehashing of progressive neoliberalism. As Charles Bettelheim argued:

> A dominated country, or a previously dominated one that does not alter its situation in the international capitalist division of labour, merely reproduces its unfavourable situation: the more it increases the production of the products that its 'place' assigns it, the more does it participate in the worsening of its own unfavourable situation.[40]

Welsh governments have not attempted to fundamentally alter Wales' position within the international division of labour, instead our unfavourable position has merely been reproduced. Furthermore, both the Welsh Conservatives and Plaid Cymru vowed to bring back a Welsh Development Agency in some form if they won the elections of 2021. There seems to be an impasse between a neoliberal incumbent on the one hand, and the recreation of an agency guided by neoliberal logic on the other. Neither future seems particularly rosy.

It is important to remember, however, that although neoliberalism is deeply embedded in our society, and a 'definite form of life' has been successfully created in Wales, we should not fall into a spiral of defeatism. We must remember that 'the materialist doctrine that men are products of circumstances and upbringing, and that, therefore, changed men are products of changed circumstances and changed upbringing, forgets that it is men who change circumstances. … The coincidence of the changing of circumstances and of human activity or self-change can be conceived and rationally understood only as revolutionary practice.'[41] Our future can be remade in the image we want.

Furthermore, neoliberalism depends on the state for its existance. Whilst capital is global, 'the world today is more than ever a world of nation states. Global capitalism is nationally organised and irreducibly dependent on national states'.[42] Transnational firms take advantage of the spaces opened to them by neoliberal governments but 'transnational firms would not be possible without a system of states maintaining stable relations of unequal influence across the globe'.[43] By reducing the role of the state solely to one of facilitator, we create an ideological smokescreen from which neoliberalism can claim legitimacy.[44] Neoliberalism is not the only game in town, nor are governments powerless to fight against it. Most importantly, we, the people, are not powerless to fight against neoliberalism nor our governments when necessary. We must remember that a better Wales is possible, and a better world.

---

[1] Rhys Jones, Mark Goodwin, Martin Jones, and Kevin Pett, '"Filling in" the state: economic governance and the evolution of devolution in Wales', *Environment and Planning C: Government and Policy* 23, no. 3 (2005), 341.

[2] Wales Act 2017 (Wales)
https://www.legislation.gov.uk/ukpga/2017/4/contents/enacted

[3] David Bailey and Nigel Driffield, 'Hymer and uneven development revisited: foreign direct investment and regional inequalities', *Contributions to Political Economy* 21, no. 1 (2002), 57.

[4] Jamie Peck, and Adam Tickell, 'Neoliberalizing space', *Antipode* 34, no. 3 (2002), 380–404.

[5] Neil Brenner and Nik Theodore, *Spaces of Neoliberalism* (Malden: Blackwell, 2002), 37.

[6] Terry Flew, 'Six Theories of Neoliberalism', *Thesis eleven* 122, no. 1 (2014): 56.

[7] Nancy Fraser, 'Progressive neoliberalism versus reactionary populism: A Hobson's choice', *The great regression* (2017), 40–42.

[8] William Gissy, 'Political Economy of Violence and Nonviolence', in Lester Kurtz, ed., *Encyclopaedia of Violence, Peace and Conflict* (London: Academic Press, 2008), 1634.

[9] Wendy Brown, 'Neo-liberalism and the end of liberal democracy', *Theory & Event* 7, no. 1 (2003), 41-42.

[10] Terry Flew, 'Six Theories of Neoliberalism', 60.

[11] Andrew Gamble, 'The free economy and the strong state', *Socialist Register* 16 (1979), 15.

[12] Mark Fisher, *Capitalist realism: Is there no alternative?* (London: John Hunt Publishing, 2009).

[13] Karl Marx and Friedrich Engels, *The German Ideology (1845)* (1965), 162.

[14] See Leon Gooberman, *From Depression to Devolution: Economy and Government in Wales, 1934–2006* (Cardiff: UWP, 2017) for a full account of Wales' economic structure.

[15] Max Munday, 'Foreign direct investment in Wales: Lifeline or leash?' in *Wales in the 21st Century* (London: Palgrave Macmillan, 2000), pp. 37–38.

[16] Calvin Jones, 'Comparative disadvantage? The industrial structure of Wales', in *Wales in the 21st Century* (London: Palgrave Macmillan, 2000), pp. 12–13.

[17] Max Munday, Annette Roberts, and Neil Roche, 'A review of the economic evidence on the determinants and effects of foreign direct investment', *Cardiff: Welsh Economy Research Unit* (2009), 84.

[18] Munday, 'Foreign direct investment in Wales', 50.

[19] Max Munday and Annette Roberts, 'Foreign Direct Investment in Wales: Past, Present and Future', *Welsh Economic Review* 20 (2008), 20.

[20] Munday, Roberts, Roche, 88.

[21] Chen Xu, Calvin Jones, and Max Munday, 'Tourism inward investment and regional economic development effects: perspectives from tourism satellite accounts', *Regional Studies* 54, no. 9 (2020), 1231.

[22] Ibid, 1231.

[23] Welsh Government, *Wales in the World: The Welsh Government's International Agenda*, Cardiff, Wales: National Assembly for Wales (2015): 4.

[24] Welsh Government, *Prosperity for All – Economic Action Plan*, Cardiff, Wales: National Assembly for Wales (2017), 1.

[25] Constantina Kottaridi, 'The 'core-periphery' pattern of FDI-led growth and production structure in the EU', *Applied Economics* 37, no. 1 (2005), 108.

[26] Ibid, 108.

[27] Munday, 'Foreign Direct Investment in Wales', 44.

[28] Jones, 'Comparative Disadvantage?', 19–20.

[29] Munday, 'Foreign Direct Investment in Wales', 49.

[30] Ibid, 47.

[31] Dennis Thomas, 'Winner or loser in the new Europe? Regional funding, inward investment and prospects for the Welsh economy', *European Urban and Regional Studies* 3, no. 3 (1996), 227.

[32] David Botterill, R. Elwyn Owen, Louise Emanuel, Nicola Foster, Tim Gale, Cliff Nelson, and Martin Selby, 'Perceptions from the periphery: The experience of Wales', *Tourism in peripheral areas* (1997), 16.

[33] Robert Rowthorn 'Combined and uneven development: Reflections on the North–South Divide', *Spatial Economic Analysis* 5, no. 4 (2010), 364–365.

[34] R.L. King, 'Southern Europe: dependency or development?' *Geography* (1982), 224.

[35] Ernest Mandel, 'Revolutionary Strategy in Europe – a political interview', *New Left Review* 100 (1976), 46.

[36] Nicholas A. Phelps and Mark Tewdwr-Jones, 'Globalisation, regions and the state: exploring the limitations of economic modernisation through inward investment', *Urban Studies* 38, no. 8 (2001), 1254.

[37] Welsh Government, *A Framework for Regional Investment in Wales Securing Wales' Future*, Cardiff, Wales: National Assembly for Wales (2020), 27.

[38] Dennis C. Canterbury, 'European bloc imperialism', *Critical Sociology* 35, no. 6 (2009), 804.

[39] Phelps and Tewdwr-Jones, 'Globalisation, regions and the state', 1255.

[40] Emmanuel Arghiri, 'Unequal exchange: a study of the imperialism of trade', *Monthly Review Press* (1972), 296.

[41] Marx and Engels, *The German Ideology*, 163.

[42] Ellen Meiksins Wood, 'Unhappy families: global capitalism in a world of nation-states', *Monthly Review* 51, no. 3 (1999), 1.

[43] Clyde W. Barrow, 'The return of the state: globalization, state theory, and the new imperialism', *New Political Science* 27, no. 2 (2005), 127.

[44] Ash Amin and John Tomaney, 'The regional dilemma in a neo-liberal Europe', *European Urban and Regional Studies* 2, no. 2 (1995), 185.

Drowned Out: Wales' Absent Public Sphere

Dafydd Huw Rees

The problem with the Welsh public sphere is that there is no Welsh public sphere.[1]

Rather than a public sphere of its own, Wales has a niche within the UK's public sphere – and a small, inadequate niche, at that. The outlines of the problem are well known. Wales has very few indigenous media outlets, and those that it does have only reach a minority of the population, whichever language they use. The majority of the population consume UK-wide media outlets – that is to say, Anglo-British media outlets, typically based in London – which give only glancing mentions to Wales. Most people in Wales inhabit an epistemic environment which is, to all intents and purposes, entirely Anglo-British.[2] Under these circumstances the prospects for Welsh democracy are poor. The virtuous circle of feedback between the public sphere and the state, vital to deliberative democracy, cannot take place. In what follows I will concentrate on news coverage, since this is most directly relevant to the political role of the public sphere. But much could also be said about how Wales' absent public sphere constrains cultural output, impedes the development of a collective civic identity, and hampers the flourishing of the Welsh language.

The facts are discouraging. According to Ofcom figures, the most widely read newspaper in Wales is the *Daily Mail*, which in its print and online forms reached 18% of adults aged over 16 in 2020, making it the seventh most consulted news source in Wales. In contrast, *all Wales-based newspapers combined*, in print and online, reached only 13% of the population.[3] It is difficult to obtain reliable figures for the *Daily Mail*'s circulation within Wales, but it is undoubtedly much, much larger than that of any Wales-based publication. The *Western Mail*, which describes itself as 'Wales' National Newspaper' despite being confined to Cardiff and the south-east, on average sold only 10,341 daily copies in 2019. The North Wales-based *Daily Post* is the best performing of Wales' newspapers, selling 16,327 daily copies in 2020, while even the healthiest of the others, such as the *South Wales Evening Post* and *South Wales Echo* hover between 10–12,000 daily copies.[4] Nearly all of these 'Wales-based' newspapers are in fact owned by three English companies, Reach Plc., Newsquest, and Tindle. Reach (formerly Trinity Mirror Group), head-quartered in Canary Wharf, is especially significant. It owns the *Western Mail*, *Wales on Sunday*, the *North Wales Daily Post*, *South Wales Echo*, *South Wales Evening Post*, and their associated websites. It has repeatedly centralised its news gathering and editorial operations in order to reduce costs and maximise profits, cutting the number of journalists it employs in Wales,[5] and has ambitions to establish a single central editorial team for the whole of the UK and Ireland.[6] It is possible that within the next few years, all of Reach's 'Welsh' titles will be not only physically printed, but actually *written and edited*, from England.

It is true that print newspapers are a declining medium, and that their circulations have been trending downwards for decades, as their readers migrate online.[7] But note that the Ofcom figures quoted above refer to both the print *and online* version of these outlets. In other words, far more adults in Wales get their news from *MailOnline* than from all the Wales-based news websites such as *WalesOnline*, *NorthWalesLive*, and so on, combined. There are no solid figures about how much coverage the *Daily Mail* and similar outlets devote to Wales, but it is reasonable to assume that it is not a large amount, and not particularly detailed.[8]

In terms of radio and television, the major UK-wide networks, above all, the BBC, are in a commanding position in Wales. In 2020, 64% of adults named BBC One as a main news source, followed by ITV at 49%.[9] The BBC is in fact *more* dominant in Wales than in any other UK nation, with 34% of adults identifying BBC One as their 'single most important source for news in general', compared to 23% in England, 22% in Northern Ireland, and 18% in Scotland.[10] These TV channels may be designated as Welsh – they are named 'BBC One Wales' and 'ITV Wales', after all – but this does not make them indigenous media outlets. Even if they have some studios and newsrooms in Wales, they are ultimately owned and managed from England. Some of the programmes produced by the BBC in Wales – such as *His Dark Materials, Dr. Who*, and *Sherlock* – have proved very successful. But they are produced with a UK and global audience in mind. In terms of their content, they might as well have been produced in London, Bristol, or

Manchester. The hours of first-run programming produced by BBC Wales *for viewers in Wales* has declined steadily for more than a decade, from 821 hours in 2006 to 611 hours in 2017.[11] Commercial broadcasting has fluctuated in Wales since its introduction in the 1960s, with the HTV franchise producing varying amounts of Wales-oriented content between 1968 and 2000. This came to an end when HTV's owner Granada merged with Carlton in 2000. The Welsh nation-region franchise was rolled into an 'England and Wales' ITV franchise, which in 2017 produced 329 hours of first-run programming for Wales, carried as opt-outs,[12] ITV having come to an agreement with Ofcom in 2009 to reduce its English-medium programming obligation to Wales by 40%.[13]

BBC Radio 2 is the most listened-to radio station in Wales, with a 37.9% weekly audience reach, followed by BBC Radio 1 (23.6%) and BBC Radio 4 (17.1%). Compare this to 12% for BBC Radio Wales and 5% for BBC Radio Cymru.[14] Three companies, Nation Broadcasting, Communicorp, and Bauer Media, own all of Wales' commercial radio stations, and here at last we encounter a Wales-based media outlet which has some reach within the country: Nation Broadcasting, which operates seven stations across Wales, is headquartered in St. Hilary in the Vale of Glamorgan, while Communicorp and Bauer are based in Dublin and Hamburg respectively. However, all of these locally based commercial stations make up only 23% of radio listening in Wales, while the BBC's UK-wide stations make up 48%, and its Wales-based ones 9%.[15] Commercial radio is also exempt from any public service broadcasting requirements, meaning that there is no legal incentive to produce Wales-oriented content of any kind. Since February 2019, Communicorp no longer carries *any* locally produced content on its stations, after centralising all of its production in London. Nation Broadcasting now broadcasts entirely in English, after closing the Welsh-medium Radio Ceredigion in 2019. The BBC, which evidently does have public service requirements, claims that local news opt-outs (i.e., broadcasting a separate Welsh news bulletin on its UK-wide stations, to listeners within Wales) are technically unfeasible. Since FM and DAB radio use the same frequency for south-east Wales and south-west England, if opt-outs were introduced, around a million listeners in England would receive the Welsh bulletins.[16] It is apparently unacceptable for 1.8% of the English population to hear news which is not relevant to them, but acceptable for 100% of the Welsh population to do so.

Much of what could be called the *material infrastructure* of the Welsh public sphere (e.g. printing presses, TV and radio studios) is located outside of Wales. Where this is not the case (e.g. TV and radio transmitters, internet exchange points), the infrastructure is typically owned and controlled from outside Wales. Reach no longer has any printing facilities in Wales, following the closure of its press at Portmanmoor Road Industrial Estate in Cardiff in 2016.[17] The *Western Mail*, *Daily Post*, and others are now printed in either Birmingham or Watford.

Wales' eight TV and radio transmitter masts (Llanddona, Moel y Parc, Long Mountain, Wenvoe, Carmel, Preseli, Blaenplwyf, and Kilvey Hill) and their subsidiary relay stations are owned by the Winchesterbased company Arqiva. Arqiva was formed in 2005 and now owns *all* of the UK's radio and TV transmitters. It acquired them following the privatisation of the BBC's network of transmitters, along with those built by the Independent Television Authority and the National Grid, in 1997. Arqiva itself is owned by a group of Canadian and Australian pension funds and investment banks, Macquarie Group, Canada Pension Plan/Régime de pensions du Canada, and IFM Investors.

The picture is different when it comes to internet infrastructure, since this is by definition decentralised and distributed. Internet traffic is routed through local exchanges (LLUs) maintained by BT Openreach, of which Wales has 213.[18] LLUs in turn connect to larger central internet exchange points (IXPs). Wales acquired its own internet exchange point, LINXWales, in 2014, located in the Stadium House data centre in Cardiff,[19] supplemented by a second location, at New Generation Data's data centre in Newport – the largest data centre in Europe – in February 2020.[20] LINXWales was set up as a subsidiary of the London Internet Exchange (LINX), the UK's main IXP, but IXPs by their nature are collectively owned and managed by the internet service providers which make use of them. Ownership and governance of internet infrastructure can thus be more or less democratic and decentralised – LINX, for instance, is a non-profit company limited by guarantee – meaning that the issues of centralised control from outside of Wales do not weigh so heavily here.

It is clear, then, that UK-wide outlets drown out indigenous Welsh outlets in terms of the news received by citizens of Wales. 20 years after devolution was imple-

mented, and despite multiple commissions and commit-
tees which have repeatedly recommended the devolution
of broadcasting and an overhaul of media in Wales, Welsh
citizens consume news and entertainment produced
outside of Wales, and aimed at a generic 'British'
audience. What is harder to quantify is the casual erasure
of Wales in this news coverage, as when outlets refer to
UK government ministers as '*the* education secretary' or
'*the* health minister', despite health and education being
devolved areas under the Welsh Government's control.
The existence of devolution is ignored, and matters
relevant only to England are spoken of as if they were UK-
wide. It is no wonder that surveys have shown the Welsh
public to be worryingly ignorant of what is and is not
under their control, with a number of surveys showing
that as many as 40% believe health, one of the core
devolved areas, to be run from Westminster.[21] This
situation may have improved since 2020 as a result of
the Covid-19 pandemic, due to the clear differences
between Cardiff and Westminster's public health policies.
But the fact remains that when the public sphere performs
so poorly that citizens do not know what they are making
decisions *about*, their decisions do not meet deliberative
democracy's basic standards of validity.

Creating a Welsh Public Sphere: An Illiberal Proposal

In discussions of the inadequate state of the Welsh public
sphere, a few telling phrases recur: the lack of Welsh

media outlets and dominance of UK-wide ones is called 'market failure', and proposed solutions are described as 'creating a level playing field'.[22] These phrases are significant because they reveal the grip of neoliberal ideology on the way we think about the public sphere, and in particular about the potential solutions to Wales' lack of a public sphere.

The term 'neoliberalism' has been justly criticised on a number of bases.[23] It is fair to say that it is often applied much too broadly and without critical thinking, but for my purposes here I will stick to a narrow definition: 'neoliberalism' is the ideological formation which accompanied the intensification of free-market capitalism in Western economies after around 1980, characterised by the belief that there is no alternative to markets, that all human social activities are best mediated by market exchange. Markets are 'natural' and 'flexible', market outcomes are efficient and just, and state action is characterised as 'intervention', something inefficient, crude, and 'unnatural'. If the operation of markets leads to harmful or damaging outcomes – too little affordable housing is produced, or too high a level of carbon emissions – this must be an example of 'market failure': the market is not being allowed to operate *as it should*. The only permissible solution is to ensure that the market mechanism operates more freely, and in the case of a 'missing market', a market must be created by fiat. The housing crisis can only be solved by help-to-buy schemes for first-time buyers, enabling them to participate in an ever-inflating housing market. Climate change can only be tackled by creating a cap-and-trade system for carbon emissions, in other words a market for emission permits. Any state 'intervention' must be minimal, light-touch, and geared towards letting markets run free.

This neoliberal ideology blinds us to an important fact: collective social problems (such as the lack of a public sphere undermining a country's democratic viability) are often the results of markets working *efficiently*, not of their *failure*. It is not 'market failure' when Welsh citizens are left ignorant of the basic facts about their own country. It is not 'market failure' when 40% of the houses sold in Gwynedd are second homes. It is not 'market failure' when fossil fuel extraction is more profitable than renewable energy. In each case, the market is working perfectly: sellers are maximising their profits, buyers are having their demands met. When Reach cuts the number of journalists it employs in Wales and centralises all its operations in England, when Communicorp removes all locally produced content from its radio stations, when Welsh citizens get their news exclusively from the *MailOnline* and BBC Radio 2, they are following market incentives precisely.

The metaphor of a 'level playing field' is inflected by the same neoliberal ideology. The assumption here is that in an entirely free and efficient 'media market', Wales-based outlets offering Wales-oriented news could compete fairly with UK-wide and global ones. It is assumed that in the long run, the preferences of Welsh 'media consumers' (never 'citizens') would win out, and an adequate equilibrium level of Wales-oriented news and culture would be produced. The problem with the current situation is that competition between Wales-oriented and UK-oriented media outlets is not, in some way, fair and equal – the media market, which should be operating in an entirely free, efficient, and fair manner, is somehow being prevented from doing so. The absurdity of this metaphor becomes clear if we think for a moment about really-existing public spheres. Is there a 'level playing field' within France's public sphere between French and German news? Are exactly half of the media outlets presenting output concentrating on France, and the other half on Germany? Certainly not. French citizens are free to access news from German media outlets if they choose – and this is an important freedom, which should never be impeded – but their public sphere is overwhelmingly oriented towards France itself, as it should be if deliberative democracy is to have a chance. We do not need a 'level playing field' between Wales-based and UK-wide media outlets. We need a very, very *uneven* playing field, tilted massively in Wales' favour. This is no more than every other functioning democracy on earth has, and it is one of the things which makes them functioning democracies.

In line with neoliberal ideology, it is assumed that the only valid solution to Wales' lack of a public sphere is to encourage the 'organic' development of indigenous media outlets, and hope that these are eventually able to compete, on a level playing field, with UK-wide ones. Proposals to enhance Wales' public sphere, such as the IWA's 37 recommendations[24] or the periodic reports of the Senedd's Culture, Welsh Language and Communications Committee[25], stick within these parameters, a typically gradualist approach of light-touch nudges. The most top-down policy that political parties and civil society groups are prepared to entertain is the devolution of broadcasting powers to the Senedd.[26] Anything more direct, more interventionist – policies to *create* a Welsh public sphere – are rarely discussed. The idea here is that a public sphere must develop 'organically', that it cannot be forced into existence, and that trying to do so would be at best ineffective, at worst a violation of liberal democratic norms.

Here, again, we can see the grip of neoliberal ideology, in the unspoken belief that markets are natural and free, spontaneously producing valid outcomes, while state action is an *intervention in* these pre-existing markets, and as such heavy-handed, artificial, and of doubtful efficacy. The truth is that most markets, and perhaps especially media markets, only exist because of some form of state action. There is nothing natural, or organic, or spontaneous about them. States create markets by making some goods and services legal and others illegal, by maintaining a legal system in which contracts can be enforced, by providing a regulatory framework for transactions, and simply by issuing a currency which can mediate between supply and demand. Neoliberal ideology acknowledges this to an extent – as noted, setting up a cap-and-trade systems for carbon credits is an example of states creating a market by fiat – but it does not let this acknowledgement affect its core tenets. If really-existing markets – not the caricatures found in economics textbooks – are created, shaped, and maintained by state action, then the dichotomy between a natural 'free market' and artificial 'state intervention' is unsustainable. Can you intervene in something which only exists because of your intervention?

This is even more true for media markets. Public

spheres exist in their current forms because of patterns of state action over time. To paraphrase a point made by Tom O'Malley, 'public interventions in print are far more numerous and nuanced than the simple awarding of grants or the regulation of content. Government policy, and indeed government spending, helps shape the media landscape in ways that proponents of the "free market" would prefer us not to think too much about.'[27] The very existence of state broadcasters is, strictly speaking, an 'intervention' in the 'market', and a heavy one at that. The BBC does not account for such a dominant proportion of Wales' television viewing and radio listening simply through the operation of market forces. The reason that Arqiva owns all of Wales' radio and television transmitters is because successive UK governments chose to privatise this formerly publicly owned utility, and Ofcom allowed a single company to buy it. States can, and do, *force* public spheres into existence. Public spheres are highly 'artificial' things, which approximately fit the borders of polities and serve their democratic needs only because of many 'interventionist' actions by states, over generations.

Once we move past the crude ontology of an intervening state and a pre-existing market, a wide range of options for creating a Welsh public sphere open up. There are good ethical and political reasons for rejecting certain types of state action in the public sphere – censorship of content, most obviously – but these are independent of any concerns about supposedly 'natural' markets and 'interventionist' states. The devolution of broadcasting powers is an obvious first step. Whatever their ideological bent, many of the changes proposed by the IWA and the Senedd's Culture,

Welsh Language and Communications Committee are very sensible. Going further, Cymdeithas yr Iaith's detailed proposal for creating a network of new TV and radio stations, based on the Basque and Catalan examples, provides an inspiring model for what could be done with broadcasting powers, once they are secured.[28] The BBC could finally be compelled to provide Welsh news bulletins as opt-outs. Yet more could be done with legislative changes. TV and radio broadcasting licences can be rewritten to include much higher local content requirements. Existing newspapers, while fully retaining their editorial independence, could be pressured to publish Wales-specific editions, as they do in Scotland. Looking further ahead, laws and tax incentives could be used to encourage the development of accessible, Wales-based, locally owned media outlets. Building a new public sphere is not simply a technical fix. It opens up radical possibilities of restructuring our collective social life, a chance to overcome the exclusions and injustices of the public sphere as it currently exists.

For deliberative democracy to fulfil its promise, we must create our own public sphere. Stepping outside the neoliberal frame of reference is the first step.

---

[1] For a historical and philosophical account of the public sphere and its role in deliberative democracy, see Jürgen Habermas, *The Structural Transformation of the Public Sphere* (London: Polity, 2003), and *Between Facts and Norms* (London: Polity, 2004).

[2] See Daniel Evans, 'Welshness in "British Wales": Negotiating National Identity at the Margins', *Nations and Nationalism* 25:1 (January 2019).

[3] Ofcom News Consumption Report 2020, p. 86. See https://www.ofcom.org.uk/__data/assets/pdf_file/0013/201316/news-consumption-2020-report.pdf

[4] Circulation figures obtained from https://www.abc.org.uk/

[5] See https://nation.cymru/news/media-wales-staff-shocked-as-70-are-told-they-could-lose-their-jobs/

[6] See https://www.pressgazette.co.uk/reach-to-create-news-wire-as-part-of-plan-for-one-editorial-team-across-uk-and-ireland/

[7] https://www.iwa.wales/agenda/2015/10/the-press-and-online-journalism-in-wales-problems-and-possibilities/

[8] This in itself is a problem. Wales is *epistemically invisible* – few institutions collect data at the level of Wales, opting instead for the UK level, or subsuming Welsh data into that of a neighbouring English region, 'Wales and West' or, in the case of YouGov, 'Midlands/Wales'. Thus, among many other gaps, there is little solid data on the circulation of UK-wide media outlets *within* Wales. The invisibility of Wales makes it difficult to work out just how invisible Wales is.

[9] Ofcom News Consumption Report 2020, p. 86. See https://www.ofcom.org.uk/__data/assets/pdf_file/0013/201316/news-consumption-2020-report.pdf

[10] Ofcom News Consumption Report 2020, p. 88. See https://www.ofcom.org.uk/__data/assets/pdf_file/0013/201316/news-consumption-2020-report.pdf

[11] Ofcom Media Nations: Wales Report 2018, pp. 21–23. See https://www.ofcom.org.uk/__data/assets/pdf_file/0010/116011/media-nations-2018-wales.pdf Discussed at https://stateofwales.com/2019/09/the-welsh-media-vii-television-film/

[12] Ofcom Media Nations: Wales Report 2018, pp. 23–24. See https://www.ofcom.org.uk/__data/assets/pdf_file/0010/116011/media-nations-2018-wales.pdf

[13] https://www.iwa.wales/agenda/2015/11/few-successes-for-english-language-tv-in-wales/

[14] https://stateofwales.com/2019/09/the-welsh-media-vi-radio/, based on 2018 Ofcom figures.

[15] Ofcom Media Nations: Wales Report 2018, p 42. See https://www.ofcom.org.uk/__data/assets/pdf_file/0010/116011/media-nations-2018-wales.pdf

[16] National Assembly for Wales Culture, Welsh Language and Communications Committee, *Tuning in: Inquiry into Radio in Wales* (December 2018) p. 35. See https://senedd.wales/laid%20documents/cr-ld11993/cr-ld11993-e.pdf, and video of the relevant exchange between Siân Gwenllian AM and Rhodri Talfan Davies, then director of BBC Wales: https://seneddhome.com/2018/09/welsh-news-opt-outs-on-bbc-radios-1-2-not-technically-possible/

[17] See http://www.holdthefrontpage.co.uk/2016/news/trinity-mirror-set-to-axe-south-wales-print-plant/

[18] See https://availability.samknows.com/broadband/llu/exchanges?filterby=r.name&filtervalue=Wales. These LLUs double as telephone exchanges, and are hyper-local – a small area such as the Amman Valley alone has two.

[19] See https://www.linx.net/about/our-network/linx-wales/

[20] https://www.linx.net/contact/linx-news/linxcardiff-becomes-linxwales/

[21] BBC/ICM St. David's Day Poll 2017, tables 9 and 10. See https://www.icmunlimited.com/wp-content/uploads/2017/03/2017_BBC-Wales_poll_2017.pdf and Roger Awan-Scully's discussion of the results: https://blogs.cardiff.ac.uk/electionsinwales/the-bbcicm-poll-1-devolution/

[22] From the IWA's Wales Media Audit 2015: 'In a situation that requires investment and coherence, overall Wales has seen market failure writ large.' (p. 2) 'In overall terms Wales is seeing market failure.' (p. 6) '23. The UK Government and the devolved administrations, together with the European Commission, should institute an urgent review of current regulations and legislation to ensure that international manufacturers can guarantee a level playing field for public service broadcasters at the sub-national level.' (p. 9). See https://www.iwa.wales/wp-content/media/2016/01/IWA_MediaAudit_v4.pdf

[23] See Rajesh Venugopal, 'Neoliberalism as Concept', *Economy and Society* 44:2 (2015), 165–187.

[24] See https://www.iwa.wales/wp-content/media/2016/01/IWA_MediaAudit_v4.pdf, 7–10.

[25] Ably summarised by Owen Donovan: https://stateofwales.com/2019/08/the-welsh-media-v-the-welsh-news-deficit/

[26] E.g. the early day motion tabled by Plaid Cymru at Westminster in 2018, 'EDM 961: The Devolution of Broadcasting to Wales' https://edm.parliament.uk/early-day-motion/51432/the-devolution-of-broadcasting-to-wales

[27] https://www.iwa.wales/agenda/2015/11/should-welsh-government-intervene-in-news-coverage-decline/

[28] 'Darlledu yng Nghymru: Yr achos dros bwerau darlledu a cyfathrebi i Gymru' (2019).

Atomic Wales:
Embracing Nuclear Colonialism

Robat Idris

Nuclear-Free Wales

Are you sitting comfortably? Read this story of the
warping of a nation's political morality and decide if you
can still sit comfortably afterwards.

Once upon a time, back in the 80s, there was a Nuclear-
Free Wales. All Welsh local authorities had signed up to
oppose not only nuclear weapons, but also the building of
nuclear power stations. It was a stance which was maintained for years, even attracting an Early Day Motion[1] as
late as 2006, one of whose sponsors was Llanelli MP Nia
Griffith, later to morph into a gung-ho Trident supporter
when Labour Shadow Defence Minister. The motion was
also signed by Adam Price, then the rising Young Turk of
Plaid Cymru. The 80s were the heady years of Wales
against Thatcher, the Miner's Strike, Welsh women spear-
heading the Greenham Common peace camp – and PAWB
(People Against Wylfa B).[2] There was strong opposition
from all political parties in Wales – bar the Tories – to a
new nuclear power plant, and by November 1989 it was
all over, as the plan was shelved.

What has happened since then to persuade Wales, now
preening itself in the glory of having its own Parliament, to

capitulate to nuclear colonialism? And not just capitulate but embrace it wholeheartedly. What does this volte-face tell us about the crumbling edifice of what masquerades as Welsh democracy? What follows isn't a polemic about the many drawbacks of nuclear power, which are analysed in the comprehensive and sobering 'Uranium Atlas'.[3] Rather this article is a critique of the political goldfish bowl in Wales. It's a story of how a powerful lobby can have excessive influence in what are mistakenly termed the corridors of power. Corridors worn smooth by the expensively shod feet of the Welsh neoliberals. Corridors of complicity. Leek-flavoured UKism, even by those who claim to back an independent Wales. There can be no independence in a dependency culture, of which nuclear is the ultimate example.

Nuclear Colonialism

Wales a nuclear colony? Really? Let's see. The concept of 'Nuclear Colonialism' was introduced by American Indian Movement members and environmentalists Winona LaDuke and Ward Churchill. It describes the way that governments and companies cause devastation to indigenous peoples and their land in a systematic way in order to enable the nuclear cycle. Native Americans have suffered disproportionately at the hands of the nuclear industry, civil and military. LaDuke and Churchill's landmark 1985 paper *'Native America: The Political Economy of Radioactive Colonialism'* should be required reading for those within the political establishment in Wales who view nuclear exploitation as economic salvation.

While it can be fairly argued that Wales has seen a diluted version of nuclear colonialism, it is here nonetheless. Its corrosive influence has permeated into the very essence of Welsh politics, the educational establishment and the media – just as plastic has not only polluted the oceans but been incorporated into the very structure of marine life. And if we happily sign the Faustian pact, seduced by the whispered promises of the nuclear serpent, then we too are complicit in the wrongs done to other people all over the world – and indeed to our own environment and communities. If Wales supports nuclear, it is complicit in the wrongs perpetrated on not only Native Americans in the USA and Canada, but also on indigenous people in Australia, Africa, Asia and, historically, in Europe. It is also agreeing to build a 'house without a toilet', as our friends in Japan describe a nuclear plant. Nowhere has a satisfactory answer to radioactive waste been found – an answer which must be secure for thousands of years. Yet from the Future Generations Commissioner, complete silence on the waste issue.

Blinded by a single word – 'jobs' – buying into this dystopia has been the hallmark of the Welsh political establishment. And this despite the compelling evidence of the dangers of nuclear from Windscale, Three Mile Island, Chernobyl and Fukushima.[4] [5] [6] Could it mark the end stage of servile assimilation into the British state, where acceptance of the crumbs of largesse from Westminster confirms us as champion practitioners of Stockholm syndrome, finding reasons to be thankful for our oppression and exploitation? Could a Plaid Cymru-run Wales ever be truly independent if it was in hock to the nuclear industry and its shadowy paymasters? And for Welsh Labour, is a neoliberal Wales, perpetuating environmental degradation and human inequality, something it really wants? Or can we learn from the nuclear tragi-comedy to fashion a new Wales based on putting environment before pollution, people before profit, and communities before corporations, as Gwynedd and Môn-based community activists SAIL argue?[7]

The Nuclear Lie

But nuclear in Wales is for peaceful purposes, surely? Scratch the surface and you see it isn't so. How did it all start?

US President Dwight 'Ike' Eisenhower delivered his 'Atoms for Peace' speech to the UN in 1953 as part of a Cold War propaganda plan to promote the idea of nuclear to the American public who were wary of its destructive potential so soon after Hiroshima and Nagasaki. Under Eisenhower and dependent on the plutonium produced in nuclear reactors, US nuclear weapons rose from 1,000 to 20,000. The impoverished UK, starting to hang on to the USA's coat-tails as the British Empire disintegrated, was an enthusiastic pupil. Now we come to the lie on which 'civil nuclear' in Wales is founded.

The UK's civil nuclear programme was sold to the public as a way of producing electricity. There was no mention of plutonium production for weapons at the time – this was only admitted years later.[8] Trawsfynydd and Wylfa were pioneer Magnox nuclear reactors, coming on stream in

1965 and 1971. Their plutonium went to Sellafield to enable warhead production. Workers were led to believe that they were doing work of 'vital national interest' in producing power. However, it was a completely different type of national interest that they were facilitating.

The continuing link between civil and military nuclear has been exposed by University of Sussex researchers Prof Andy Stirling and Dr Phil Johnstone.[9] Rolls-Royce, who are leading the charge to develop a Small Modular Nuclear Reactor at Trawsfynydd, and possibly Wylfa, make no secret of the need to maintain nuclear skills for 'defence' purposes.[10] Military Wales and Nuclear Wales are inter-linked for the benefit of the UK, and both are welcomed by Welsh Labour's Government and the Welsh political class in general.

Fission Refreshed

The first generation of UK reactors slid quietly into the background. Thatcher's dream of building a reactor every year for 10 years was never realised. For a time, nuclear more or less disappeared from the political arena. It was not considered as essential to future energy needs as late as Blair's Cabinet Office Energy Review in 2002.[11]

Never a man to be put off by an inconvenient report, Blair got his way in a subsequent Energy Review in 2006.[12] Nuclear was back big time, with an ambition to build several new reactors. The green light had been given to the loftily termed 'Nuclear Renaissance'.[13] However, given what we now know, this seems a ridiculously naïve statement:

It will be for the private sector to initiate, fund, construct and operate new nuclear plants and to cover the full cost of decommissioning and their full share of long-term waste management costs.

It is hardly irrelevant that two years of relentless lobbying by the nuclear industry had been instrumental in producing such a turnabout in official government policy.[14] Such lobbying has continued ever since. The Planning Act 2008 under Brown removed obstacles and delays for 'Nationally Significant Infrastructure Projects' like nuclear and HS2.[15] The 'Nation' being the UK of course.

Chain Reaction

Wylfa was back on the agenda. This triggered a house-of-cards-collapse of our Nuclear-Free Wales, and ultimately gung-ho support for new nuclear. The efforts of Welsh Government, Ynys Môn and also Gwynedd Council were concentrated on lending political, financial and logistical resources to back Wylfa B from then on. The Joint Local Development Plan for Gwynedd and Ynys Môn adopted in July 2017[16] and the North Wales Economic Bid prepared in 2018[17] and signed off in December 2020[18] were written based on the expectation that Wylfa B would, indeed, be built. The politicians chose to ignore those of us locally and indeed worldwide who warned early on that the economics of nuclear didn't stack up. There was no Plan B if Wylfa B failed to materialise. PAWB's pioneer 2012 publication, largely the work of Dr Carl Clowes, offered an alternative route to employment on Ynys Môn.[19] It was totally ignored by politicians.

Massive political capital was invested in Wylfa, with further reserves ploughed into Trawsfynydd. Here's a brief timeline:

November 2009: Westminster announced a new fleet of nuclear reactors were to be built. First Minister Rhodri Morgan remained opposed to nuclear,[20] and so did the Welsh Government. Labour's Westminster Welsh Secretary and Welsh MP Peter Hain was predictably in favour, as were Ynys Môn's Labour MP Albert Owen and Plaid Cymru AM and then party leader Ieuan Wyn Jones.

December 2009: All change for Welsh Labour, as Carwyn Jones succeeded Rhodri Morgan as First Minister. Strongly pro-nuclear, having backed Wylfa in his leadership campaign,[21] he then took the Welsh Government with him. Conveniently, Ieuan Wyn Jones was Deputy First Minister in the Labour–Plaid coalition from 2009 to 2011, thus it was imperative that dissension within Plaid ranks was stifled.

March 2011: The Fukushima nuclear disaster. This catastrophic event heralded the start of the long, slow march back from nuclear worldwide – but not in the UK, or its fawning acolytes in Wales.

September 2011: At Plaid Cymru conference an anti-nuclear motion (opposed by Ieuan Wyn Jones) was defeated by one vote – a vote which was hotly disputed.[22]

The current position remains unchanged since then – in essence, Plaid claims to oppose nuclear, but not on sites where it has previously been established. As Jill Evans, former Plaid MEP and consistent anti-nuclear campaigner said at the time: 'People are confused on how we stand. If we oppose all new nuclear power stations we should say so clearly. Our own members aren't clear about where we stand.'

September 2011: The Jones family who have farmed Caerdegog for seven generations refused to sell land to Horizon. A rally in support was held in Llangefni in January 2012 organised jointly by PAWB and Cymdeithas yr Iaith (Welsh Language Society) and backed by Greenpeace.[23] [24] Horizon reeled from the adverse publicity. The Caerdegog family had no support from any political party.

March 2012: The German consortium of RWE/Eon, who had set up Horizon Nuclear Power in July 2008, gave up on nuclear and sold Horizon to Hitachi from Japan in October 2012.

June 2013: Ieuan Wyn Jones stepped down as Plaid leader,[25] soon to head up the establishment of Menai Science Park (M-SParc), an offshoot of nuclear partisan Bangor University.[26] New leader and anti-nuke Leanne Wood commissioned a discussion paper 'An Energy Policy for Wales' which specifically warned against the dangers of new nuclear.[27] This paper sank without trace as far as the nuclear element is concerned.

June 2014: Albert Owen MP and Jones' successor as Ynys Môn AM, the Wylfa backing Rhun ap Iorwerth, went to Japan on a trip paid for by Hitachi,[28] but didn't go to Fukushima. (To the best of my knowledge, not a single Welsh politician has visited Fukushima.)

February 2015: Naoto Kan, Japanese Prime Minister at the time of Fukushima, visited Wales, hosted by PAWB, and warned against the dangers of nuclear at Wylfa.[29] Welsh politicians failed to take heed.

May 2018: Hitachi realised that nuclear economics make no commercial sense and tried to de-risk the project financially by seeking assurances from May's Tory Government.[30] [31] A PAWB delegation visited Fukushima, Tokyo and Osaka and campaigned against Wylfa with FoE Japan and Naoto Kan, generating more Japanese media interest in the anti-nuke viewpoint in a few days than there has ever been by Welsh media here, in over a decade.

Meltdown

Following weeks of speculation, on 17 January 2019 Hitachi announced the 'suspension' of the Wylfa nuclear project.[32] A death in the family would hardly have met with more wailing and gnashing of the collective political teeth in Wales.[33] Ashen-faced emergency meetings were held to discuss what wasn't an emergency at all, but a collective failure to read the runes over several years.

Last-ditch lobbying and PR by Horizon Nuclear over the summer of 2020 came to naught.

On 16 September 2020 Hitachi announced that it was going to 'end business operations on the nuclear power plant construction project in the United Kingdom'.[34] On 27 January 2021 Horizon withdrew[35] its application to the Planning Inspectorate for a Development Consent Order, also announcing that Horizon itself was to be wound up by 31 March 31 2021. On 4 February 4 2021 it was revealed that the Planning Inspectorate would have recommended that the application be refused by the Secretary of State.[36]

What should be by now the Wylfa death rattle is being drawn out yet again. One prospective saviour already named by Skates is the recently bankrupt Westinghouse and its failed AP1000 reactor, now owned by Brookfield Business Partners, who have connections with the Saudi regime, potentially leading to Saudi nuclear weapons. [37] Nuclear colonisation indeed!

Another hat was thrown in the ring by Shearwater Energy, fronting a bid for twelve (yes, twelve!) SMNR's at Wylfa. It was investigative journalism by *Voice Wales*' Mark Redfern that showed that Shearwater Energy is headed by a loan shark.[38] Yet again, no such scrutiny was provided by mainstream media.

'Future Wales – the National Plan 2040'[39] still supports nuclear at Wylfa and Trawsfynydd. Predictably, the regular politicos backing Wylfa and Trawsfynydd now pin their hopes on one or both sites being selected as an experimental site for the untried, unproven, uncommercial and potentially dangerous so-called Small Modular Nuclear Reactors (SMNR).

Fallout

Over 10 years have been wasted by politicians across the political spectrum in backing Wylfa, with no apology forthcoming for this monumental error. The reality is this: the economic future of Ynys Môn, and the wider economic plans for the north of the country were placed in the hands of a room full of people in a boardroom in Tokyo. Prostration before the capitalist behemoth came to naught.

A generation of youngsters were drip-fed the prospect of well-paid jobs for life, from the educational establishment, from Horizon, and from the politicians. While the kids have been hung out to dry, many of the nuclear backers earned a good wage and many continue to do so. The bloated recipients of largesse from the nuclear bandwagon – much of it publicly funded – continue to thrive, for example at the Nuclear Futures Institute at Bangor University.[40]

Meanwhile as the Nuclear Neros fiddle, the kids drift away, the economy and language decline, and the housing market increasingly excludes local people. Wylfa's political supporters claimed to be acting to prevent the loss of youngsters, but it was their failure as a political class and the flaccidity of our political institutions which have led to this perfect storm of hopelessness. The siren call of nuclear drowned out every other sound. The need to develop a diverse economic base was neglected. Without a murmur of objection from any political party, many properties in Cemlyn next to Wylfa were demolished after the residents felt they had little option other than selling up to Horizon. At Tryweryn, a similar act of vandalism was objected to by all Welsh MPs bar one. Wales didn't have a Senedd then, but it did have a conscience.

Nuclear Bunker Mentality

The Tories, with current Boris acolyte and new Ynys Môn MP Virginia Crosbie to the fore, continue to salivate in public at the thought of Wylfa. As Dan Evans says: 'Welsh Labour's fixation with nuclear power is the inevitable, tragic outcome of their wholesale conversion to the rules of neoliberal capitalism.'[41] Moreover, oppressed by trade union support for nuclear, Welsh Labour continues to make encouraging noises with Ken Skates leading the charge, fully supported by Gwynedd Council leader Dyfrig Siencyn of Plaid Cymru. One wheeze is to establish a company called Cwmni Egino to 'help exploit the economic benefits of small modular reactors and associated technologies for Trawsfynydd in the Snowdonia Enterprise Zone'.[42]

Plaid Cymru, led by the 'economist' Adam Price, continues to be all things to all men regarding nuclear. Stating that he was against Wylfa B during his leadership campaign, he did this on the grounds that an independent Wales couldn't afford the consequential costs of the huge Hitachi project. By not taking a view on the principle of nuclear, he left the door open to smaller nuclear developments at Wylfa and Trawsfynydd, as favoured by elected Plaid politicians Rhun ap Iorwerth and Liz Saville Roberts. In a setback for Plaid grandees, anti-nuke candidate Mabon ap Gwynfor has been selected to stand in the Senedd election in 2021. The major abrogation of responsibility in Plaid is that those elected politicians amongst them who are known to be anti-nuclear continue, with few exceptions, to be silent. Since January 2019 PAWB and CADNO (who oppose Trawsfynydd) have thrice requested a meeting with Price to discuss nuclear, without the courtesy of a reply.

At the time of writing (February 2021) Welsh Government is reinforcing its nuclear fanaticism. It has signed a Memorandum of Understanding with the Sizewell C nuclear consortium in Suffolk.[43] Most bizarre of all, at a time of unprecedented pressure on public finances, undenied reports say that it is in talks to buy the Wylfa site from Hitachi.[44] [45]

Toxic Repository

What does the Wylfa saga tell us about our Welsh political process? It has shown itself to be in thrall to multinational corporations, subject to the economic whim of Westminster, and totally unwilling to engage and discuss nuclear other than in narrow economic terms – i.e., jobs. Environmental concerns, health worries, social infrastructure pressures, language issues have all been marginalised. The inclusion of civic society in consultation after consultation with few, inevitably cosmetic changes to plans, feeds into the wider disillusion with politics. The Hinkley nuclear mud saga is a case in point.[46]

The lack of independent Welsh media, and the incessant barrage of pro-nuclear messaging which has only been superficially interrogated by journalists, has meant that the general population has been deliberately led away from informed decision-making.

The wilful Canute-like obstinacy in the face of mounting evidence that nuclear is a technology of the past and rapidly being overtaken by renewables is a symptom of a malaise in the body politic – a manifestation of lack of self-belief, of capitulation to vested interests, of failing to recognise that big capitalism is inherently destructive.[47] This does not inspire confidence that the profits from a proper green energy revolution would not be exported to multinationals.

A democracy based on ignorance is no democracy. Our manipulated faux-democracy suits the political elite and their corporate backers as they pursue a failing neoliberal agenda on a wounded planet. An agenda embraced across the party, class and language spectrum at all levels of government in Wales. Culpability with no contrition. Failure with no flak. Hubris with no humility.

If this is what the Welsh state looks like, independent or not, then it is a failed state. Failed as a democracy, failed as an economy, failed as a guardian of citizens and the environment, and yes, failing future generations. Thirty-five years ago, LaDuke and Churchill concluded their paper 'Native America: The Political Economy of Radioactive Colonialism' with prophetic wisdom:

The new colonialism knows no limits. Expendable populations will be expended. National sacrifice areas will be sacrificed. New populations and new areas will be targeted, expended and sacrificed. There is no sanctuary. The colonialism is radioactive; what it does can never be undone. Left to its own dynamics to run its course, it will spread across the planet like the cancer it is. It can never be someone else's problem; regardless of its immediate location at the moment, it has become the problem and the peril of everyone alive, and who will be alive. The place to end it is where it has taken root, where it disclosed its inner nature. The time to end it is now.

---

[1] https://edm.parliament.uk/early-day-motion/29997/keep-wales-nuclear-free-campaign

[2] https://www.stop-wylfa.org/about-us/

[3] The Atlas provides an authoritative current overview of the whole nuclear military-industrial complex and says: 'Uranium has been extracted from the earth since the 1930s. It has left a lethal trail of radioactive contamination and waste.' There can be no justification for jobs if our greedy, needy hands are tainted by accepting an industry which has proved so destructive worldwide. https://beyondnuclearinternational.files.wordpress.com/2020/07/uraniumatlas_2020.pdf

[4] https://www.thelancet.com/journals/lancet/article/PIIS0140-6736(15)61106-0/fulltext

[5] https://www.nationalgeographic.co.uk/environment/2019/05/chernobyl-disaster-what-happened-and-long-term-impact

[6] https://311mieruka.jp/index_en.html

[7] https://www.sail.cymru/en/home/

[8] http://drdavidlowry.blogspot.com/2015/12/wylfas-secret-role-in-nuclear-warhead.html

[9] http://www.sussex.ac.uk/spru/newsandevents/2017/findings/nuclear

[10] https://www.rolls-royce.com/~/media/Files/R/Rolls-Royce/documents/customers/nuclear/a-national-endeavour.pdf p. 22.

[11] http://www.gci.org.uk/Documents/TheEnergyReview.pdf

[12] https://assets.publishing.service.gov.uk/government/uploads/system/uploads/attachment_data/file/272376/6887.pdf

[13] https://politics.co.uk/news/2008/03/26/hutton-calls-for-nuclear-renaissance

[14] https://www.sourcewatch.org/index.php?title=Energy_Review_(UK_2006)

[15] https://infrastructure.planninginspectorate.gov.uk/

[16] https://www.gwynedd.llyw.cymru/en/Council/Documents—Council/Strategies-and-policies/Environment-and-planning/Planning-policy/Anglesey-and-Gwynedd-Joint-Local-Development-Plan-Written-Statement.pdf

[17] https://northwaleseab.co.uk/sites/nweab/files/documents/growth_plan_doc_5_final.8.feb_.2018english.cleaned_0.pdf

[18] https://northwaleseab.co.uk/resources/north-wales-growth-deal

[19] https://www.stop-wylfa.org/wp-content/uploads/2019/02/Maniffesto-Mon.pdf

[20] http://news.bbc.co.uk/1/hi/wales/north_west/8351874.stm

[21] https://www.walesonline.co.uk/news/wales-news/carwyn-jones-backs-nuclear-part-2078172

[22] https://www.dailypost.co.uk/news/north-wales-news/plaid-cymru-split-over-plans-2684713

[23] https://www.youtube.com/watch?v=AjyOfyIFgTQ (In Welsh – worth learning the language for this alone!).

[24] https://www.youtube.com/watch?v=xF5ItE_oaOM (In Welsh).

[25] https://www.bbc.co.uk/news/uk-wales-22990696

[26] http://www.m-sparc.com/bangor-university

[27] https://issuu.com/plaid/docs/an_energy_policy_for_wales_-_unders

[28] https://www.bbc.co.uk/news/uk-wales-north-west-wales-27954336
http://democracy.anglesey.gov.uk/documents/s4730/Japan%20-%20Learning%20Journey.pdf

[29] https://www.bbc.co.uk/news/av/uk-wales-31651846

[30] https://electricityinfo.org/news/wylfa-74/

[31] https://beyondnuclearinternational.org/2018/05/01/welsh-anti-nuclear-activists-to-japan/

[32] https://www.hitachi.com/New/cnews/month/2019/01/f_190117.pdf

[33] https://www.youtube.com/watch?v=xzFk4QPdtxg&t=282s

[34] https://www.hitachi.com/New/cnews/month/2020/09/200916.pdf

[35] https://infrastructure.planninginspectorate.gov.uk/wp-content/ipc/uploads/projects/EN010007/EN010007-003962-DCO

%20Withdrawal%20Letter%20Horizon%20Nuclear%20Power%20-%20PINS%20January%202021.pdf

[36] https://infrastructure.planninginspectorate.gov.uk/wp-content/ipc/uploads/projects/EN010007/EN010007-003948-Recommendation%20Report%20-%20English.pdf

[37] https://www.business-live.co.uk/economic-development/interest-reviving-wylfa-nuclear-plant-19023018?utm_source=businesslive_newsletter&utm_medium=email&utm_content=BL_Wales_smallteaser_Image_Story1&utm_campaign=wales_newsletter https://www.world-nuclear-news.org/Articles/Westinghouse-sale-to-Brookfield-completedhttps://www.chooseenergy.com/news/article/failed-v-c-summer-nuclear-project-timeline/
https://www.theguardian.com/commentisfree/2019/mar/10/us-saudi-arabia-trump-kushner-mohammed-bin-salman

[38] https://www.voice.wales/wylfa-b-payday-loan-shark-behind-new-bid-for-nuclear-plant-in-anglesey

[39] https://gov.wales/sites/default/files/publications/2020-09/working-draft-national-development-framework-document-september-2020.pdf

[40] https://nubu.nu/

[41] Dan Evans, 'Nuclear Capitalism and the Welsh State', *Planet* 237 (February–May 2020).

[42] https://gov.wales/future-potential-trawsfynydd-site-strengthened?fbclid=IwAR0DOaCVuKekGOU4jOX5ZaPbvmi_V8AiXHVOxyGidViw1gYZtiZocrnt6sQ

[43] https://gov.wales/welsh-government-signs-mou-sizewell-c-consortium

[44] https://www.thetimes.co.uk/article/wales-bids-for-hitachi-nuclear-site-dj8vgj6lm

[45] https://www.bbc.co.uk/news/uk-wales-55970394

[46] https://nation.cymru/news/petition-against-dumping-nuclear-mud-off-cardiff-reaches-5k-threshold-for-senedd-debate/

[47] https://www.worldnuclearreport.org/IMG/pdf/wnisr2020_lr.pdf

In What Sense Sustainable?
Wales in Future Nature

Calvin Jones

Wales and the State of Nature

The entire world is awakening. Awakening belatedly and
slowly, partially and problematically, but awakening – to
the deep and comprehensive impacts that human activity
has had on the functioning of ecosystems, levels and
diversity of planetary natural capital, and the operation
of the Earth's climactic system. In few cases are these
impacts in any way positive. In most cases they are
traceable to the operations of markets that notionally add
economic 'value', whilst actually destroying complexity,
damaging function and turning discrete, beautiful and
perfectly fit components of unimaginably intricate natural
systems into waste and slag. If our intention had *actually
been* to increase the level of irreversible entropy in this
special corner of the Universe, we could scarcely have
done a better job. Wales is (politically at least) in the
vanguard of this realisation, and promising to do
something about it, through Acts of government that
require the public sector to take account of the environmental impact of policies, and of the well-being of future
generations – not just in Wales, but globally.

One can argue that this focus on sustainability arises

from an economic history that has shaped political preferences, individual identities and community values. The economic history of Wales is narrow, uncomplicated and (to broad-brush) binary between urban and rural. It is peripheral to UK and global cores in terms of control and capital accumulation. Wales' place in the history of capitalism is, with a few exceptions, that of a sometime-important but largely passive enabler. This history is also resource-focused, whether that resource is the coal of South Wales, the slate of the Gogledd, the landscapes and waterscapes of everywhere else, or the relatively cheap labour that filled the Asian-owned factories of the 1980s and 1990s. Small wonder, perhaps, that when Wales thinks of itself, the physicality of the country is recognised as important.[1] Also, perhaps importantly for future direction, the inability under either Victorian laissez-faire, social-democratic or neoliberal regimes to translate natural resources into widespread and enduring prosperity relative to other UK and European places is obvious – even as those resources become depleted and degraded.[2]

Is this then the worst of all worlds, economically and environmentally? Certainly not compared to much of the Global South, but sufficiently (and visibly) dysfunctional enough to drive a narrative of stewardship and responsibility within Wales' centre-left which syncs with more radical voices railing against the exploitation of resources by 'others' within commodified and poorly regulated systems – be these Severn Trent Water, property-hungry and monied immigrants, or tourists flooding from England to Eryri in Covid lockdown. Twin this with a desire for positive global engagement, and a sense of community and social justice that is strong in Wales (although perhaps in decline), and the positioning of Wales as a leader in environmental management, sustainability transition and post-carbon social organisation seems possible if not yet natural.

There is, however, a long way to go. The reality of Wales' position and role within global value chains is not magicked away by the Future Generations Act. The Environment Act will not offset the millions of tonnes of CO_2 emitted from the Tata steelworks at Port Talbot. And the *Size of Wales* does not halt the import of coltan-laden smartphones. The legal requirement to be globally responsible places burdens on Welsh policy that are hard to shift without a radical reassessment of how we obtain and use the resources that protect and enhance well-being in Wales – and indeed a reassessment of what well-being requires.

What the Environment does for Wales ... and what Wales does to it

It is fair to say (without seeking to claim equivalence) that Wales has developed economically in ways that echo those experienced in 'resource peripheries' subject to (and following) European colonisation.[3] Without wishing to diminish the activities of pre-industrial farmers and herdspeople, the story of modern Wales is one of immigration (and within-Wales migration) driven by for-export natural resource extraction, and by the development of industries (again, usually export-oriented) that gained an advantage from being close to such resources (like steel and heavy manufacturing).[4] This is not a 'finished' story. Through the twentieth century 'resources' become in part more human and less natural – critically relating to the excess (and hence cheaper) labour 'left over' from earlier resource booms, which became an attractor for both government-directed branch plants and investment from multinational enterprises. Still, however, the physicality of Wales is an important part of the economic story, for example both in terms of the energy and tourism industries which are embedded in the intrinsic nature of Wales.

In both these cases the nature of employment, value-added and economic embeddedness also brings to mind debates about resource-based 'enclave' industries in the Global South – in terms of processes, if not severity of negative impacts. Whilst the energy industry in Wales has important impacts socially, politically and environmentally it is owned and controlled almost wholly by non-Welsh entities, working within pricing and regulation systems that are also mostly non-Welsh in origin.[5] Whilst this is in part true of the majority of regions, Wales is unusual in that its economic peripherality means that it (or rather, 'Welsh' entities) lack the political, financial or social capital to engage in and control either the nature of its own energy economy, or to conversely exercise control over anybody else's – with key important outcomes.[6] Moving to tourism, we see an industry where local (within-Wales) ownership is more prevalent – contributing around half of economic supply – but where there is a distinct differential within the industry. Welsh-owned businesses tend to activities that are lower value added, (relatedly) lower wage and more precarious and higher turnover (B&Bs, taxis and restaurants) whilst 'non-local' (including rest of UK) firms are concentrated in areas which are more capital intense and at 'larger scale', such as larger hotels, coaches, ferries and (until recently) rail and air transport. This concentration of inward investment in capital-intense sub-activities, contributes to the fact non-Welsh-owned tourism activities are much more 'productive' in terms of value added per employee: they also display lower levels of local (within-Wales) sourcing.[7] In both of these examples, mirroring findings from 'less-developed' nations, limited 'value-added' processes happen within Wales – which remains at the wrong end of the value chain and with constrained economic (or developmental) benefit, yet with these industries having important impacts on landscape and people.[8]

This exploitation of the natural environment for little economic gain is then a notable characteristic of Wales, and one which raises serious questions about just how far Wales is away from genuine national sustainability and global responsibility, albeit with responsibility for this shared with non-national entities. To take the climate, we have a productive economy that is high-carbon, a public transport system not fit for climate purpose, a housing stock that is amongst the worst in the UK, and with key firms – Tata, Airbus, Aston Martin (but not, in the end Ineos) – engaged in hugely problematic activities.[9] We justify subsidising such activities financially to support jobs – because *of course* Wales cannot create its own, or do with fewer, and using the rationale that were they not in Wales, they would simply emit greenhouse gases from plants elsewhere (despite each of these industries suffering from structural oversupply in Europe). Twin this dysfunction with an apparent inability to keep our own environmental house in order, even where we have the legal competency and local audit, and we are long way from fulfilling our commitments on environment and climate responsibility.[10]

Despite this less-than-ideal starting position, there does seem some prospect of a more sustainable – and well-being aware – approach to economic development finding its feet in Wales, at least compared to that across our only border; additionally, the recognition that our resources are exploited 'on behalf of' others, is growing, linked often to the (at time of writing) growing support for Welsh independence. Politically however, there seems limited appetite to address the elephant in the room: that our environmental impacts are centrally driven by our participation in a poorly organised and deeply imbalanced global economic system that forces us to both produce and consume in ways that are not only climate and ecologically destructive, but also destructive of well-being.

What then is in Near Prospect?

Within Wales, the UK, the US and Europe the hope is to respond to the climate and (less talked of) nature emergency via a programme of adapting production and distribution systems within our existing economic model. These 'Green New Deals' are pitched as the 'other' game in town; a counterpoint to the wilful, greedy destructiveness of our current policies that is also a 'job creation' bonanza. They are, however, unlikely to work.

Firstly, a set of issues relate to the ability of capitalist agents – be these firms or governments – to act in ways which deliver necessary aims. It is chastening to think that even under a green-left government in the UK, the reshaping of our transport, broadband and energy systems would necessarily, given the almost impossible climate timescales and consequent inability to move actual activity in-house, have been delivered by Capita, Openreach and Serco under the for-profit model that is centrally implicit in the problem we are seeking to solve. More broadly, chasing ecological ends using capitalist means confronts the issue that the core requirement of private capital – generating not just a return, but the *maximum* return, on investment – is antithetical to sustainable behaviours. An obvious example is the private transport sector, where we have seen the Dieselgate scandal,[11] the massive growth in sales of heavy and polluting but profitable) SUVs, the success of rarely charged but very tax-efficient 'plug-in hybrids', and the market leadership of two-tonne-plus super-performance battery electric vehicles: all during a decade where the eco-climate catastrophe was clearly evident and urgent. No matter the sector or industry involved in any green new deal, in the absence of wholesale nationalisation or mutualisation, implementation actions are doomed to gaming, regulatory capture and outright fraud as agents fulfil their central objective – profit not planet.[12]

Even if the above problems were solved in a timely and holistic fashion, the Green New Deals proposed during the late teens would not suffice to address our natural crises. There is a problem with the scope of the current debate, which focuses on the role of industry and production in adapting to our ecologically straitened circumstances, whilst downplaying the radical changes necessary in wider lifestyles and behaviours. Proponents of investment to 'green' the economy rarely draw out the necessity for people to consume in far less destructive ways, and indeed far less overall. This means that Jevon's Paradox will come into full effect: savings from energy-efficient housing will be pumped into more stuff and more holidays, and better public transport systems will help already large cities grow even larger, sucking in more people to work there (and requiring more food and energy to sustain them). This lack of holism is stark. And without a wider, deep-green framing for why a green new deal is necessary, arguments for wider lifestyle change are harder to make.

This last point illustrates the most fundamental issue with positioning green new deals or tweaked neoliberal capitalism as the solution to our interrelated natural crises. Capitalist systems rely on an ever-growing economic base to reward investors and owners of capital (including almost everyone with a pension). Money, and hence the resources it commands, must multiply, and the lack of adequate multiplication is decried as recession and stagnation. Indeed, green new deal proponents often couch green investments in terms of kickstarting anaemic economic growth in Western democracies, with an old-fashioned Keynesian injection addressing this issue of 'secular stagnation' or the Covid recession. But a focus on 'jobs and growth' ignores the incompatibility of ever-growing economies with our ecological limits. What is pitched as more jobs and more prosperity is actually an ever-faster and ever-greater transformation of (largely) natural resources into useless waste; despite some improvements in the relative efficiency of resource use, the world has failed to decouple economic growth from resource throughput at the rate needed (or perhaps, really at all).[13] Energy saved as developed economies move from manufacturing to services is replaced by that used (and coal-powered) in Asian economies to manufacture goods that are shipped thousands of miles to Western consumers; smokestacks are replaced by server farms, and 'two weeks in Tenby' with multiple short breaks here there and everywhere. This is a circle that cannot be squared – or if it can, only within timescales orders of magnitude longer than those that we have imposed upon ourselves with our prior climate-impacting behaviours.

What should we do?

Debates around the greening of national or global capitalism are fundamentally flawed. They address *how* we do things, not *why* we do them; they focus on intensity and efficiency, not the absolute scale of activity generated by society and economy – but it is the latter that is the core problem. In Wales, however, we have, with the Future Generations Act especially, begun to address the 'why'. Perhaps what follows will be a focus on the real solutions: to restructure our economy to be respectful of global limits; to persuade and regulate against the unthinking purchase of consumer goods; to eat more locally and parsimoniously (and probably more plant-based); to scale back new physical investment in favour of climate-adapting existing structures; and to abandon hyper-mobile lifestyles for local work and fun. Of course, rather a lot of this is difficult given the limited devolved competence of the Welsh Government (and the rather problematic reality of Senedd elections) – but this is not to say that progress is impossible.

First, our elected officials might consider stopping doing obviously damaging things in pursuit of unattainable economic development or ephemeral voter approbation: the abandonment of the M4 relief road was a decent first step, although continued and non-transparent support for high-carbon inward investment projects is of some concern. Second, Welsh Labour in particular might seek to lead the uncomfortable discussions and decisions that are necessary to transform Wales into a more sustainable and fair society: their (still) relatively dominant political position perhaps allows a little more uncomfortable radicalism. Additionally, the implementation – the *real* implementation – of policies that further the Future Generation goals would seem to be an ideal mechanism for build of an alliance of left-oriented parties in Wales (either formal or informal) that perhaps avoids some of the electoral pain associated with speaking truth to voters, whilst testing mechanisms to address the imminent requirements to find a new way of doing business.

The even easier part comes first of course, as the ideas are there. Disinvestment of public sector investment and pensions from fossil fuels and other damaging industries, and towards (local) renewables, social housing and transport that pays back moderately but for the long term. A four-day week (not ruinous to productivity[14]) implemented across the public sector and encouraged in the private with whatever devolved tools we have to hand; a commitment to universal basic services (in the absence anyway of our ability to implement universal basic income). And a commitment to only enact government policies, programmes or projects that are *at least* demonstrably carbon-neutral: carbon budgeting that means something.

A general de-emphasis of paid work would seem to be a pre-requisite for genuinely greening the economy. Even if we take at face value the partial 'de-coupling' of economic growth from material throughput (although we shouldn't), and the reduction in commuting forced by the pandemic, the tools of work are still environmentally damaging, and more importantly, the consequences of (access to) work as currently structured are over-consumption, time-poverty and burn out for some, and actual poverty, insecurity and poor well-being for many, many more. This de-emphasis of course requires the thing that politicians and capitalists dread the most: (p)redistribution, and a significant reduction in material consumption, especially at the top end of the income scale. Only by reducing the frivolous consumption of (almost wholly imported) consumer goods could Wales hope to retain enough financial wealth (and, more importantly, people's time) to properly address the deficits in key, well-being-vital assets such as decent housing, transportation and public services – as well as the rebuilding of communities.

Hoping that national politicians will engage with this low-consumption, effectively degrowth (or rather, growth-agnostic) model[15] is perhaps optimistic. None of this will, or perhaps can or should, happen 'top down'. There is a strong argument that economic direction should be set at a much more local level where radical but embedded and bespoke solutions might emerge, crowdsourced and with firmer local support given their bespoke characteristics, but 'bounded' by the key red lines of the Future Generations Act. The political consensus in Wales has failed to produce the radical change that Wales and the World requires. It is perhaps time to give dissensus a chance.

Conclusion: What chance of any of this?

We can see Wales as a very atypical territory and nation in terms of how it has engaged internationally during the capitalist era; relatively poor and functionally narrow, and bereft of almost all power, except as a minor part of a UK that has spent the majority of the last 300 years either making the international economic order or helping the US to do so. In Wales, the neoliberal 'settlement' was not cast anew in 1980 but reflected and reinforced a relative economic weakness that stretches back to at least Henry Tudor, if not further; related closely to the resource-based nature of economic activity, lack of further local process-ing of those resources that would help command more of the value chain and critically, and increasingly over time, lack of ownership of resources by genuinely local and embedded agents. None of the ameliorative policies enacted by UK and Welsh governments or the EU, in good or not-so-good faith, have managed to address, or in some cases even understand these central problems.

Wales has not prospered (relatively) in the laissez-faire pre-war period, under post-war interventionist social democracy, in the Thatcherite consensus of 'competitive regions' that dominated from 1980 until recently, or under the whatever-it-is-we-have of now. This is an opportunity as well as a weakness. The physicality of economic activity in Wales, and the impact it has on territorial landscapes and water has opened the debate on how the perceived natural 'richness' of Wales has not translated to incomes or wealth – and indeed, how this follows from Wales' position in the UK and (perhaps less so) the international financial-economic order. There is also an emergent debate about how far the correct response to this imbalance is to fight for a (marginally?) better settlement, for example following independence, or to declare a plague on all capitalist houses and find a way of living that brings reasonable comfort for all, and is moderate, growth-agnostic, dependent on renewable resources and critically, globally just. At time of writing the latter prospect seems the less likely one, particularly within relevant climate timelines. However, the relevant legal frameworks are already (in part) in place in Wales, and there is a fast-increasing likelihood of catastrophic natural events and losses that bring home to 'normal people' just how much damage is associated with business as usual. It is a cliché no doubt, but Wales could and should be an important part of the process that moves humankind beyond the world-spanning, intrinsically inequitable and deeply ruinous capitalist system – just as we were in its beginnings.

[1] D. Llewellyn et al., 'Transforming landscapes and identities in the south Wales valleys', *Landscape Research* 44.7 (2019), 804–821.

[2] Natural Resources Wales, *State of Natural Resources Report (SoNaRR) for Wales 2020* https://naturalresources.wales/sonarr2020?lang=en

[3] See, for example, Eduardo Galeano, *Open veins of Latin America: Five centuries of the pillage of a continent,* (New York, NYU Press, 1997).

[4] C. Jones, 'Comparative Disadvantage' in *Wales in the 21st Century*, ed. by J. Bryan & C. Jones (London, MacMillan, 2000).

[5] J. Bryan, et al., 'Regional electricity generation and employment in UK regions', *Regional Studies* 51(3) (2017), pp. 414–425.

[6] Calvin Jones and Max Munday, 'Capital ownership, innovation and regional development policy in the economic periphery: an energy industry case', *Local Economy* 35(6), (2020), 545–565.

[7] Full detail of these results can be found in C. Xu et al., 'Tourism inward investment and regional economic development effects: Perspectives from tourism satellite accounts', *Regional Studies* 54(9) (2019) pp. 1226–1237.

[8] Interestingly, the landscape of Wales is both post-industrial and post-economic, with even locally controlled activities like farming and forestry only (just) viable via direct and hidden subsidies, and having deleterious impacts on local environment and the climate.

[9] Calvin Jones, 'Less and less favoured? Britain's regions in the energy crunch', *Environment and Planning A* 42(12) (2010), 3006–3022.

[10] Natural Resources Wales, *SoNaRR*.

[11] See https://en.wikipedia.org/wiki/Volkswagen_emissions_scandal

[12] M. Reynaert, 'Abatement strategies and the cost of environmental regulation: Emission standards on the European car market', *The Review of Economic Studies*, 88(1) (2021), 454–488.

[13] Q. Wang and S. Min, 'Drivers of decoupling economic growth from carbon emission – an empirical analysis of 192 countries using decoupling model and decomposition method', *Environmental Impact Assessment Review* 81 (2020): 106356.

[14] See, for the case in favour, A. Barnes, *The 4 Day Week: How the Flexible Work Revolution Can Increase Productivity, Profitability and Well-being, and Create a Sustainable Future* (London, Piatkus, 2020).

[15] See https://steadystatemanchester.net/ for developments across the border.

The New Dissent: Neoliberal Politics and the Welsh Way

Huw Williams

The structural upheavals of the pandemic, which have deepened capitalism's current crises, could be an opportunity for dramatic political change here in Wales. Possibilities abound, and a casual observer might suppose it is an opportunity for the Labour Party to reappropriate Welsh radicalism in a genuine way, and undo years of neoliberal politicking. The following analysis outlines why currently this outcome is at best unlikely.

Power in Denial

A prevailing attitude during the pandemic has been the defeatism, impotency and denial of responsibility that has typified Labour politics in Wales in particular since Carwyn Jones' ascendancy to the leadership. It also speaks of the hypocrisy at its heart. For example, after years of ignoring calls for the devolution of broadcasting, the complaints about the difficulty in engaging the Welsh public on Welsh terms during the pandemic are on a par with the well-worn tactic of Labour politicians campaigning against local NHS closures in Wales.

Installing Mark Drakeford as leader may have been

perceived as a wish on behalf of the majority of the party to develop a more ideologically robust politics that would bring practice somewhere closer to the well-worn yet empty rhetoric of radicalism. Some of his bolder moments during his management of the pandemic have been suggestive of this. After all, this is a man who came to power with a promise of twenty-first century socialism and a campaign supported by leftist Welsh Labour Grassroots – the home of Momentum in Wales and the group that has, since devolution, been the biggest champions of devolution and advocates for the One Wales coalition with Plaid.

However, in practice, this caucus may well complain that their service has been poorly rewarded by what has in effect been a continuity administration; despite some movement in the latest reshuffle, there is a major question around the decision not to radically reform the present group of ministers and advisers that has shown little sign of staking out a new direction for Wales, either before or during this crisis. Lee Waters, hardly a prophet of the left, might be seen as the minister pushing the envelope most during these past two years, with his mission of reducing urban speed limits to a default 20 mph. No mean task, but not exactly a programme of a twenty-first century socialist vanguard.

There are, however, deeper conditioning issues here than Jones' lack of politics and Drakeford's conciliatory personality. Hegel's analysis of the state and civil society, for example, encourages us to reflect on the conditioning nature of individuals' roles in society. He discusses the different classes and the manner in which their role elicits certain behaviours; it is difficult not to consider his thoughts on these conditioning factors without the Welsh Government coming to mind.

Specifically, it leads us to reflect on our politicians and how the lack of power and autonomy the Senedd wields may have inevitably created a political class that is less inclined to lead, because in practice policy-making has never been about staking out a truly different path for Wales (for all the talk of clear red water) but rather adding a Welsh veneer to Westminster policy-making. This technocratic approach, materially rooted in a comparative lack of economic, financial and legal levers, has become painfully exposed during this time of crisis, where the incompetence and inhumanity of Westminster policy is clear and we are willing our politicians to take a different approach.

There are also reasons to suppose that these attitudes have other, wider influences, in particular the general political culture that has emerged, in particular in the west, over the last quarter of a century. David Chandler's argument in his book *Empire in Denial*[1] was premised on the idea that the state-building programmes applied to failed states in the international context – like the social inclusion agenda in the domestic context – were nothing more than 'therapeutic' measures that were put in place to give the impression of politicians taking genuine action. In reality, however, they did nothing to address the deep, structural conditioning factors that create failed states.

This failure of statesmen and women to embrace their power and to set out a truly political agenda that seeks to reform basic structures – such as a global economic order dominated by the US – is in Chandler's view, a symptom of our time. Politicians in the West are presented as incapable of taking a political rather than technocratic approach, ultimately because they no longer take an ideological, transformative approach to politics where there resides a belief that underlying conditions can actually be changed. This is despite them still benefiting from a neo-imperialist world order that endows them with great power.

Ultimately, this is of course because a majority of western politicians and those who hold power are beholden to the neoliberal hegemony, and therefore have no wish to challenge the status quo, and act according to its diktat that the state must divest itself of as much influence as possible and allow the market to work its magic instead. Neoliberalism itself, if it offers any sort of guidance to politicians as an ideology, demands at best – in its 'progressive' form – types of action that expand inclusion and participation on a purely meritocratic basis and thus will never be reconciled with the type of far-reaching policies that are required in order to tackle inequality and marginalisation in a meaningful way. This aversion to state interventionism is sometimes reflected in the manner in which the Welsh Government, when not simply funding the private sector directly, 'outsources' even some of its most mundane tasks in an attempt to cloak its own actions and influence.

This speaks to the ideological vacuum at the heart of contemporary politics in Wales and beyond. Without bold, steadfast and principled beliefs, a politician's interest will not be to lead and tackle the relevant underlying factors, but in fact to deny responsibility whilst appearing concerned through applying measures that treat symptoms rather than causes. This pervasive culture is perhaps one of the reasons the actions and attitude of Jacinda Ardern, Prime Minister of New Zealand (former President of the Internationalist Union of Socialist Youth), have appeared so stark, in her principled, uncompromising and unremitting response to the pandemic. In Wales we talk of radicalism and twenty-first century socialism, but our political institutions seemingly defy the rhetoric at every turn.

Non-nationalists

Given Welsh Labour's very firm roots in the project of New Labour – that Chandler uses as his domestic analogue of political power in denial – it is worth considering how this cautious, managerial, technocratic approach is characteristic of the party, in particular when it is coupled with the perception that a more transformative politics is less of an expectation within a devolved context (although we should not forget that power over education and other policy areas could, in fact, be transformative – look at how certain areas, such as Preston,[2] have changed politics fundamentally at a local level).

However, there are other, deep-lying historical and cultural factors particular to Wales that are worth reflecting upon, as other causes of a seeming unpreparedness to grasp and wield power. This relates in particular to Welsh Labour's unwillingness to embrace the majority of support amongst its own voters for independence with a far-reaching ambition for at least a Confederal Britain. Whilst it has not launched itself on the same path to oblivion taken by the trenchantly unionist Scottish Labour, it has always been Welsh Labour's way to try and strike a balance between soft nationalism that allows them to assert their Welsh identity and claim to being the party of Wales, whilst at the same time being free to accuse Plaid Cymru of narrow nationalism.

Part of this reflects a genuine historic tie to the union and the idea our interests ultimately lie in our contribution to the UK. Part of it also reflects complex internal contradictions about how far it should exercise a more identitarian and aggressive politics. The performative contradiction is most obviously illustrated in the current complaints from Labour about the lack of a Welsh media, and it often puts Wales in a perceived weaker position – as when the First Minister himself claimed in Brexit negotiations that the lack of a bigger indy lobby weakened his hand.

What the crisis in particular has highlighted is that despite its best efforts to appeal to ideas like 'Welsh values', when push comes to shove the Welsh Labour party does not have within it the makings of a genuine spirit and national consciousness strong enough or sufficiently self-informed to provide the basic psychological strength and steadfastness to drive a forceful change of direction. One might, of course, pass a similar comment with respect to our self-professed nationalist party and the question of a unifying narrative.

There has been some controversy recently over the relevance or aptness of postcolonial studies to Wales, and without wishing to wade into that debate about the obvious limitations, it is very difficult not to read Frantz Fanon's reflections on the frailty of national consciousness in the Global South following decolonization without thinking that some of the comments are insightful with regards to a 'national' government that is in perpetual service to its superiors. What Wales has in common with some of those nations is that, until recently, national consciousness has not been tied to autonomous, national state structures in meaningful ways. Moreover, Fanon's insights into the ruling bourgeois raise difficult questions for our wider intellectual culture that informs our politics.

When Labour make yet another passing reference to Welsh values, without any notable substance, Fanon's words ring true: 'National consciousness,' he says 'instead of being the all-embracing crystallisation of the innermost hopes of the whole people, instead of being the immediate and most obvious result of the mobilization of the people, will be in any case only an empty shell, a crude and fragile travesty of what it might have been.'[3]

Fanon is fairly blunt about where the problem lies. It is: 'the result of the intellectual laziness of the national middle class, of its spiritual penury, and of the profoundly cosmopolitan mould that its mind is set in.'[4] These words bring to mind the type of clichés we seem to hear so often around Welsh 'radicalism' and 'internationalism' that are accepted but rarely interrogated, imbibed as they are from histories that are given elevated status in our public sphere. Moreover, when we consider the hackneyed old stereotypes that are taken to represent us (post-industrialism, rugby, a nation of singers and fire-breathers ...), and whilst we continue with our unwillingness even to accept the idea of a national history in our schools' curriculum, his words have a particular resonance:

> A national culture is not a folklore, nor an abstract populism that believes it can discover the people's true nature. It is not made up of the inert dregs of gratuitous actions, that is to say actions which are less and less attached to the ever-present reality of the people. A national culture is the whole body of efforts made by a people in the sphere of thought to describe, justify, and praise the action through which that people has created itself and keeps itself in existence.[5]

The New Dissent

The morbid intellectual and spiritual condition of Wales that can be read into Fanon's descriptions are clearly gestured towards in the late work of Gwyn Alf Williams, when he was responding to the devastation of the 1979 referendum in Wales, Thatcher's election, and of course the Miners' Strike.

An important symptom of 'The Welsh Predicament'[6] for him was the rejection of what he called – following Gramsci – our organic intellectuals. These were the people 'who exercised some organising, planning, expressive function – anyone in truth who was a 'worker by brain' ... Those people who whatever else they did, expressed, made historically operative, the consciousness of groups and classes coming into historical existence' in opposition to 'the kind of moral hegemony which was as all-engulfing as the air *we* breathe ... which made some thoughts virtually unthinkable.'[7]

When Gwyn Alf speaks of the Welsh organic intellectual, he speaks of a group that have been essential to the history of the Welsh – he speaks of the Gogynfeirdd, the Tudor humanists, Iolo Morgannwg and the Gwyneddigion, and the 'overproduction' of ministers, writers, teachers and industrial leaders in the modern age. 'It is possible,' he says, 'and, I believe, necessary to write the history of the Welsh in terms of their organic intellectuals'.[8]

For Williams, the No Vote in 1979 and the general elections of 1983 were votes that were the political manifestation of no less than the elimination of Wales and the Welsh from history through the developments of late capitalism. The rejection of its intellectuals was one of the more obvious symptoms, 'along with the concurrent bankruptcy of every political tradition to which the modern Welsh have given their allegiance, of the terminal nature of the crisis which now faces the Welsh nation and even more catastrophically, the Welsh people.'[9]

To survive, Williams believed that we needed a movement that would restore organic intellectuals, those that could fight back against the hegemony through our reconstruction and retranslation. It is here that his famous characterisation of the Welsh comes to the fore: the idea of us as a people constantly in crisis since AD 383, who have survived through our constant reinvention.

Was the campaign for, and then the creation of the Assembly ever the grounds for such a reinvention – a genuine intellectual and spiritual recovery? It is difficult to believe so if we look at what has followed since. Yes, there has been incremental increases in the powers of the Assembly, and recently of course a new name, but much of that smacks of an attempt to make good the shortcomings of the original institutional settlement rather than a desire for power to fundamentally change Wales. Neither has there been a groundswell of grassroots political activity or the reinstatement of the organic intellectual that suggests anything close to what Gwyn Alf thought was required.[10]

Instead, in fact, we seem to have the opposite – the denial of the will, a desire to turn away from the possibility of remaking the history of Wales and a thoroughgoing anti-utopianism. To call it *the New Dissent* mimics the manner in which we are always so keen to attribute our traditions and assumed values to the present but in a way that rings hollow. Rather than a dynamic, creative movement and crucible for the reinvention of the nation (as Gwyn Alf describes the form of Dissent that emerged around the turn of the nineteenth century) – in actual fact it describes a dissent *against* politics that has emerged in our era; a rejection of its core activity, which is the wielding of power, and the transformative potential therein.

It is also a reference to the old dissent of the Baptists and Independents – *Yr Hen Ymneilltuwyr* – as characterised by Iorwerth Peate, who argued it was reformed beyond recognition by the Methodists.[11] To him, the Methodists performed a corruption of tradition, in particular in their aspiration to engage with the world, reform it and transform it. The true spirit of the original

Nonconformity was to distance oneself from the world, seek salvation in the next life, and carry the burden of this life with dignity and patience.

This spirit seems to typify our contemporary response to the ongoing crisis of capitalism: an acceptance of the system and the circumstances it creates, a rejection of the idea that we can engage and transform the world leading us only to work within its constraints, and a pervasive attitude that we are seeking only some form of individual contentment. We see only occasional exceptions to this attitude: a display of the will to struggle, an acceptance of responsibility, and attempt to try to bend the world to our will. And of course, whilst the old dissenters crucially held to a justificatory belief in the promise of the afterlife and the eternal soul, no such salvation is offered up in the New Dissent. Just a meek, arid acceptance of a materialism that permeates all aspects of our lives through the neoliberal hegemony, one that offers nothing but spiritual penury.

Now or Never?

It should be recognised that this is not an affliction merely of the Labour Party. One of the most deflating examples of the ubiquity of this condition was Plaid Cymru's response in Gwynedd and Ynys Môn when the Local Development Plan was under review.[12] The justifications for supporting housing schemes shown to be potentially damaging for the Welsh language community reflected either a tendency to deny responsibility or to bow to the inevitable predominance of the market: some argued there was little that could be done to rail against the Welsh Government's diktat, while others argued that thousands of houses were required, in order for the market to operate for the benefit of local people by maintaining a large supply that would lower prices.

If our opposition party, borne from a single-minded desire to protect and maintain our language and identity, can be prepared to subside to the apparently predetermining forces of neoliberalism, one is left asking the question raised by Gwyn Alf Williams: 'whether any kind of real Wales and real Welsh can survive?'[13] The polarization of politics in Wales, the emergence of an independence movement with the vitality to take on a revanchist British nationalism, expressed most recently through calls to abolish our parliament, suggests we are on the precipice of yet another final reckoning. For that movement to succeed, it must also recognise that it is the capitalist core of Britishness that renders it a mortal enemy. It would be no small irony if this small collection of people, bound together by a millennium and a half of perpetual crisis, should lose its will to endure at the very moment a global crisis enables the supplanting of those structures that has kept it on the brink, for so very long.

A version of this essay first appeared on the website of O'r Pedwar Gwynt.

---

[1] David Chandler, Empire in Denial: The Politics of State-Building (London: Pluto, 2006).

[2] Matthew Brown and Rhian E. Jones, *Paint your town red: How Preston took back control and your town can too* (London: Repeater, 2021).

[3] Frantz Fanon, *The Wretched of the Earth* (London: Penguin Classics, 1990 [1961]), p. 19.

[4] Ibid.

[5] Ibid, p. 188.

[6] Gwyn A. Williams, *Sardinian Marxist and the Welsh Predicament* (Radical Wales, 1985).

[7] Ibid, p. 19.

[8] Ibid.

[9] Ibid.

[10] All of which suggests the acuity of Dan Evans' deployment of another Gramscian concept, *'passive revolution'*, to understand devolution. See 'Devolution's Passive Revolution' IWA, 31 October 2015. https://www.iwa.wales/agenda/2015/10/devolutions-passive-revolution/

[11] Iorwerth C. Peate, *Y Meddwl Ymneilltuol,* Efrydiau Athronyddol, XIV, 1951, 1–11.

[12] Huw L. Williams, 'Building 8000 new homes in Gwynedd and Môn is a defeat for Welsh Democracy' in Nation.Cymru https://nation.cymru/opinion/new-homes-gwynedd-mon-plaid-cymru-welsh-democracy-labour/

[13] Williams, *Sardinian Marxist and the Welsh Predicament,* p. 21.

POLICY FIELDS

Standardising Wales: Divergence and Convergence in Welsh Education Policy

Dan Evans

Every three years, the Programme for International Student Assessment (PISA) ranks seventy-two national educational systems from across the world. The United Kingdom originally appeared on the list as a whole, and it scored respectably. However, when the results separated the four UK home nations in 2006, they showed that Wales was performing very badly. Welsh children lagged behind the rest of the United Kingdom – and indeed much of the world – in literacy, numeracy, and science.

There hasn't been much improvement since then. Wales scored the lowest in the UK in 2009, 2012, and again in 2016 and 2018. Because of Covid, the PISA assessments scheduled for 2021 have now been delayed until 2022.

Successive low scores have created an existential crisis within Welsh education and within the country more generally. The idea that our kids are thick and our schools are useless has rapidly become the national common sense. The Welsh media participates in the ritual by enviously comparing Wales to countries with semi-militarized education systems, which, despite their success in literacy and numeracy, push children to breaking point.

PISA as an Example of Soft Power Neoliberalism

PISA appears to have entirely benign goals. Its introductory video explains that the program determines 'whether fifteen-year-olds are acquiring the social and emotional skills they will need to thrive, like knowing how to work and communicate with others'. Its ranking system helps PISA identify good practices in education in order 'not only to show how these systems are constructed, but to encourage countries to learn from each other's experience in building fairer, more inclusive school systems'.[1]

This façade masks a number of serious issues. First, the program suffers from quite basic and well-documented sampling problems, including its use of imputed scores and the fact that it doesn't produce truly longitudinal data.[2] More than that, however, PISA simply doesn't measure like with like. Is it valid to compare an extremely deprived country of three million to the world's sixth wealthiest country with 53 million people?

Dissatisfied with PISA, Rees & Taylor came up with an alternative model for measuring educational attainment. When they compared Wales to a composite nation comprised of English counties facing similar social problems wrought by similar deindustrialisation, Wales did relatively well.

Yet PISA's issues run deeper than sampling or method. For all its egalitarian rhetoric, it symbolises the deep structural changes that have occurred within world education since the neoliberal turn.

Starting in the 1970s, the basis of the world economy shifted. Advanced capitalist economies moved away from manufacturing and resource extraction, and those sectors migrated to poorer countries. Places like the United Kingdom and United States began to measure their economic growth and success on 'knowledge', which was subsequently transformed into a commodity. The population's 'intelligence' and 'skills' became a country's main natural resource, and governments started prioritising information, technology, and education over production.

Education is now central to the global capitalist economy. However, this is rarely done with local interests in mind. Companies looking to invest require knowledge about the labour pool in each country: what sort of jobs can this population do? Are they smart enough to do research and design, or are they just good for assembling things on a conveyor belt? Will they ask for high wages, or will they be happy with nothing? Are they likely to unionise and cause problems for us? As part of the Organisation of Economic Co-operation and Development's educational component, PISA fills this need to quantify and profile different countries for companies looking to invest. This is its main function: a vital pillar of global capitalist trade and investment. Moreover, higher-level skills are rarely taught for the benefit of local communities. Instead, neoliberal universities champion the idea of higher education as a shared pool of globalised knowledge, with academics free to travel peripatetically around the world being experts, with little intellectual allegiance to the communities in which they work.

Thatcher famously claimed that neoliberal economic policy was not the end in itself, but rather a way of changing a society's heart and soul, of altering its *values*.

Nowhere can we see this more clearly than in education, where neoliberalism's seductive logic has fundamentally altered both its purpose and its nature. While education has always been linked to the economy to some extent, society's understanding of *why* education matters has fundamentally changed since the neoliberal turn. Today, it is commonsensical that the sole purpose of education is to give children 'skills' to grow the 'knowledge economy', which helps explain why bosses' organisations like the CBI routinely weigh in on school reform. Individuals are encouraged to accrue qualifications to build capital that will help them find a job. Education no longer appears as a public good in its own right; if it doesn't benefit the economy, narrowly defined, it is pointless. Notions about cultural development, personal fulfilment, and civic participation seem outdated. This is particularly painful to reflect upon in Wales, a country with a long and proud tradition of workers' and adult self-education: industrial communities in the past clubbed together to build libraries and miner's institutes, where working-class people came together to learn about the world – not to advance their career, but to help their community and to help the cause of socialism.

If education's function has changed, so too has its *content*. Subjects that add no tangible value to the economy – like art, music, and sociology – have been marginalised in favour of hard sciences. The world needs engineers and web developers, not sculptors, poets and theorists. In a world where everything is quantifiable, teaching and education now focus on producing *data*. Schools test children to track their progress, and schools and teachers themselves must be tested to ensure that they are delivering high-quality services. This culture forces schools and schoolchildren to compete with one another. It discourages solidarity and encourages over-whelmed teachers to begin 'teaching to the test'. In this standardised model, coursework is designed only to prepare children to pass exams. It no longer imparts an in-depth understanding of or deep interest in the topic. These unquantifiable achievements don't improve league-table standings, after all.

All this is why the Finnish educator Pasi Sahlberg clas-sifies PISA-driven global reforms by the acronym GERM: Global Educational Reform Movement, characterised by privatisation, market-driven reforms, free school choice, competition and test-driven accountability.[3]

Devolution and Education

In Britain, as the economy moved toward services, inno-vation, and culture, Tony Blair and New Labour enthusiastically embraced the 'knowledge economy' and became obsessed with using education to drive economic growth. Although New Labour retained residual elements of old Labourism, its approach to the school system faith-fully followed Tory reforms, espousing a managerial, conservative ethos, personified by the scarily right-wing education minister, David Blunkett. They retained school league tables to ensure efficiency, and launched the Private Finance Initiative (PFI) to allow private providers to enter the educational sector. Under New Labour, education focused on delivering higher standards to parents and children, who were clearly positioned as *consumers of a product*, and teachers buckled in for a tougher life. Parental choice – which often set parents against teachers and staff – became the new mantra. The government and media began treating educators as a vested interest that selfishly refused to be held accountable for their performance, and Blunkett repeatedly attacked progressive forms of pedagogy, insisting instead that schools return to traditional, whole-class teaching and emphasise the 'three Rs' to raise standards.

Before 1999, the Welsh education system, with some significant exceptions, closely resembled England's. After devolution, however, Welsh ministers became responsible for every element of education except for teachers' pay. They made the most of their new freedom: Jane Davidson, the Minister for Education and Lifelong Learning from 2000 to 2007, explicitly linked education to social justice, clearly departing from the path taken by New Labour in England.

The Welsh Government established a children's commissioner, stating that it intended to put children and education at the heart of society. In 2001, it abolished school league tables and, in 2004, got rid of the national standardised text, a move which teachers' unions welcomed.[4]

A firm belief in its comprehensive-school system means that Wales resisted the introduction of so-called free schools, and today has no selective grammar schools, and no 'academies'. In 2005, the government introduced school councils to give students an active role in their school's management. On top of this, the Welsh Government developed initiatives, including Flying Start (2006–7) and the pupil deprivation grant (launched in 2012), designed to help the most deprived students. Davidson, herself a former teacher, adopted a more conciliatory tone with teachers and teaching unions than her English counterparts.

Davidson also oversaw curricular revisions. Drawing on progressive experiments from across the world, the government introduced their flagship Foundation Phase for children aged three to seven, a play-based program meant to replace the more formal key stage 1. In 2003, Wales piloted its new baccalaureate qualification, which offered a broader curriculum that encouraged community service and 'soft skills'.

In the early years of devolution, no field personified the concept of 'clear red water' better than education.

Counter-revolution

PISA changed all of this. In 2006, following the Daugherty Review's recommendations, Davidson entered Wales into the PISA program. Before the first report came out, however, Jane Hutt had taken over as minister.

In the first PISA scores, Wales didn't score exceptionally well, but it also didn't rank significantly lower than the other home nations. Hutt reacted to the news coolly. She claimed that her priority was 'to secure better outcomes for learners, not just to score highly in PISA rankings,' but she also acknowledged 'the importance of PISA as a yardstick against which we can measure our progress.'[5] During her two years in office, Hutt made no changes to Davidson's programs, explaining that she wanted to give her predecessor's policies time to work.

Her short tenure was the calm before the storm. In late 2009, she was replaced by Leighton Andrews. The PISA results that came out in 2010 – in which Wales scored poorly – had a profound impact on Andrews' time as education minister and on the Welsh educational system.

In contrast to Hutt's sanguine reaction, Andrews called the results 'a wake-up call to an education system in Wales that has become complacent, falling short of being consistently good and not delivering the outcomes our learners deserved.'[6] Rather than consider the low baseline from which Wales started or focus on relatively high levels of student well-being, or indeed the broader evidence regarding deindustrialisation and poverty and its inevitable impact on educational attainment, Andrews became fixated on climbing the PISA league tables. He ambitiously promised that Wales would become one of the top twenty nations for reading by 2015.

Andrews set about his task with a fanatical sense of purpose, initiating a wide-ranging set of reforms and dismantling many of Davidson's initiatives. He introduced a twenty-point plan, 'driven by performance' and guided by the OECD. Advisers who disagreed with him left the government quickly. Andrews prioritised 'performance', which he narrowly defined as literacy and numeracy scores measured against international peers.

Crucially, two years into Andrews' tenure, Labour won a majority in the 2011 Welsh elections. As a result,

Andrews no longer had to appease Plaid Cymru, who had been dragging Welsh Labour to the left, giving him free rein to implement his 'vision'. Shortly after Labour began to govern alone, Andrews reintroduced the hated school league tables, now called banding. He also reinstated literacy and numeracy tests and frameworks, with the explicit aim of driving up Wales' PISA score.

While these reforms were very much neoliberal and in keeping with the strategy adopted by New Labour in England, in a case study of Welsh Labour's MO, Andrews continuously deployed progressive rhetoric to justify them. He dismissed initiatives he did not agree with as 'libertarian', contrary to Wales' 'communitarian' Labour traditions.

He applied this logic selectively, however. Allowing children to develop at their own pace (pupil choice) counted as a 'libertarian' program, while league tables, which foster parental choice, were progressive because they inform working-class parents about their child's education. The Welsh media adored Andrews, smitten by his confrontational style. Every fight he picked gave them good copy, and they enthusiastically backed his reforms, claiming that Davidson had removed key 'accountability mechanisms' and had given 'complacent' teachers too much autonomy. The BBC billed Andrews' agenda as 'one of the most radical and ambitious reform programmes that Welsh education has ever seen'.

Surrounded by special advisers drafted in from New Labour in England, Andrews became obsessed with the notion that 'better teaching' could solve all the nation's problems. His school improvement program, which focused on reforming teaching, crystallised these illusions.[7]

Andrews' initiatives put immense pressure on belea-guered teachers, who began to suffer from 'initiative fatigue', as the government impatiently introduced, then quickly revised, new programmes before they had a chance to take root, leaving schools and teachers reeling.[8]

Unions argued that the increased workload, pressure, and scrutiny was crushing morale and pushing teachers to the breaking point.[9] Schools felt stigmatised by the new league tables, and teachers shelved community engage-ment and extracurricular activities in order to teach to the test and get children to meet the new standards. WISERD's (Wales Institute of Social and Economic Research) survey of Welsh teachers in 2014 painted a picture of a profession in crisis, struggling to cope with Andrews' neoliberal reforms.[10] 63.5% of teachers surveyed claimed that the Welsh Government did not listen to teachers, while 52.3% said they felt demoralised. This was unsurprising: the Jones government slashed the education budget. From 2010 to now, schools lost 9% of funding – equivalent to £500 per pupil.[11] Thus Andrews was asking beleaguered teachers to do more with less.

Predictably, Andrews' punitive reforms failed to raise standards. In fact, when the 2012 PISA results came out, Welsh scores in maths and science had actually *decreased*.

Andrews banked on winning political capital by improving the nation's educational system and taking on the so-called 'vested interests' who were blocking progress (i.e., teachers). As each passing year brought no miracu-lous breakthroughs, his tone became more confrontational, angrily blaming teachers for letting his project down. Eventually, Andrews suffered a farcical demise when he resigned after being caught protesting the implementation of his own school closure policies – a hubristic fall from grace that could only happen in Wales.

Conclusion

The trajectory of Welsh education is a tragic metaphor for the failures of devolution and the hollowness of Welsh Government claims of radicalism. Progressive, albeit moderate reforms in the early years of devolution were rapidly abandoned in favour of a wholesale internalisation and embrace of the neoliberal model of education by the Welsh Government, although this was, as usual, camouflaged by radical rhetoric and the Welsh tendency to only compare ourselves to England.

As reams of empirical research demonstrates, the reality behind the rhetoric is overstretched, overstressed teachers, cuts to education budgets, unhappy, over-tested children, exemplified by a huge demand for educational psychiatrists.

This reality, which is glaring for those engaged in frontline education work, has been masked by the conscious marginalisation of the dissenting voices of teachers' unions and the voices of children in particular by a Welsh political and media class which has bought in wholesale to neoliberalism. Andrews may have left government, but he managed to shift Wales' education paradigm, bringing it in line with the new global common sense regarding what education looks like and is for.

Another 'modernizer', former teacher and Blairite Huw

Lewis, took over from Andrews in June 2013, and continued his reforms, although also commissioned a review of the Welsh curriculum – led by Graham Donaldson – which has led to the new 'Successful Futures' curriculum.

Lewis stood down in 2016. His replacement, the Liberal Democrat Kirsty Williams, was tasked with implementing this new curriculum, which constitutes the biggest structural change to education since devolution.

Despite being hailed by the supine Welsh media and political class, teachers' unions and academics have expressed serious concerns with the new curriculum, including that it removes teacher autonomy; that it clashes with the existing neoliberal 'accountability' framework of examination and inspection; and that it is unclear how it is going to be actually implemented.[12]

Another WISERD teacher survey from 2017 echoed these concerns. 53.6% of teachers felt the Welsh Government did not listen to them; 56.1% felt that new initiatives were not based on the views or input of teachers; 46.7% felt undervalued in Welsh society; 54.9% felt that new initiatives were not accompanied by enough guidance from the Welsh Government; 62.2% felt PISA had been unhelpful to them as teachers; 56.3% felt they did not have enough non-contact time for preparation. Incredibly, nearly 30% felt they would leave the profession within 5 years. Follow-up qualitative interviews with head teachers demonstrated huge anxiety about the implementation of the new curriculum, a lack of clarity of its purpose and a lack of funding and guidance. Power, Newton and Taylor have argued that without specific guidelines about implementation and care, the new curriculum may entrench existing inequalities in the education system.[13]

Significant concerns have also been raised about how the new curriculum will be resourced in the face of year-on-year funding cuts to education in Wales. Jones for example writes that

> delivery of the vision for schools ... significantly exceed the current resource base of the sector. This would be true in all probability even without a decade of austerity and consequent per pupil funding reductions. Increasing spending on schools is not easy, especially when the spending in prospect is largely ongoing wage spend rather than one-off capital spending ... It is our firm opinion therefore that increased resource will need to be found from within Welsh budgets, and further, that due to the critical importance of high-quality school education for the well-being of future generations, that money should be ringfenced to ensure the structures and delivery described in this report can be properly funded. Given current budget conditions this will need to be new money ... a 10% increase in schools budget would require in the region of £200m per annum.[14]

These concerns provide a sobering counterpoint to the hyperbole and back clapping and talk of 'radicalism' and being 'world leading' within the political sphere regarding the new curriculum. The new curriculum contains some progressive and ostensibly laudable ideas, pledging to develop young people as 'ethical, informed citizens of

Wales and the world' and 'healthy, confident individuals, ready to lead fulfilling lives as valued members of society'. These promises come with commitments to focus on the arts and humanities alongside science and maths.

Yet there is fundamental contradiction at the heart of the initiative. The Welsh Government remains committed to moving up the PISA rankings, and individual schools want to move up the league tables. Thus the new curriculum, for all its good intentions and progressive rhetoric, is simply being overlaid on a neoliberal skeleton. The Welsh education system still retains the punitive testing and inspection regime, excessive data-isation, i.e., the *logic* of neoliberalism education. The 'radical' curriculum is being imposed on a profession which is at breaking point, who will not be given any extra money to implement it, and who have already repeatedly stated they do not feel that guidance has been adequate.

During Covid, the true nature of Wales' education system was repeatedly exposed: teachers' unions were attacked in the media for resisting Welsh Government plans to send children back too early;[15] the Welsh Government attempted to force children to accept lower A-level grades. Yet the crisis also showed that change is not impossible: the government were eventually forced into a humiliating U-turn on A-level results after students and teachers mobilised *en masse* and protested in front of the Senedd.

Robert Cox argued that across the world, world leaders and politicians, whether ostensibly progressive or conservative, essentially share a common ideology of how the world should be ordered.[16] PISA represents a case study in how transnational hegemonic ideology can operate. It does not force its reforms on countries; it does not force anyone to sign up for the program or follow its advisers' suggestions. Everything PISA produces is, simply, advisory. In this way, the program represents an all-pervasive hegemonic ideology, a commonsensical understanding of how education should work. There is no alternative. This soft power, imported through advisers and experts, smooths out the hard edges of neoliberal hegemony.

Indeed, neoliberal educational reforms are actively implemented by reformers in each country – like Leighton Andrews – who consider themselves to be progressive. Kirsty Williams was a self-styled progressive, and so is the new education minister, Jeremy Miles, installed in May 2021. But what Wales' convergence with the rest of the world shows that it is eminently possible to accept, promote and use neoliberal methods and norms even when one is ostensibly motivated by social justice. In some ways it is easy to understand this impulse: when PISA publishes its league tables, even high-achieving countries internalise the belief that their education system is failing. They feel pressure to steer their national education systems toward an internationally recognised standard. The irony, of course, is that no one wins under this system. While Wales faces incredible pressure to move up in the rankings, top-performing countries must continually ensure that they don't slip down. Even if Wales did climb the ladder, it would simply trade one kind of stress for another. Challenging what has become commonsensical will be difficult. It is difficult to imagine a scenario in which a Welsh leader could withstand the political fallout from pulling out of PISA, scrapping league tables, and reducing testing.

---

[1] https://www.oecd.org/pisa/aboutpisa/

[2] https://www.oecd-ilibrary.org/docserver/9789264081925-2-en.pdf?expires=1623226097&id=id&accname=guest&checksum=6D036CCD57381F5B0D74B30CAF5F34B1

[3] https://pasisahlberg.com/text-test/

[4] https://www.theguardian.com/uk/2004/nov/10/schools.sats

[5] http://news.bbc.co.uk/1/hi/wales/7127718.stm

[6] https://www.bbc.co.uk/news/uk-wales-19899357

[7] https://www.southwalesargus.co.uk/news/10971631.education-file-all-change-again-for-wales-school-system/

[8] https://www.bevanfoundation.org/wp-content/uploads/2017/01/After-PISA-Report.pdf

[9] https://www.walesonline.co.uk/news/wales-news/teaching-unions-attack-education-minister-2031317

[10] https://wiserd.ac.uk/news/teachers-wales

[11] https://www.bbc.co.uk/news/uk-wales-47828736

[12] https://www.nasuwt.org.uk/uploads/assets/uploaded/47a240ea-2836-4f3d-b768d6a258e3d217.pdf

[13] https://www.bera.ac.uk/blog/curriculum-reform-and-inequality-the-challenges-facing-wales

[14] https://www.futuregenerations.wales/wp-content/uploads/2019/10/2019-10-16-Fit-for-the-Future-Education-in-Wales-1-1.pdf

[15] https://www.bbc.co.uk/news/uk-wales-55518121

[16] Robert W. Cox with Timothy J. Sinclair, *Approaches to World Order* (Cambridge: CUP, 1996).

The Neoliberal University in Wales

Joe Healy

In early March 2020, after a cold day on the picket line with the University and College Union (UCU), I asked a worker how they thought their employer, Cardiff University, would respond to the industrial dispute. 'I don't think they'll take much notice,' they told me. 'The bigger problem the university's gonna have over the next few months is coronavirus.' I laughed. 'Nah, you think so?'

In my defence, at the time it was difficult to imagine the situation getting much more chaotic. This was UCU's third round of strike action in three years. A union formed of academics and support staff, they had struck in 2018 over proposed changes to their pension scheme, action which swiftly developed into further disputes resisting not only the attack on pensions but other ongoing changes to their pay and conditions, clear symptoms of a higher education model infected by neoliberalism.

Unsurprisingly, the marketisation of universities took off in the 1980s with Thatcher, but, as in countless areas of Welsh society, neither Westminster nor Cardiff Bay has sought to undo her legacy. They have only deepened it over time, with students, staff and knowledge itself now simply playthings for the grasping hand of the market as it exposes every inch of higher education to the logic of competition, with predictably disastrous consequences.

Welsh Universities: Little England

The university in Wales was founded and funded by the Welsh people themselves for a very different purpose. By the early twentieth century, the University of Wales (under a federal model uniting Bangor, Aberystwyth and Cardiff) formed one of three major Welsh cultural institutions, alongside the National Library and National Museum, which had at their heart a will for knowledge and national educational development.

In the neoliberal university, though, the aspiration to education as a common good is little more than a rhetorical device. The past 40-odd years have ensured that the motives of modern Welsh higher education align much more closely to those of private businesses than to those of the quarrymen and farmers whose monthly donations gave birth to Prifysgol Bangor.

This is a product of Thatcher but also of her heirs. As ever, it's useful to recall that she herself named New Labour as her greatest achievement. In spite of some notable successes (devolution not least among them), Blair's tenure (1997–2007) brought the private sector into areas that even the Conservatives would never have dared touch. Hence the introduction, for the first time, of university tuition fees.

Fees were defended by Labour with recognisable Thatcherite logic: as an economic necessity to which there was no alternative. Their espoused goal was to get as many young people as possible to go to university (all part of 'education, education, education'), and it was proclaimed that this commitment to expand higher education could never have been funded through general taxation. Instead, individual students needed to bear a financial burden in exchange for a broadening of their opportunities.

What went unspoken was that alternatives for young people had already been decimated. With manufacturing jobs largely destroyed and other facets of Thatcher's legacy (such as the selling off of council housing via Right to Buy) beginning to take effect on younger generations, expanding university entries seemed a quaint way of creating a 'knowledge economy', papering over the cracks of neoliberalism without ever attacking the root cause.

Moreover, the UK Government's argument – that, in order to get university entries up, students would have to pay – was always a fiction. With education now devolved, the Scottish Government rejected tuition fees. In Wales, they were not only introduced but subsequently raised from £1,000 to £3,000 per year. Yet, the percentage of young people attending university in Scotland has kept pace with Wales since, and Scottish students continue to be free from tuition debt.

To its credit, Welsh Government deviated when, in 2011, the newly elected Lib Dem-Tory coalition in Westminster moved to raise fees further in the name of austerity. It was decided that tuition fees for Welsh students would remain at around £3,000, whilst their English counterparts had theirs tripled. As a member of the very first cohort of English students to incur £9,000 fees, I saw the relief of my Welsh peers in Cardiff at not having this brought upon them. But, having spent several subsequent years at the same institution, I've also observed Welsh universities' absorption of the wider process of neoliberalisation of which fees form an integral part.

Just as Asad Haider wrote that neoliberalism is 'an ideology of generating market relations through social engineering', tuition fees – whilst of huge individual concern for those with stratospheric debts, I can attest – are not only an issue of personal finance but of a changing economic conditionality. They are an individual financial stake in higher education, transforming the relationship between students and educators into that of customers and service providers. The student becomes a consumer, putting money into their future and expecting a return on investment.

Welsh students are not spared this simply through accumulating lower levels of debt, and it is no less damaging, but far more frustrating, that this is the case after more than two decades of devolution. Higher education is as good an example as any of Welsh Labour's insistence that minuscule deviations from Westminster's failed policies are in fact major successes. The result is that Welsh institutions are plagued by almost identical problems to English ones, yet those responsible for their oversight baulk at the idea that things could be done differently. Blairism, it seems, is difficult to shake off.

Education over the Counter

The introduction of fees is best seen as a large step in the privatisation of universities. Rather than receiving stable streams of money from government, institutions' funding now flows from their ability to attract students away from their competitors.

For Welsh, English and Northern Irish students, their respective government covers their individual tuition, which they then pay back via debt over the course of their lifetime, meaning that the money universities receive upfront depends on the number of students they bring in. The cap on annual intake levels (intended to prevent institutions from being overwhelmed by large cohorts) has also been lifted to allow a fully-fledged market to develop. Each enrolment is a cash sum, and universities jostle for every last student.

More lucrative still are international arrivals, who pay astronomical amounts in tuition. Thus, universities are financially reliant on their ability to entice students from abroad, and internal funding decisions are made with this in mind. Millions are set aside for huge new state-of-the-art buildings, which look good on brochures and can be advertised across the globe. Glossy new projects decorate urban skylines, not only for learning facilities, but for housing. Cardiff's seemingly unstoppable germination of overpriced student accommodation, for instance, has rendered the city barely recognisable to a decade ago, as the campus spreads ever further upwards and outwards.

All the while, the university is plastered wherever it can be seen: on tote bags, pens, train station platforms. In 2020, Swansea University was signed as Swansea City FC's official shirt sponsor, with its advertising also visible at every home game and press conference, as well as on the club's livestreaming site, meaning it is perfectly placed to take advantage of football's international fanbase. In search of cash, the university brand is pushed to a global audience.

The rise of this funding model is supplemented by the prominence of university league tables. *The Times* and *The Guardian* run highly detailed, annual features listing universities from best to worst, based on all manner of criteria from teaching quality to sports facilities. The National Student Survey (NSS), filled out by thousands each year, acts as the primary data source for these rankings, and is the chief determinant of its single most important value: the student satisfaction rating. Universities know that, in order to climb the table, they must keep their students happy, and so find themselves operating under the insidious retail motto that the customer is always right.

Those working in higher education are therefore constantly required to help their employers look good. Many lecturers are encouraged to artificially inflate grades: since league tables reflect how many first-class degrees each institution grants, higher average marks attract students who, understandably, want the best qualifications money can buy.

It is further expected that staff will sacrifice their free time to partake in extravagant promotional events like open days, aimed at reeling in clients, and, in the interests of student satisfaction, that they will be subject to ever more changes to their working environment based on internal feedback and, of course, on increased student numbers.

Welcome to the Uber-versity

Yet, as funds are funnelled away from labour costs and towards marketing, these workers are not nearly compensated for their extra efforts. Wages have been squeezed for several years, and the perception of academia as a stable and well-paid career is falling into obsolescence.

The university has become a hotbed for the exploitative employment practices of the modern service sector. Fixed-term and zero-hours contracts abound in almost all Welsh universities, often leaving workers struggling to get housing and going weeks or months without pay. Cardiff University, meanwhile, maintains that it does not indulge in zero-hours contracts, but it has been instead offering contracts guaranteeing two hours per year – less than three minutes' work a week.

This is not to say that hours are thin on the ground, because the reality is quite the opposite: the work is mounting. Rather, these precarious working conditions are geared to grant university management the power to decide workers' hours and income at short notice, according to the whims of the market.

To deal with the higher workload, institutions are reliant on low-paid agency workers, as well as on PhD students, many of whom are not even recognised as employees, so are not entitled to working rights such as sick pay. The precarity of the sector also leaves it exposed to vast inequalities, overwhelmingly disadvantaging women, people of colour and workers with disabilities or health conditions. Cuts are not only brought upon lecturers, but on support staff and Student Union funding, leaving all sides of the university stretched to their limit. All sides, that is, other than management: the average salary of a University Vice Chancellor in Wales is well over £200,000 per annum.

As part of these new gig economy-style conditions, work itself is systematised and downgraded, forcing staff to do more with less. One example of many is the marking of assessments, where pay is often calculated by algorithm. Rather than self-reporting how long tasks take to complete, staff have it dictated to them how long they *should* take, set at a rate with which it is impossible to keep pace. Even for large projects on which students have spent weeks, it is calculated that to read, give detailed feedback, grade and return the work to the student through the appropriate bureaucratic channels requires only a few short minutes.

Staff are given an impossible choice: rush through, skim-reading each submission, unable to provide adequate comments; or give students' efforts the time and attention they deserve, but do so unpaid, using their evenings and weekends. They almost invariably choose the latter, but were they to choose the former, they would face the wrath of management following poor feedback from short-changed customers. If they are employed on a casual contract, as is increasingly common, this may affect whether or not they remain in a job. In this way, the entire edifice of the neoliberal university is sustained on the one hand by coercion, and on the other by the boundless goodwill of staff members committed to what remains of their vocation.

The Impact Agenda

Of course, universities are not only places of learning but of research, and academics' ability to carry out this second task is tightly governed by an ideological bent which again takes us back to Thatcher. New Public Management in the 1980s relied on an insistence that public services should be subjected to private rationale, and whilst universities did not go the same way as the rail network and telecoms in being fully privatised, they were subject to an agenda of 'accountability', needing to demonstrate their worth to the government, at risk of having their funding removed. This ideology, which continues in only more crystallised forms in academia today, comes with layers of bureaucracy which add to mountainous workloads. More fundamentally, it forces a market into knowledge production and acts as a smoke-screen for the removal of public funding, compelling academic colleagues to compete with each other over scarce resources.

The Research Assessment Exercise (RAE) was intro-duced by Thatcher's government for this purpose in 1986, and in 2014, it was updated to the Research Excellence Framework (REF). The REF is a 'performance-based research funding system' to which all UK universities have to submit. As well as emphasising the now longstanding desire for accountability and competi-tion in research, the REF also includes an 'impact assessment' which is supposed to judge research's contri-bution to the economy and society outside academia.

According to the logic of accountability, research

deemed most 'impactful' is delivered funding at the expense of that – largely in the arts and humanities – which relies on a commitment to 'knowledge for knowledge's sake', and so struggles to demonstrate benefit beyond pure human enrichment. The filtering of funding away from these fields restricts their ability to produce research, and so the cycle continues until less 'impactful' endeavours are cut out altogether. This systematically disadvantages more theoretical, critical, or even simply enjoyable scholarship in favour of that which produces demonstrable, measurable effects.

As money is directed away from certain fields, competition in these areas – for research funding and, consequently, for jobs – becomes overwhelming. Pressure to produce and advertise output – journal articles, conference papers, 'networking' events – necessarily leaves researchers, particularly younger, more precariously employed ones, dedicating almost all their time to their careers. The social media accounts of academic workers become billboards for the brand. The boundary between the personal and the professional is ever more blurred, as the need to constantly reproduce oneself gives rise to a new generation of 24/7 academics. In the neoliberal university, everyone is an entrepreneur.

Who Confronts the Crisis?

The woes of higher education – from which only university management, local landlords and property developers are immune – embody the structural contradictions of neoliberalism. Education is of course not something which cannot be comfortably subjected to capitalist pressures, and, just as with schools, the increasing emphasis on testing and monitoring, alongside financial cutbacks, have piled stress and bureaucracy on staff and students alike, restricting their ability to flourish.

Staff, as we have seen, are required to cope with rising student numbers, intrusive parameters for their research, higher expectations and worsening pay and conditions, and yet are expected to be more productive than ever. For those who refuse to play this game, who do not play it well enough or those deemed to be insufficiently 'impactful' or 'agile', there are cuts to funding. Hence, pay downgrades, precarity, redundancy and, even where these are avoided, workloads which are simply unmanageable. Staff are alienated from the profession, with many abandoning it altogether.

Students face tuition debt and ballooning living costs, meaning they are materially and emotionally ever more invested in their degrees. Due to the precarious and low-paid nature of work after graduation, growing numbers of them will end up with jobs for which they are massively overqualified, rendering their qualifications increasingly meaningless.

This only increases the pressure to succeed. In a carbon copy of their experience at school, the system encourages students to focus on exam technique. They become experts at meeting the 'learning criteria'. Intellectual development is sidelined in pursuit of value for money, and genuine fulfilment is found only in those fleeting minutes of escapism. The change of mood towards learning when students know that 'this won't come up in the assessment' is palpable, but such instances are exceedingly rare.

The tragic result of this unrelenting pressure on all sides is an exploding mental health crisis. Perhaps neoliberalism's greatest contradiction is the sheer amount of suffering and, ultimately, death that it is willing to tolerate in the name of supposed freedom. The modern Welsh university is adorned with memory of students and staff who have taken their own lives in recent years, many of them explicitly citing work-related stress in their final thoughts.

Recognition of the collective suffering in academia was one of the driving forces behind the UCU strikes. Many picketers have personal experience with these darkest of consequences and saw no option but to push back. Marketisation, after all, relies on finding new resources to exploit, or new ways to exploit the ones it has. Where it cannot expand outwards, it must turn inwards, finding ways to stretch and pull. Whilst the higher education marketplace remains, universities will only descend further in this race to the bottom, facing resistance from staff who, to their immense credit, make huge personal sacrifices to oppose the systemic mistreatment to which they are routinely subject.

It would be impossible to believe that the Welsh Government does not realise the extent of the crisis in universities. It has the devolved power to do the necessary institutional work to undo much of this suffering, including through the abolition of tuition fees, regulation of student numbers, the extension of maintenance grants for poorer students, the elimination of performance-based research funding via the REF, and rent caps on the private rental sector. It should be lobbying for a ban on zero-hours and casual employment contracts, not just in higher education but across the board. It should pressure institutions themselves to grant full working rights to graduate students and to take serious action to iron out pay inequalities, including vast reductions in management pay.

This would only be the beginning of the end of higher education marketisation in Wales, but the reluctance to take up any of these fights demonstrates complicity in the neoliberalisation of Welsh public institutions. Caught between alleged radicalism and deeply held unionism, the Welsh Government rocks the boat as gently as it possibly can, and in so doing flattens any possibility of an alternative.

Everything Must Change: Welsh Language Policy and Activism

Angharad Tomos

Two visits to Europe have stayed in my mind. One was my first time abroad on a family camping holiday when I was in my early twenties. Staying in France, I was sent to the shop, equipped with my CSE French, and a shopping list that included the bare minimum. Having tried, and failed with my knowledge of French, I resorted to my second language, and spoke in English. 'Quoi?' replied the man behind the counter. I stood there, silently, and realised that English was not as universal a language as I had believed. That it did not take you everywhere in the world, as everyone had taught me it would. That it couldn't even buy me half a pound of butter in France.

The second visit was several years later when I went with two friends to Barcelona. All three of us were members of Cymdeithas yr Iaith (The Welsh Language Society), and we went on a five-day visit to see how they campaigned for their language. It was to be an eye opener. In the mid-1980s, the new Catalan government was promoting the Catalan language. For us, who had spent more than ten years trying to get the British government to concede the basic rights for Welsh, this was a totally new scenario.

During the five days we spoke to so many different people that understood exactly what we, as Cymdeithas, was struggling for. There was no need for much introduction, they knew where we were coming from. That has struck me on all the different delegations I've been a part of, whether in Ireland, the Basque country, Nicaragua or Palestine. We're on the same wavelength. But in Barcelona in 1986, that's where I experienced solidarity for the very first time. As Welsh campaigners, it was not a small country against one of the most powerful in the world. We were part of an international campaign of nations fighting a universal fight for justice. As CIEMEN (Centre Internacional Escarré per a les Minories Ètniques i les Nacions), one of the movements in Catalunya said, 'It is a house of freedom which welcomes in, shares and blends together the desires and aspirations of all the ethnic and national groups.' I went to Barcelona as a campaigner who carried on because I believed in the cause. I returned from Barcelona having seen bilingualism in action. I saw what was possible if a government wanted to see a real change in society.

Not that I had not seen the results of campaigning in my own country. In 1982, after ten hard years of petitioning, letter writing, delegations, protests, sit-ins, climbing masts, occupying studios, court cases, prison sentences, and the famous proposed hunger strike of MP Gwynfor Evans, the Tory government made a U-turn and promised that the fourth TV channel in Wales would be a Welsh language channel.[1] As I sat watching S4C on the first night in November 1982, it was strange to see what we had daubed on walls looking so professional on a TV screen. Sianel Gymraeg – there it was. Change was possible. My question was why did it take so long? Why did such an elementary right need ten years of campaigning? Didn't we have better things to do with our lives?

That was forty years ago, and I'm still asking the same question. Nowadays, I'm feeling that we're taking one step forwards and two steps back. Forty years ago, I never dreamt that nine members of the Catalan government would be in their third year in prison for their stand on independence. On the bright side, I would never have believed that a solid majority of the people of Scotland would be in favour of independence.

So, how are things in Wales now? Many are asking this question and I'm often asked, 'Was it worth it? The years of campaigning … are things better now, is there ground for hope?'

Saunders Lewis gave an interesting reply to this question, the question of hope, in 1962 in his famous BBC lecture, 'Tynged yr Iaith' ('The Fate of the Language' that inspired the formation of Cymdeithas yr Iaith). 'Is the situation hopeless?' he asked, before offering his own answer: 'Yes of course, if we decide to lose hope. There is nothing more comfortable than giving up hope. Then we can get on and enjoy life.'

That has struck a chord with me. Losing hope is an easy option, an option that is not a choice to many. I have asked the same question myself to people in Nicaragua, asking, 'How can you carry on?' And they look at me with a smile, replying, 'And what is the alternative?'

So we carry on, but it's harder. Not only because cynicism tends to overtake the blind optimism of youth, but because the attitudes of those in power have changed. Or have they? One thing that you can be certain of. The

Welsh language is always at the bottom of the list of priorities. No change there.

After the manifesto of 1982, when Cymdeithas declared itself a socialist movement, the slogan was 'Rhaid i bopeth newid' (Everything must change). For the language to survive, every aspect of society had to change. In a capitalist society, the Welsh language was worthless. Since 1972, the movement had campaigned against second homes and outward migration, but it had been a single-issue movement mostly because so many resources had gone into the campaign for a Welsh television channel.

While I was chair of Cymdeithas following the S4C victory, there were two ongoing campaigns, the ever-present one for a Language Act and one for Welsh-medium education. We had the 1967 Language Act giving Welsh equal validity to English, but nothing more. Welsh-medium education was growing in spurts, whenever a group of parents set up a fight to ensure such education for their children. The campaign for a Corff Datblygu Addysg Gymraeg (a Body to Develop Welsh-medium Education) would ensure constant development until every child in Wales had access to Welsh-medium education.

My experience is that the government will finally respond to your calls by giving you the least possible. By 1993, we secured a new Welsh Language Act and a Welsh Language Board. Things would be in Welsh if there was 'enough demand', and if that demand was 'reasonable' (a free-market trope that remains a foundation stone of the approach to Welsh in today's neoliberal Wales, most notably in education). That was a far cry from the Catalonian pattern – that the Catalan government actively promoted the Catalan language. In Wales it was an uphill struggle, and you always had to prove your point and persuade that it was a 'reasonable demand'. I used to think of Owain Glyndŵr and his letter to the King demanding a university for Wales. He'd have been kicked out immediately for being so unreasonable. Ditto for the campaign for a body to develop Welsh-medium education. Yes, it was set up eventually, but without funding. We shook our heads in despair – and carried on.

Regarding Welsh-medium education itself, there are still hundreds of parents with children on waiting lists, a new generation – the children or grandchildren of those who went to the first Welsh-language school. And why are they called Welsh schools? Are there English-medium schools in England? Why not ensure that all schools in Wales teach children to fluency in Welsh? Why is the English language still crucial for every job, but not Welsh? This situation still exists although we have had our own Assembly (now Senedd) since 1999.

We cannot blame all the problems on Westminster anymore. The Senedd must share the blame. They still have to understand how crucial it is to make the Welsh language a cornerstone of their policies – in every field.

There have been victories, and notable ones, I must keep reminding myself. The one in 2011 to establish Y Coleg Cymraeg – to plan and support Welsh-medium higher education – is one that Glyndŵr would have been proud of. It ensures that research is done in all kinds of fields through the medium of Welsh, and it provides lecturers that can teach in Welsh. Since 2016, it is responsible for post-16 education as well. Following its success, a Welsh medical school should have been set up in Gwynedd a long time ago, but we are still waiting. Actually, Vaughan Gething vetoed the school, ignoring clinical advice on helping recruitment of medics to the area. There are students who want to be doctors in Welsh-speaking areas of Wales, and a medical school in North Wales is vital. But until then ...

In that same year we had another Welsh Language Act – that ensured that the official status of the Welsh language had a legal effect and that it should be treated no less favourably than the English. This changed the act that Henry VIII passed in 1536 that the Welsh language was not an official language. Four hundred years is a long time to wait, and it would have been good if this had been passed in 1967 rather than 2011. The 2011 Act also gave us a Welsh Language Commissioner, and language standards. Unsurprisingly, in a society that places the market on a pedestal, beyond reach, it does not cover private companies, and that is a major problem.

Four years later, in 2015, the Welsh Assembly passed the Well-being of Future Generations Act for public services to work together to achieve long-term goals, and to produce a more inclusive and empowered society, particularly for younger generations. Sustainable Development is at the heart of this bill, and is a step to be welcomed. But this Act is glaringly more ambitious than anything concerning the Welsh language. Again in 2015, we had the Planning Act, and this would be considered a major milestone by Cymdeithas. For the first time the Welsh language would be a consideration when giving planning consent. For decades, we had seen contractors buying land and building unnecessary housing estates with the sole purpose of making profits. These houses were beyond the reach of local people, and so the buyers were people from outside the area and this weakened the situation of the language. Now, the language would be a factor they had to consider. The weak spot? There was no legal obligation for them to do so. Worse than not implementing their own laws, they actively undermine them. The Policy Planning Wales (Welsh Government 2016a) document states that 'policies must not introduce any element of discrimination between individuals on the basis of their linguistic ability, and should not seek to control housing occupancy on linguistic grounds'. Once more, a classic example of doublespeak.

And so the trends of the twentieth century continues in modern Wales. Pass laws, but always ensure that there's a loophole, thus rendering the laws ineffectual. Pass progressive sounding laws and trumpet your own radicalism for doing so. Give in to campaigners, but make sure the free market can continue to thrive. Thus, the slogan 'Rhaid i Bopeth Newid' is as relevant as ever. All over Wales, communities are fighting large developments on a local basis. Some succeed, most do not.

A year later, in 2016, we had the Welsh Government presenting its vision of 'A Million Welsh Speakers by 2050'. A Labour Welsh Government, I may add. To my generation, who remember the violent anti-Welsh language stance of Leo Abse, George Thomas, Neil Kinnock and the like, this was unheard of. I sat through enough meetings of the

Labour-led West Glamorgan Council, listening to councillors spit their hatred of the Welsh language more times than I care to mention. To be Labour for a long time meant you took an anti-Welsh language stance as a matter of course. That was the only thing to define you as different to Plaid Cymru. That is not the case today, it appears.

The million speakers is a nice idea, but if their policies are too weak to keep the present percentage of Welsh speakers, where will the government find the extra 400,000? Maybe a better idea would be to stop the cuts on the Welsh language (such as Welsh for Adults, Twf and the Welsh Language Commission etc.) which have been deep and constant. Maybe the government's budget on the Welsh language should be slightly higher than 0.16%.

Have we reached the Catalonian paradise I got to see back in 1986? Has the aims of Cymdeithas yr Iaith been achieved? Is there a need for Cymdeithas any longer? Or is it time to sit back and watch the Welsh Government realise its ambitious vision? I think not. That is why we still need movements such as Cymdeithas yr Iaith.

The million Welsh speakers is not too radical a goal. It could be achieved, if the will was there. But the present conditions make the goal totally impossible. I say that as a person who lives in a village with over 80% of its people Welsh speaking. Whatever happens here, I can be more or less certain that in other places, the situation will be worse regarding the Welsh language. If it cannot thrive in Dyffryn Nantlle, it will certainly cease to be a living language in other places in Wales. We are at a crossroads in Dyffryn Nantlle. It could go either way. That is why the challenge is exciting, but also full of worry.

In recent years, my campaigning has been on a more local basis, and the council for our area is Plaid Cymru-led Gwynedd Council who have – as they always like to remind us – the best Welsh-language policies of all councils in Wales, as if that was difficult. Many of their main councillors and officers are men and women who have been members of Cymdeithas in the past, and who believe they know the movement well, and feel they've matured since their heady days when they painted road-signs. 'Things are much more complicated now' is the mantra they keep repeating in their patronising tones. I think they feel it is a complicated, mature feat to keep the beliefs of Plaid Cymru whilst operating Tory policies of economic cuts. 'If we didn't do it, somebody else would,' they say, 'people with much less sympathy with your aims.'

And so in Gwynedd, like the rest of Wales, we've had a decade of Tory policies, except here they are being delivered through the medium of Welsh, which is frustrating to say the least. One of the earliest was the unpopular policy of closing small rural schools in Gwynedd, when we saw a fierce protest outside the county council, with people in tears because of the situation. Small schools had 'too many empty spaces', so in the name of economic common sense, they were closed. Sometimes brand-new schools were built to compensate, but people remember, and thus Llais Gwynedd (The Voice of Gwynedd), a new political party to challenge Plaid was formed, although they are down to only half a dozen councillors by now,

'Tai a Gwaith i gadw'r Iaith' has been an old slogan, (houses and jobs to keep the language) and that is so true in Gwynedd. The heavy industry – slate mining – has long gone, and nothing has really taken its place. A factory here and there, tourism which is seasonal, and a nuclear power station, endorsed by the local political establishment. The factories came when Labour was in power in Gwynedd, and now they're fifty years old. When they close, nothing takes their place.

Thus, the only thing that Gwynedd could come up with was to support Wylfa B, or Wylfa Newydd – new Wylfa in neighbouring Ynys Môn. For the past thirty years, all hopes have been placed on this project. Grants have been given in the hope that young people will be able to work in this field, and the new M-SParc was set up in Gaerwen. When Hitachi recently pulled out of the deal, the councillors could not believe their ears, but that is the nature of the capitalist beast.

After Covid, the paper factory in our village has closed, bringing redundancy to 94 families. In a crucial area like Dyffryn Nantlle, that could be the last straw for the future of the language here.

Too much is being left to fate. The Million Welsh Speakers by 2050 rings hollow here. Every week, a hundred teenagers come to the local youth club. They talk Welsh naturally to one another. It's a Language Commissioner's dream. Gwynedd's policy? We cannot support youth clubs in Gwynedd, there is no money there. We have a lively library, as many villages in the county have. Here, in a public space, people communicate and meet one another. It's a vital place where the Welsh language is naturally used. Yet, this library and others have been under the threat of closure due to economic cuts. Schools, post offices, libraries, youth clubs – all the organic, working-class public sphere where Welsh is being used as a natural medium of communication, exactly the right conditions you need to produce your vital percentage of the million Welsh speakers, they are all under threat.

When the young people want to buy a house, they have no chance at all. They are priced out of the market. For a long time, it's been known that 10% of Gwynedd's housing stock are second homes. But things are reaching crisis point: in 2020, 38% of the houses sold in Gwynedd were sold as second homes.

What is to be done? Giving up is not an option, however disheartening the situation may be. We have to carry on the fight, because as my Nicaraguan comrade said, there is no alternative. But if the Johnson regime has highlighted anything, it's shown more blatantly than ever before the destructive effect of Conservative policies, in the extreme.

We have been here before. Some of us still remember Thatcher. No one personified selfishness and greed as much as she did. And in response, we had a united front of language activists, anti-apartheid supporters, CND stalwarts, union members, church movements coming together to form a left front to fight their unionist policies. We can do it again. Seeds of that coming together have been sown in the Yes Cymru movement.

That is what gives me hope, as well as my angry seventeen-year-old son who's had enough of Covid and whose generation is so angry with the British elite for making such a mess of ordinary young people's exam results (as well as everything else). They were angry in May 2020 because of the killing of George Floyd, they were angry two years ago because of climate change. They are used to being on the streets as they have no vote and no other chance of showing their discontent. These young people have to be supported, and it's our duty to march along with them. As Greta Thunberg said when she was sixteen, in a most prophetic way, 'Change is coming, whether you like it or not.'[2] It has come, and we have to accept the challenge.

As I see them coming out, even in the middle of a pandemic, masked and socially distanced, I watch the youthful faces protesting about racism and second homes, and I feel hope. There is a desperate need for something to be done, and the political establishment have not achieved it. It is back onto the streets and highways once more and political agitation is once again on the menu.

---

[1] See Elain Price, *Nid Sianel Gyffredin Mohoni!: Hanes Seflydu S4C* (Cardiff: UWP, 2016).

[2] https://www.youtube.com/watch?v=qWEpTok6AJo&ab_channel =NBCNews

The Housing Crisis

Steffan Evans

The coronavirus pandemic and its resulting nationwide lockdowns have starkly highlighted the importance of a warm, affordable, safe home. Yet while many take such a home for granted, thousands of people are left without. The average rent on a two-bedroom property, both social and private rent, is unaffordable to the lowest quartile of earners in every local authority area in Wales.[1] This pushes people into poverty, leading to households having to cut back on heating, food, and other essential items. At its extreme, this lack of affordable housing can push people into homelessness: 12,000 households were made homeless in Wales in 2018/19.[2] Yet these problems are not new. The current crisis is a result of decades of policy failure, the lessons of which we are still too slow to learn.

The Rise and Rise of the Private Rental Sector, Wales' Growth Sector

The key feature of the Welsh housing market over the past two decades has been the rise of the private rental sector, with the sector doubling in size. Back in 2001, around 90,000 homes were privately rented in Wales – around 7% of the total housing stock.[3] By 31 March 2020 the figure stood at over 200,000, accounting for 14% of all housing stock.[4]

This growth has come at the expense of both the owner-occupied and the socially rented sector. Whilst the overall number of owner-occupied homes in Wales has increased by around 60,000 over the past two decades, the sector now only accounts for around 70% of Welsh homes, down from 74% in 2001.[5] The number of social homes in Wales has actually declined by around 12,000 over this period, with the sector now accounting for around 16% of the total housing stock, not dissimilar to the proportion that are in the private rental sector.[6]

This change in the composition of Welsh housing stock has serious implications for Welsh society. Renters are significantly more likely to live in poverty than owner occupiers. 13% of owner occupiers in Wales live in poverty; by contrast, the same is true for 41% of private renters and 49% of social renters.[7] The growth in the private rental sector at the expense of the owner-occupied sector is therefore putting more families at risk of poverty.

The growth of the private rental sector at the expense of the social rented sector also has severe social implications. Despite significant increases in recent years, social rents remain cheaper than private sector rents. Social housing tenants also have greater protections from evictions providing families with security, whilst there are far more stringent regulations in place in the social rented sector around housing quality standards than in the private rental sector.

Supporting the Growth

Instead of challenging the growth of the private rental sector, the Welsh Government's focus over recent years has been on 'professionalising' the sector. In numerous Welsh Government policy and research papers from 2002 all the way through until 2020, the need to 'profession-alise' the sector is a common theme.[8] Some of the measures that have been taken as part of this process are to be welcomed. The introduction of landlord registration and the introduction of legislation to strengthen housing quality standards are positive steps, but these stop short of providing private rental sector tenants with the same protections that are offered in the social rented sector. The calls to 'professionalise' the sector and the timidity to take substantive action appear to be based, in part, on the belief that the growth of the private rental sector is an in-evitable process. There appears to be limited consideration, however, that both UK and Welsh govern-ment policy may in fact be contributing to the sector's growth.

There are numerous reasons why the private rented sector has grown in Wales over the last two decades. The availability of cheaper credit through 'Buy to Let' mortgages in the 1990s and 2000s paved the way for thousands of people to develop their very own 'property portfolios'. In more recent times, investment from insti-tutional investors such as pension funds in student accommodation and new 'build to rent' schemes has seen the sector grow in new ways. Instead of countering this shift, however, the policies of the UK and Welsh governments have facilitated the growth of the private rental sector.

Each year, millions of public funds are diverted straight into the pockets of private landlords. In August 2020, nearly 40,000 households living in the private rental sector in Wales were in receipt of housing benefit. With each household receiving an average of £87.52 a week, that's over £180m a year of private rents directly funded by the UK Government in Wales alone.[9] With over 50,000 other households who live in the private rental sector being in receipt of the housing element of Universal Credit, the total spent subsiding private sector rents is significantly higher.[10]

It is not just the UK government that is subsiding the profits of private individuals. The Welsh Government also spends vast amounts of money supporting tenancies in the private rental sector. The most recent example of this is the creation of the Tenant Saver Loan Scheme. Through the scheme the Welsh Government provides loans to tenants who have or who are expected to fall behind on their rent due to the impact of the pandemic. A tenant who is successful in their application will see the funds paid directly to their landlord, with the tenants having five years to repay the loan at 1% interest. Whilst the aim of scheme is ostensibly to assist tenants affected by Covid-19 job cuts and prevent homelessness, in practice it provides a bail out to private sector landlords.

The reason for this significant public investment is clear: with a shortage of social housing, tenants who would otherwise be living in the sector have no option but to look at the private rental sector. With many of these tenants being unable to afford private rents or having housing needs that the sector would struggle to accommodate however, they would be faced with eviction and homelessness if the taxpayer did not supplement their rents. But these measures are in fact facilitating the growth of the private rental sector and exacerbating the problem. These payments are directly transferring money from the state to private landlords, allowing them to pay off their mortgages and purchase more properties, further driving up house prices and housing costs – and all this within a context where the neoliberal paradigm has perversely conditioned us to accept that rising house prices is tantamount to a public good.

The Social Housing Crisis

Despite the fact that the UK and Welsh governments are spending millions facilitating the rise of the private rental sector each year, underinvestment continues to be a problem for our social housing sector. Approximately £200m has been spent by the Welsh Government on constructing new social housing over each of the last three years. Whilst this is not an insignificant sum of money, it is nowhere near enough to fund the significant development that is needed to meet demand. This underinvestment affects people in Wales in a number of ways.

The most obvious implication from the Welsh Government's underinvestment in social housing is its shortage. There are 70,000 fewer social homes in Wales today than there were in 1981.[11] At the same time, there are an estimated 67,000 households on social housing waiting lists across Wales.[12] This huge reduction can, in large part, be attributed to the introduction of the Right to Buy in the 1980s, but this problem has been exacerbated by the slow progress made in building new social housing over the past two decades.

More than 4,000 new social homes were built in Wales every year between 1974/5 and 1980/81.[13] In 1975/76 alone, over 8,000 new social homes were built. For the first fifteen years of the new millennium, however, fewer than 1,000 new social homes were built annually.[14] In nine of the last twenty years, no new social homes at all were built by local authorities.[15] Whilst progress has been made to increase these numbers recently, it remains painfully slow with only 1,289 new social homes built in 2018/19.[16] At current rates it would take the Welsh Government over 50 years to construct enough new social housing for everyone already on the waiting list, and unless the prevailing ideological climate changes, the prospects will not greatly improve.

Rising Rents

A lack of social housing is not the only problem caused by the Welsh Government's lack of investment. Social housing has become increasingly unaffordable over recent years.

Social housing in Wales refers to two types of housing. Traditional council housing, meaning homes owned and managed by local authorities, and homes that are rented and managed by housing associations which are private, independent organisations that are run on a 'not for profit' basis. Two decades ago, almost all social housing was council housing. Now, the opposite is true with 10% of people in Wales living in housing association owned homes and 6% living in homes owned by local authorities.[17]

The primary reason for this change is the stock transfer policy pursued by the Welsh Government towards the end of the first decade of devolution. In 2002, the Welsh Government introduced the Welsh Housing Quality Standards, a set of minimum standards all social homes were expected to comply with. Following decades of underinvestment in existing social housing, many homes were in a poor condition and the standards were an attempt to improve this. It was clear that this would be a significant cost for the public purse, so in an effort to push the borrowing off the public balance sheet, the Welsh Government gave local authorities the right to transfer all their council housing to newly created housing associations, who would be free to borrow from the private sector to fund this work. Half of all Welsh local authorities transferred their entire stock, meaning they now own no council housing. This has become a model upon which the Welsh Government's attempts to build new social housing has become to rely upon with a devastating impact on social rents.

Historically, new social housing had been overwhelmingly financed by the state either through direct construction of local authority housing, or in the form of Social Housing Grant which was paid to housing associations to build new homes on behalf of the Welsh Government. In recent years, however, with the Welsh Government reluctant to invest the sort of public funds required to construct social housing at the rate required to meet its own targets, attention has turned to finding new 'innovative' forms of finance to construct new social housing whilst reducing the direct contribution made by the state. This has inevitably meant seeking greater private investment. This has seen housing associations borrowing ever larger sums of money from a range of private sector institutions such as banks, institutional investors and (especially in England) from the bond markets.

This shift to private finance has placed new pressures on housing associations and increased the need for social landlords to boost incomes to service this new debt. Inevitably, with rents being their largest revenue stream, this has led to pressure to increase social housing rent. The Welsh Government has actively facilitated this process through its adoption of a new rent-setting mechanism.

The rent-setting mechanism introduced by the Welsh Government sets out the maximum amount by which social landlords are permitted to increase their rent each year. Between 2014/15 and 2018/19 social landlords (both housing association and local authorities) were permitted, by the Welsh Government, to increase their social rent by CPI inflation + 1.5 per cent, plus an additional £2 per week. In 2019/20 this was changed to a cap that was in line with CPI inflation, before being amended again in 2020/21 to CPI inflation + 1%. This new cap is due to remain in place for the next five years.

In practice this means that thousands of social renters

in Wales have seen years of above inflation rises in their rents at a time when wages have been largely stagnant and welfare reform has seen the amount of benefits many families receive reduce. Recent research by the Joseph Rowntree Foundation has found that social rents have raised by 8% in real terms over the last five years, an increase that has pushed 40,000 people into poverty.[18]

The result of this process has therefore been transferring the cost of constructing new social housing from the state onto individuals who already live in social housing. With 49% of social renters living in poverty, this means that in practice that the Welsh Government's pursuit of 'innovative' funding models and market solutions has shifted the burden of funding onto some of the poorest people in society, leading them to disproportionately shoulder the financial burden for the construction of new housing whilst wealthier owner occupiers and private landlords remain unaffected. Here we see at work a particularly invidious and damaging form of 'trickle-up' neoliberal economics.

Time for a Reset

Housing policy over the last two decades has been a process of transferring wealth from the poorest in society to the wealthiest. Whilst private landlords have received billions in public funds, 40,000 social housing tenants in Wales have been pushed into poverty due to the failure to adequately invest in a new generation of social housing, with thousands more forced into unsuitable private rental sector properties. There are funds available to make a difference.

It is not just private landlords who have benefited from regressive housing policy. Each year, the Welsh Government invests £70m into the Help to Buy Scheme, an investment that has questionable benefits for boosting the supply of affordable housing, but which does have some clear benefits for property developers. The Welsh Government's decision to temporarily raise the threshold at which Land Transaction Tax would be paid to £250,000 last year amounted to a £77m[19] giveaway to the middle classes at a time that thousands of Welsh households were struggling to pay their rent and bills.[20]

The recovery from Covid-19 provides us with an opportunity to change. It is clear that we will not be able to end our reliance on the private rental sector to house people on low income overnight. Constructing the number of new social housing we need in Wales and buying up empty properties and returning them to the social sector will take years. But unless we start on that process, things will never improve.

That process must include moving away from a system that subsidises rents to a system that subsidises house building. Back in 2016 the Bevan Foundation calculated that £1 billion was spent in Wales each year on Housing Benefit between the social and private rental sectors.[21] If such funds were invested in social housing construction this would represent a five-fold increase on current spending, transforming both the number of homes that could be built and the need to rely on private sector borrowing and ever-increasing social rents to fund their construction.

An opportunity was missed in 2016 to push for

Housing Benefit to be devolved. With Housing Benefit now incorporated into Universal Credit, it will be harder for the Welsh Government to get their hands on this substantial amount of money that could transform the Welsh housing sector. This is not a reason to avoid pushing for change however, and the case for the devolution of the housing element of Universal Credit and investing in construction rather than in rents has arguably increased in strength over the past five years. There are steps that the Welsh Government could take in the interim, however, to boost the construction of social housing, whilst also capping social rents to ensure they do not rise above inflation.

The Welsh Government should immediately stop spending public funds investing in types of housing that has little to no impact on improving the supply of affordable housing. Scrapping its investment in the Help to Buy Scheme and transferring all the investment over to the Social Housing Grant would be an easy first step.

The Welsh Government also does have powers over taxation. These could be used to raise funds to finance the construction of new social housing in a more redistributive way than the current system that burdens the poorest in our society with a disproportionate share of the bill. Rather than cutting land transaction tax, the Welsh Government could look to increase it to ensure that those who are in the fortunate position to be able to buy a home are paying their fair share. Far more could also be done to raise funds by raising taxes on second homeowners, including landlords.

This process will take time, it is therefore also vital that we strengthen and tighten legislation that controls the private rental sector in the interim. The motivation for such action, however, should be protecting tenants not 'professionalising' the sector.

The long-term ambition for any Welsh Government must be that there is a social home available for everyone in Wales who should want one. State wealth should not be being used to allow private individuals to be get richer at the expense of the poorest people in Welsh society. Now is the time to turn the tide on our failing system.

---

[1] Bevan Foundation, *Solving poverty: Reforming help with housing costs* (May 2020) https://www.bevanfoundation.org/publications/solving-poverty-reforming-help-with-housing-costs/

[2] Undod Cymru, *Solving the housing crisis in Wales* (July 2020) https://undod.cymru/en/2020/07/03/tai-housing/

[3] Stats Wales, *Dwelling stock estimates percentages by year and tenure* https://statswales.gov.wales/Catalogue/Housing/Dwelling-Stock-Estimates/dwellingstockestimatespercentages-by-year-tenure

[4] Ibid.

[5] Ibid and Stats Wales, *Dwelling stock estimates by year and tenure*

[6] https://statswales.gov.wales/Catalogue/Housing/Dwelling-Stock-Estimates/dwellingstockestimates-by-year-tenure

[7] Stats Wales, *People in relative income poverty by tenure type* https://statswales.gov.wales/Catalogue/Community-Safety-and-Social-Inclusion/Poverty/peopleinrelativeincomepoverty-by-tenuretype

[8] Welsh Assembly Government, *Review of the Private Rental Sector in Wales* (February 2002) https://gov.wales/sites/default/files/statistics-and-research/2019-06/020201-review-private-rented-sector-en.pdf; Welsh Government, *Understanding the Tenant Experiences of the Private Rental Sector* (June 2020) https://gov.wales/sites/default/files/statistics-and-research/2020-08/understanding-tenant-experiences-of-the-private-rented-sector.pdf

[9] Housing Benefit Caseload data via Stat-Xplore.

[10] Household on Universal Credit, month by housing entitlement via Stat-Xplore.

[11] Dr Bob Smith, *Social Housing in Wales,* (UK Centre for Collaborative Housing Evidence, October 2018) https://housingevidence.ac.uk/wp-content/uploads/2018/10/R2018_SHPWG_04_Bob_Smith.pdf

[12] Shelter Cymru, *A good home for everyone* https://sheltercymru.org.uk/politicians-have-listened-to-our-social-housing-campaign-now-its-time-for-them-to-take-action/

[13] Stats Wales, *New dwellings completed by period and tenure* https://statswales.gov.wales/Catalogue/Housing/New-House-Building/newdwellingscompleted-by-period-tenure

[14] Ibid.

[15] Ibid.

[16] Ibid.

[17] Stats Wales n(3).

[18] Joseph Rowntree Foundation, *Poverty in Wales 2020* (November 2020) https://www.jrf.org.uk/report/poverty-wales-2020

[19] https://twitter.com/Guto_Ifan/status/1281235246915166210?s=20

[20] Shelter Cymru, *Briefing Paper: Life in Lockdown in Wales* (November 2020) https://sheltercymru.org.uk/wp-content/uploads/2020/11/Life-in-lockdown-in-Wales_Nov-2020.pdf and Bevan Foundation, *Differing experiences of poverty in Winter 2020* (February 2021) https://www.bevanfoundation.org/publications/differing-experiences-of-poverty/

[21] Bevan Foundation, *Making welfare work for Wales: Should benefits for people of working age be devolved* (June 2016) https://www.bevanfoundation.org/publications/making-welfare-wales-benefits-people-working-age-devolved/

No Progressiveness in Practice: Health and Social Care Policy Since Devolution

Georgia Burdett

Since devolution, the Welsh Government has demonstrated an inability or unwillingness to make the radical
ideology of its health and social care policies a reality.[1]
The first Government of Wales Acts (1998) legislated for
the establishment of the Welsh Assembly, and health,
social care and education were some of the twenty areas
devolved to Wales. A second Act in 2006 brought about
the separation of the executive body (the government)
from the legislative body, and provided enhanced legislative powers for the Welsh Assembly Government. This Act
also legislated for the future acquisition of full law-making
powers for Wales, without the need for further legislation.
In 2011, following a referendum, the Welsh population
voted to bring primary law-making powers to Wales. Wales
now, therefore, has its own law-making process in twenty
devolved areas, including health and social care. However,
significant aspects of health and social care remain beyond
Welsh Government control, including welfare benefits.
Within the context of the Welsh Block Grant, which
Westminster Tories believe to be largely overpaid by the
much-scrutinised Barnett formula, the Welsh continue to

argue for a 'needs-based' system, which takes into consideration an 'older, less healthy, less wealthy demography,
and a mountainous, more sparsely populated geography'.[2]

Since 1998 therefore, legislation and policy in regards
to health and social care in Wales should have been
allowed to have developed a distinctive Welsh perspective.
In 2011, in *Social Policy for Social Welfare Practice in a
Devolved Wales,* Charlotte Williams refers to how devolution had created a unique environment in which the
'Welsh Way', the tradition of participation and working in
partnership in health and social care policy development,
could move forward and flourish, providing 'Welsh
solutions to Welsh problems'.[3] Since 2007, former Health
Minister Mark Drakeford has claimed that such services
in Wales are moving away from a market model of social
care provision that has historically prevailed in the United
Kingdom, and are instead aspiring towards a model of
'Progressive Universalism'.[4] Under such a model there
should be services for all citizens, and all citizens are
'stakeholders' in such services, with particular emphasis
on greater provision where there is greater need for it.
This philosophy, the 'Welsh Way' is claimed to be woven
into all health and social care policy and legislation
produced by the Welsh Government. This sort of 'groupthink' rhetoric is propounded by ministers, and usually
accepted and perpetuated uncritically by academics.

On a positive note, since devolution there has been greater
incorporation of the principles of the United Nations
Convention on the Rights of the Child. For example, The
Children's Commissioner for Wales was the UK's first independent human rights institution specifically for children.

Two further Commissioners have since been appointed – the Older People's Commissioner for Wales and the Welsh Language Commissioner. The role of all three commissioners includes promotion of citizens' rights in Wales.

The White Paper *Sustainable Social Services: A Framework for Action* (Welsh Assembly Government, 2011) clearly sets out the Welsh Government's priorities for action to bring about 'high quality responsive, citizen-centred social services'. This took into account demographic and financial changes, and placed the 'professional contribution of social workers and social care workers even more at the heart of services'.[5] Furthermore, the aspiration was that working in partnership with service users and carers in the design and delivery of services would ensure that their voices were heard at this stage of service provision. In this way, service users and carers could be seen as partners with local government, engaged in co-production, rather than being mere consumers of what was provided. Furthermore, The Social Services and Well-being Act (2014) aimed to address the issues raised in the White Paper, and to transform care and support in Wales. This would be achieved through working in partnership with service users to identify their needs and decide what kind of services would best maintain and enhance their well-being and promote their independence (Welsh Local Government Association, 2012). This outcomes-focused, partnership approach, concerned with well-being for people as individuals, as part of their family, and as part of their community, would be a distinctive feature of the policy and legislative agenda in Wales. It all sounded a bit too good to be true.

There are historic and systemic problems in the translation of a more progressive agenda into the everyday working practices of children's, disability, and adult social care services departments in our local authorities. The buzzword vocabulary trickles down into leaflets, workshops and consultations, but something gets lost before the point of delivery. For the vast majority of service users, experience does not live up to expectation, and the promised outcomes are very rarely delivered. Over the past decade, several Welsh local authorities have had their social services departments threatened with being placed under 'special measures' for failing to meet the very basic, regulatory standards expected of them.[6] There seems to be enormous difficulty in recruiting and retaining social workers across the board, but particularly in areas where services are under the most public and professional scrutiny. In local authorities like Powys, where social services have been hugely reliant on agency workers to fill posts, qualified social workers are extremely wary of taking up permanent posts in notoriously failing departments.[7]

Huge turnovers in staff, and widespread dependence on agency workers means that many service users will only meet an individual once before being passed on to another's caseload. The experience is demoralising for all involved. To have to explain the complexities of an individual's case and personal history over and over again without seeming to make any gains for that person can be exhausting and infuriating. Being subjected to endless box-ticking exercises and assessments on the arrival of each and every new social worker is both time- consuming and debilitating for service users and carers alike. In this way, a positive relationship between service user and social worker is at risk from the very outset. There is now a systemic and inherent lack of trust and the relationship dynamics between service user and social worker is irreparably damaged; social workers appear not as enablers or advocates, but as gatekeepers to much-needed resources and services.

Under these working conditions, the real 'work' of the social worker goes unfinished; emails and telephone calls are unanswered; documents are lost in the system and have to be rewritten; panel meetings are unsuccessful for both the representative and the represented, as professionals simply do not know the service user well enough to fight their corner adequately. Needs are constantly identified through 'assessment', then re-identified and 'reassessed' by someone else (sometimes several times), but these needs typically remain unmet. In this chaotic system, many vulnerable people routinely fall through the net.

The experience of living through a pandemic has exacerbated the problems even further. It is now even more permissible for professionals to be physically and technologically absent. Annual reviews are not undertaken, interdisciplinary meetings do not take place, or if they do, they are inaccessible to many service users and their carers. It takes a particular set of personal resources (emotional resilience, physical energy, patience, and sometimes money) for the service user or their supporters to keep asking their local authority for the resources that they know they should be entitled to. In this respect, personal outcomes in health and social care are largely dependent on where you live, and how well your local authority is practically meeting ideological objectives. The answer is, usually: not very well – it is a postcode lottery.[8]

Combatting Crisis, Deprivation and Poverty: a Lack of Pace and Impact

In 2011 the UK government established the Silk Commission to review the financial and constitutional arrangements in Wales. After consideration of the issues around social security they decided not to recommend devolution. The Commission agreed with the evidence they received that the risks and financial costs could not be justified.[9] This viewpoint was largely reinforced by the purported need to adhere to a 'parity principle' with the other nations of the United Kingdom 'as people across the United Kingdom pay the same rates of National Insurance and non-devolved taxation, they should be entitled to the same rights and benefits.'[10] It should be noted that in 2013 HM Treasury found that spending per head on social protection in Wales was 13 per cent higher than the national average.[11] Given the importance of the social security system in Wales, it is hugely significant who controls it.

In 2019 the Senedd's Equality, Local Government and Communities Committee published an in-depth report, *Benefits in Wales: options for better delivery*,[12] investigating further the various support and criticisms of devolving benefits.[13] The Wales Governance Centre examined the financial implications to Wales of devolving the same package of benefits that have been devolved to Scotland since 2016.[14] They found 'no evidence to suggest that devolving these powers' would be 'fiscally unsustainable'.[15] In fact, they said that, dependent on the Barnett mechanism used, and the nature of the inter-governmental agreements, 'the Welsh Treasury could stand to benefit considerably from the devolution of welfare powers'.[16] In their deliberations on the devolution of benefits, Oxfam Cymru noted that the Scottish Government had significantly more civil servants at 15,960 than the Welsh Government, who had just 5,290.[17] The Welsh Government would therefore have to consider carefully and comprehensively how it would meet the required staff and skills gap whilst continuing to meet that level of responsibility.

There are reasons to believe that some form of devolution in regards to benefits could result in an inherently more compassionate system that is better aligned with Wales' devolved policies, like health and social care, housing, employment, and other local services.[18] Wales could design a person-centred system, removing the stigma and prejudices that benefits claimants face by changing perceptions that access to social security is a fundamental human right. The social security system should put the needs of those who require assistance first, and advance equality and non-discrimination. A campaign to increase the take-up of existing benefits should precede the devolution of benefits, so that an accurate picture reflecting the number of potential claimants could be produced. This is precisely the kind of fundamental cultural change that is intimated in the Well-Being of Future Generations (Wales) Act 2015.

One aspect of the Scottish approach that warrants further investigation in Wales is that of removing the private sector from the benefits assessment process. Benefits to support people with disabilities or sickness usually involve an assessment before an eligibility decision is made. There has been widespread negative publicity attached to these processes and their administration, and there is a level of public concern regarding humane aspects of the system. Frequently, these assessment processes do not work properly and there have been a high level of successful appeals. Swansea Council has suggested devolving the assessment process and giving it to the NHS, who would have access to a person's medical records which would enable a more accurate assessment of their needs.[19] The Bevan Foundation also supported better integration of assessments with other elements of health and care to avoid a person having multiple separate assessments.[20] The front-end, human-facing aspect of the benefits system could be devolved relatively easily, and provide an opportunity for the integrated approach between health and social care that is such a predominant feature of the Social Services and Well-being Act (2014). In considering the movement of disability benefits assessments away from the private sector, members of the Equality, Local Government and Communities Committee voiced their concerns about the complexities between administration and the costs of the benefits system; and, in particular, that a more sympathetic approach to disability assessments (PIP) 'could lead to more applications being successful and asked, "who bears the financial consequences of that more generous assessment process?"'[21]

Although they would need to seek assurances that sufficient funding would be attached, there should be a clear commitment from the Welsh Government to consider the future devolution of sickness and disability benefits. This may not be immediately possible, given the complications around contracts entered by the UK government with the private sector to deliver these services, but it would certainly be the most marked sign of progression in their health and social care policies since 1997.

Rhetorically at least, Wales has long voiced a keen interest in the rights of carers to be heard, respected and valued. Yet, the current devolved social care system routinely fails them. At present there are over 370,000 adults and children in Wales (more than the population of Cardiff) who support a loved one who is older, disabled or seriously ill. Wales' ageing population, or 'silver tsunami' means that as people continue to live longer, more than three in five people will become carers at some stage during their lives.[22] Caring can be tough and have a huge impact on life plans. For some it's sudden: a loved one is taken ill or has an accident; a child is born with a disability. For others it creeps up unnoticed: their parents cannot manage on their own any longer, or their partner's health deteriorates. These unpaid carers provide over 96% of care in Wales, and despite the catastrophic impact on them posed by a loss of personal time, they enable their loved ones to get the most out of life, hold families together, and make an enormous contribution to society.[23]

The devolution of benefits in Scotland has allowed for supplementation of top-up payments for claimants of Carer's Allowance. This equates to an extra £221 payment automatically paid to carers, twice a year. By 2024, Scotland intends to replace Carer's Allowance with Carer's Assistance, and to allow for flexibility for claimants who care for more than one disabled person.[24] If Wales could adopt a similarly discretionary and flexible stance, its health and social care policies would start to align with a theme that is becoming increasingly prominent in cultural representations of care – that of mutual dependency. Individual potential can only be realised by accepting and leaning into our human interdependence. Critics like Eva Feder Kittay repeatedly refer to dependence as a foundational human characteristic, and that it should therefore be recognised as part of what it takes to be a citizen and a full person.[25]

While caring is an important part of life and being human, it also saves the economy billions of pounds.[26] In 2018, 223,000 people in the Welsh workforce identified as carers, which equates to one in seven workers having caring responsibilities.[27] At present, carers are eligible to claim Carer's Allowance of £66.15 per week if they care for someone for more than thirty-five hours a week – the equivalent of a full-time job. However, if they do so, their earning from any other form of employment must be less than £123 per week after deductions. If you work more than sixteen hours per week at minimum wage, you are over the limit. If you care for more than one person (say an elderly parent and a disabled child), you must choose one person to claim for, as you can only get one payment of Carer's Allowance. This leaves more and more people with no choice but to try to juggle paid work with an unpaid care role, often for multiple people. Intensively caring for another person is a psychologically-testing experience. Indeed, in 2017 a survey by Carers Wales found that over 75% of carers in Wales said that they were experiencing mental health problems.[28] Caregiving demands intense levels of feeling, exertion, and endurance that can have a detrimental effect on physical and mental health. Carers can be so involved in the lived bodily experience of their loved ones, that they begin to fall ill themselves.

In addition, state-funded care is in a dire state in Wales. At present the state, through local authorities, provides care for those who are unable to fund it themselves. In recent years, public expenditure on adult social care has been put under significant pressure. As a consequence, the fees paid to care homes by local authorities have been squeezed and are often insufficient to cover the homes' basic costs. There is therefore no incentive to modernise existing facilities or to expand in terms of capacity, and in time many care homes will be forced to close. As most care homes serve a mix of funded and self-funded residents, the sector has to some extent maintained provision by charging self-funders higher fees (in Wales, this is an average differential of 36%).[29] This model is unsustainable and the implications are ethically catastrophic; there are very few examples of new care home capacity focused on the local authority sector. An ageing population with an increasing acuity of care needs means that in future Welsh local authorities will be unable to meet demand for care home spaces regardless of eligibility.

Since 2015, Plaid Cymru have called for a national care service, pledging to abolish care charges for the elderly and those with dementia if they had taken power in the 2016 election. Delivering social care to those who need it, free at the point of delivery and funded by general taxation would be a seismic and truly progressive development. Helen Mary Jones has said that the current 'part-public, part-private, part-charitable social care system is delivering an inefficient and unjust service', and that it is now high time to 'finish what Aneurin Bevan started' and create a national care service fit for the twenty-first century.[30] Plaid will continue to push for this radical workable solution for social care as a policy for the May 2021 election. While supported by many Labour backbenchers, Plaid have historically accused the party, under the leadership of former First Minister, Carwyn Jones, as lacking a clear, long-term vision for social care, accusing them of instead fire-fighting a 'series of short-term pressures' like accident and emergency waiting times, health board scandals and a declining number of GPs.[31] Instead, Carwyn Jones, and now Mark Drakeford (who trained as a social worker) have preferred to prop up the 'new', joined-up approach between health and social care referred to incessantly in the Social Services and Well-being Act (2014), saying that it needs more time to bed-in. The First Minister, believing Wales to already exceed the social care standards that exist across the border, is still highly invested in the distinctive, 'made in Wales' ethos of this Act, at the expense of any immediate overhaul.[32] Tensions between Jeremy Corbyn and Drakeford on the subject of Labour's policy on free social care were publicly denied by Drakeford in 2019, with the Welsh manifesto simply pledging further engagement with 'people and communities' before 'extending' free social care.[33]

On paper, Wales has solutions to many of its health and social care problems, problems that play out in contexts of rurality, multiculturalism, widespread deindustrialisation and poverty. The opportunities afforded to policymakers to institute changes have been many, but in reality, much has been promised and little delivered. Successive Labour-led Welsh governments marketed devolution as something that would protect the population from the severest austerity measures of any national Tory government. But despite the much-asserted social democratic pedigree, the rhetoric of 'progressiveness' remains just that – rhetoric, not backed with any substantive policy change.

The Social Services and Well-being Act (2014) or the Well-being of Future Generations (Wales) Act 2015 have not yet transformed care and support in Wales. Indeed, there is an inherent reluctance on the part of Welsh Labour Government to even recognise the specific inequalities in current systems, for this would be tantamount to admitting culpability for systemic failures. This head in the sand approach was exemplified by Labour's 2019 rejection of The Autism Bill for Wales that proposed a particular set of protections for the 34,000 autistic people in Wales. Ministers are apparently still keen to 'give the Social Services and Well-being Act' a chance to embed itself, rather than act responsively to further specific health and social care issues brought to their attention in the five years since its unveiling. This, combined with the continued systemic failings of social services departments, and the fact that Wales does not yet manage the most fundamental of its social security benefits, compounds the issues faced by the hundreds of thousands of people who are attempting to access these services. The sheer human cost of these failures means that the risks of *not* changing Wales' current health and social care systems outweighs the risks of the further devolution. While devolution does not improve things automatically, Wales has a particular opportunity to do things differently, and the ability to create a fairer and more compassionate system. Indeed, the devolution of benefits could lead to improved alignment with devolved policies more generally, like health and social care, housing, employment and other local services – this would work with Welsh Government policies and be easier to achieve than across the UK as a whole. Yet, ultimately, there is still a huge degree of reticence in terms of the Welsh Government taking power or imposing urgent systemic and practical interventions in areas of policy that are crucial to the well-being of the population.

---

[1] https://www.legislation.gov.uk/anaw/2014/4/contents

[2] Peter Daniels, 'It's not Westminster's money: Why we should stop believing the myths about Wales' "block grant"' (6 November 2020) https://nation.cymru/opinion/its-not-westminsters-money-why-we-should-stop-believing-the-myths-about-wales-block-grant/

[3] Charlotte Williams ed., *Social Policy for Welfare Practice in a Devolved Wales 2nd edition* (British Association of Social Workers, 2011).

[4] Mark Drakeford, 'Social Justice in a Devolved Wales', *Benefits* 15:2 (2007).

[5] The White Paper *Sustainable Social Services: A Framework for Action* (Welsh Assembly Government, 2011).

[6] In 2009, Swansea County Council's Children Services department was given two weeks to respond to the Welsh Assembly Government about concerns of its handling of children's services.

https://www.communitycare.co.uk/2009/03/04/welsh-government-hands-ultimatum-to-swansea-childrens-services/ Similarly, Powys County Council has been the subject of damning reports and received threats of Government intervention due to the state of its children's services since 2017. https://www.bbc.co.uk/news/uk-wales-politics-41651441

[7] BBC News, 'High staff sickness at troubled Powys children's service' (10 March 2018) https://www.bbc.co.uk/news/uk-wales-mid-wales-43333355

[8] An example of this is in the local authorities' allocation of direct payments to service users in order for them to manage and organise their support in the way that suits them best. The take up for this initiative, rolled out in 1997 across the UK is still extremely low in many parts of Wales.

[9] Commission on Devolution in Wales, *Empowerment and Responsibility: Legislative Powers to Strengthen Wales*, paragraphs 11.3.7–11.3.11, March 2014.

[10] Ibid.

[11] HM Treasury (2013) Public Expenditure Statistical Analyses.

[12] National Assembly for Wales, *Benefits in Wales: options for better delivery* (Equality, Local Government and Communities Committee, 2019).

[13] At the outset of its enquiry the committee ruled out a number of devolution options, including the devolution of: the entire welfare system, Universal Credit in its entirety, and all sickness and disability benefits. These were ruled out for a variety of reasons, including: complexity of such devolution, the financial implications, and risks involved in such major scale change to the welfare system.

[14] Since 2016, the benefits devolved to Scotland were disability benefits (Disability Living Allowance, Personal Independence Payment, Attendance Allowance, Severe Disablement Benefit and Industrial Injuries Disablement Benefit; benefits for carers (Carer's allowance); payments related to cold weather; the social fund funeral expense payment; welfare foods; certain payments for maternity expenses. Full roll-out is expected by 2024.

[15] Guto Ifan and Cian Sion, '*Devolving Welfare: how would Wales fare? Assessing the fiscal impact of devolving welfare to Wales*', Wales Governance Centre, April 2019, p. 48.

[16] Ibid.

[17] Oxfam Cymru, in *Benefits in Wales: options for better delivery,* p. 32.

[18] It is interesting to note that in the Silk Commission's 2011 assessment of the possibility of devolving social security benefits to Wales, the Bevan Foundation submitted evidence that highlighted 'the risks of devolving social security, stating 'financial constraints and the current process of reform of social security benefits make devolution of almost all aspects of the benefit system virtually impossible in the short to medium term'. (https://assets.publishing.service.gov.uk/ government/uploads/system/uploads/attachment_data/file/310571/ CDW-Wales_Report-final_Full_WEB_310114.pdf , p. 129). By 2020 the impact of widespread poverty in Wales, exacerbated by the coronavirus pandemic, had led the Bevan Foundation to make a U-turn on its prior position. It is now advocating for a Welsh Benefits System that would enable the Welsh Government to assist people trapped in poverty, those who are currently 'locked out' of the benefits system by 'arbitrary and inadequate eligibility criteria'.
https://www.bevanfoundation.org/commentary/case-for-welsh-benefits-system

[19] Swansea Council, in *Benefits in Wales: options for better delivery*, p. 57.

[20] The Bevan Foundation, ibid., p. 57.

[21] ELGC Committee, 3 July 2019, RoP [70] ibid., p. 57.

[22] The Carers Trust https://carers.org/around-the-uk-our-work-in-wales/our-work-in-wales

[23] Carers Wales https://www.carersuk.org/wales/about-us

[24] Social Security: Benefits for carers,
https://www.gov.scot/policies/social-security/benefits-for-carers/

[25] Eva Feder Kittay, 'The Ethics of Care, Dependence and Disability,' in *Ratio Juris*, Volume 24, Issue 1, pp. 49–58, 2011.

[26] Carmarthenshire Carers Forum
http://ccf.wales/#:~:text=Carers%20save%20the%20Welsh%20econ omy,to%20be%20found%20through%20taxation.

[27] Employers for Carers https://www.employersforcarers.org/about-us/wales-hub

[28] State of Caring in Wales Report, 2018
https://www.carersuk.org/files/section/6055/carers-wales-state-of-caring-2018-final-report.pdf

[29] Competition and Markets Authority, 'Care Homes Market Strategy Report, Welsh Summary'
https://assets.publishing.service.gov.uk/media/5a1fdf8eed915d458b 922ec2/wales-short-summary-care-homes-market-study.pdf

[30] Helen Mary Jones, 'A national care service is long overdue'

https://www.iwa.wales/agenda/2019/09/a-national-care-service-is-long-overdue/

[31] Dai Lloyd, 'Why I am calling for the establishment of a National Care Service for Wales' (23 April 2018)
https://nation.cymru/opinion/why-im-calling-for-the-establishment-of-a-national-care-service-for-wales/

[32] Adrian Masters, 'Drakeford denies being "bounced" into social care pledge by Corbyn', ITV Cymru Wales (8 December 2019)
https://www.itv.com/news/wales/2019-12-08/mark-drakeford-denies-being-bounced-into-social-care-pledge-by-corbyn

[33] Standing up for Wales: Welsh Labour Manifesto 2019
https://www.welshlabour.wales/wp-content/uploads/sites/183/2019/11/Welsh-Labour-Manifesto-2019.pdf, p. 40.

Policing in Wales in the Age of Neoliberalism

Mike Harrison

> Policing needs to be reformed. We do indeed need new training regimes, enhanced accountability, and a greater public role in the direction and oversight of policing. We need to get rid of the warrior mindset and militarized tactics. It is essential that police learn more about the problems of people ...[1]

Alex L. Vitale's 2017 analysis of policing in the United States gave a damning verdict of what policing had become under the neoliberal state. The author presents a convincing argument that police exacerbate problems and tensions in communities through their dispassionate regard of people they encounter, and their enforcement of the law is overwhelmingly supported by liberal America. Any attempt at police reform within the neoliberal state is typically met with hostility due to entrenched conceptions of police work that focus on defending 'quality of life' issues.[2] Threats to the quality of life, such as how public space is occupied need to be protected, and it is no coincidence that police powers to curtail this have increased exponentially in recent decades.[3]

The role that the police officer plays can facilitate the continuation of neoliberal practices in terms of preserving a certain type of social order.[4] Whilst a key emphasis of neoliberalism is on stripping back the influence of the state – and one could be forgiven for thinking that this could include the police force – it is the actions of the so-called 'front-arm of the state' that can safeguard neoliberalism through increased punitive policies. Therefore, in addition to the impact of the neoliberal order on the nature of the police, it is its constitutive role in administering that order that is of interest here. In this respect, policing in Wales is no exception.

A Welsh Policing Identity?

One might question the specificity of Welsh policing when, organisationally speaking, it is not any different to forces in England, since policing and criminal justice are not devolved to the Welsh Government. However, this does not mean that police forces are not shaped by their local environments, and regional or national identity.[5] Indeed, my research in 2020 identified that Welsh officers were keen to define their style of public order policing as typically 'Welsh'. What exactly does this mean?

The idea of a unitary, overarching Welsh identity has been a highly contested idea. However, a popularised or stereotypical identity certainly exists. Dan Evans, for example, has suggested that this identity is 'reinforced by pop culture representations of Wales such as *Gavin and Stacey*, *Stella*, and MTV's *The Valleys*. Furthermore, it is 'synonymous with a working-class habitus' and includes characteristics such as, 'friendliness, openness, collective-ness, [and being] community-orientated'.[6] It is these characteristics that many Welsh officers in my PhD research identified with. When describing what shaped their approach of policing crowds in public order contexts such as sporting events, music festivals and protests, many argued that they would draw upon their Welsh cultural instincts and simply be 'friendly' and 'engage' in conversation. As one ground officer remarked in an interview, 'I genuinely think it's a part of being Welsh. I genuinely think it is within our culture that we speak to people.'[7] This perception was also reflective of many senior command officers as well. One commander claimed that their genial policing approach was reflective of Wales being a 'working-class-type orientated country'.[8] However, beyond these personal – and perhaps idealised – descrip-tions of how officers thought they policed, actual policing somewhat differed.

In my fieldwork, I observed that at sports events and festivals, officers positively engaged with crowds through lengthy and jovial conversations with sports fans or festival attendees. Officers posed for photographs, and even danced with entertainers and attendees at festivals. Admittedly, most of these events posed a low risk of disorder, meaning that officers could afford to act and engage in this way. They were only ever met with minor confrontations during these events, and they managed these in ways that resembled their description of Welsh identity. For example, when a unit of officers was met by an inebriated football fan who rung his sweat-soaked football shirt into their faces, one of the officer's grabbed the shirt and did the same to the fan. This resulted in a rupture of laughter from both parties, followed by a conversation about the game. This style of policing is advocated in guidelines as it supposedly deescalates, what could be considered, tense situations.[9] However, the police claimed that this was an intrinsic Welsh response rather than it being a direct impact of enforced policy.

At protests, police remained distant from activists and did not engage attendees. Of course, the context at protests was quite different, but with that aside, interaction was at a premium. An explanation for this came in police briefings before events. Commanders suggested that ground officers were more intimidated at protests because they felt their presence could be challenged, and that they could be 'caught out' because they did not know the law as well as activists did. Despite the police's role as antagonists at many protests around the world, this avoidance of confrontation is known in police parlance as 'on-the-job' trouble.[10] This suggests that police purposively avoid some incidents with the public as it can be cumbersome and challenging. Instead, the preferred mode of action, on some occasions, is to just not get involved. This could perhaps explain why officers I observed generally avoided engaging in conversation with activists. Furthermore, activists were sometimes 'othered' by police, and engagement in the alleged 'Welsh' style of policing described to me in interviews would not take place on the ground because it was unlikely to be reciprocated.

The 'friendly' Welsh identity that police so passionately believed influenced their style of policing was therefore only expressed at events that were low risk. However, an alternative explanation of the force's friendly approach (at low-risk events) was that it was a deliberate tactic of 'winning over' crowds that would make it easier to enforce more stringent policing if there was a need.[11] Whilst officers believed that their policing was connected to a friendly Welsh identity, it was the performance of this role that made it easier for them to exert a more quintessential policing characteristic, that of taking control.

The Neoliberal Turn

Policing approaches have gradually become more accommodating to protecting the materialistic interests of neoliberal capitalism in recent years. This has translated into more acute focus on policing street-level deviance and crime. Furthermore, it has normalised intrusive forms of policing, and eroded privacy.

Kaplan-Lyman suggests that zero-tolerance policing (ZTP) practices that emerged in New York City (NYC) in 1990s enabled the New York Police Department (NYPD) to 'clean-up' the streets and 'nip crime in the bud'. Initially, this form of policing was premised on the idea of Broken Windows Thesis (BWT), which suggested serious crime could be prevented if less serious crimes were tackled from the onset.[12] However, as Kaplan-Lyman suggests, 'cleaning up the streets' through increased 'stop and frisks',[13] and tougher policies on vandalism and graffiti could also facilitate a more marketable NYC. In recent years, NYC has seen significant gentrification across its boroughs, which has either displaced low-income communities or put others that live in these areas under severe financial constraints.[14] It was NYPD's hard-line policing approach that not only aimed to prevent crime but paved the way for more secure private investment in the boroughs of NYC. An additional consequence of ZTP has been the ability of police to practise more intrusive forms of policing. NYPD's use of stop and frisk increased considerably in the 1990s and the first two decades of the twenty-first century. In 1999, NYPD performed 175,000 stop and frisks.[15] This increased to 700,000 in 2011, before rates started to drop after a federal court ruled that NYPD's use of stop and frisk was unconstitutional, violating civil rights.[16] In the same ruling, Judge Shira Scheindlin had indicated that NYC's Black and Latino population had been disproportionately affected: in 2011, 84 per cent of those stopped were Black or Latino.[17] Kaplan-Lyman suggests that NYPD's use of stop and frisks was not based on BWT's supposition of 'nipping crime in the bud', but rather on 'order-maintenance policing'. In effect, it was used to increase NYPD's physical surveillance capabilities, that Kaplan-Lyman suggested 'dovetailed with the neoliberal ideology around individual responsibility'.

Policing in Wales has not been immune to the neoliberal influence of policing. This has been practised in the explicit ways, but also in ways that are less obvious. In my public order research, an analysis of friendly Welsh policing could be interpreted as a ploy to earn the trust of crowds that made it easier to exert control. Explicit forms

197

of power, such as using force in public order contexts would be viewed as disproportionate, and could potentially generate disorder and harm the reputation of 'Welsh' policing and Wales' 'welcoming' reputation and image.

Automated Facial Recognition

It is not always the case that police will attempt to conceal their intentions in the way described above. SWP was one of the first police forces in Wales and England to use Automated Facial Recognition (AFR). This enhanced and sophisticated surveillance technology has predominately been used in public order settings. It captures images of people and then compares these with a database of people who have been suspected of committing a crime or are people of interest.[18] Notwithstanding the historic controversy of police storing personal information on activists who have not committed any offences,[19] the use of AFR has been shown to incorrectly identify law-abiding citizens as criminals.

When SWP first used AFR at the UEFA Champions League final in Cardiff in June 2017, it recorded a measly 3% of 'true-positives' (i.e., correctly identifying suspects or people of interest). During an extended trial period of AFR in the spring of 2017 to spring of 2018, this increased to 26%. In explanation for its staggeringly low success rate at the Champions League, it was suggested that the unusual high volume of people that attended the event caused the AFR system to freeze and crash – which begs the question of its utility at public order events that typically attract large crowds. Moreover, as natural daylight fades the system struggles to successfully identify people, and at night it completely fails.[20]

Nevertheless, AFR has been used by other forces; according to *The Independent*, the Metropolitan Police Service (MPS) spent over £200,000 on purchasing the AFR software and hardware from its developer, the NEC corporation (Dearden, 2019).[21] The MPS deployed AFR on six occasions from August 2016 to July 2018. During this period, two people were stopped by police and then subsequently released. By contrast, SWP have deployed AFR 70 times from its first use at the UEFA Champions League (UCL) final in June 2017 to its last recorded use at a Slipknot concert in January 2020.[22] It has helped with the arrests of 60 people, although it is not clear what further action was taken against these. SWP has deployed this controversial technology at a higher rate than any other force in the UK, even at events that would usually be considered low risk.[23]

Proportionality is a term that police in Wales and the rest of the UK often use to reconnect officers with their founding mantra of policing by the consent of communities.[24] SWP has always stressed that the use of AFR has been 'proportionate', claiming it was governed by the Protection of Freedom Act 2012 as well as having oversight by a strategic partnership board and a surveillance camera commissioner.[25] Despite these layers of accountability, SWP's claims of AFR's proportionate 'legal' deployment was challenged by Cardiff resident, Ed Bridges.[26] In the first challenge, the High Court ruled that SWP's use of AFR was legal, concluding that SWP had complied with equality laws, and that the force had processed personal details in a lawful manner (R [Bridges] v CCSWP and SSHD, 2019 EWHC 2341).

However, Bridges challenged the High Court decision in the Court of Appeal and this time was successful (R [Bridges] v CCSWP & Ors, 2020 EWCA Civ 1058). In this ruling, the court found that using AFR had breached Bridges' right of privacy due to the discretion that SWP officers were afforded in terms of where AFR cameras were positioned. Additionally, the court ruled that SWP also breached their public sector equalities duty as they had not sufficiently checked to see whether using AFR cameras were biased in terms of race or sex (R [Bridges] v CCSWP & Ors, 2020 EWCA Civ 1058). This ruling was based on AFR's general inaccuracies of disproportionately selecting people of colour (and in particular, women of colour) as people of interest. In an article published in the *New York Times*, it was found that AFR technology made significant and worrying mistakes: darker-skinned men were 12% incorrectly identified, whilst that figure rose to 35% for darker-skinned women. For light-skinned women the system made errors 7% of the time, while for white men the error rate was 1%.[27]

SWP did not appeal this ruling, with its Chief Constable at the time, Matt Jukes indicating that the force would address its AFR policies.[28] However, the fact that SWP did not consider AFR's inaccuracies when it came to identifying race perhaps is representative of institutionalised thinking when it comes to people of colour.

Discriminative Policing

Supposedly, citizens of any neoliberalist state can, regardless of their background, be financially successful, simply because they are less constrained by government regulation. Individual entrepreneurism is strongly advocated by neoliberal orthodoxy, meaning that failure is attributed to the individual that did not work hard enough. However, pre-existing prejudices are, of course, absent from neoliberal thinking which means that 'members of poor and minority communities are [perceived] as *dangerous* not disadvantaged'.[29] One of the most notable trends that has accompanied neoliberal policing is that it has led to a substantial increase in practices that are prejudice. People of colour, and 'feckless and undeserving' populations such as the homeless are those often targeted.[30]

In the first few months of 2021, both SWP and Gwent Police had been accused of taking a heavy-handed approach towards young black men. Mohamud Mohammed Hassan was arrested outside his home in Cardiff on 8 January for 'breaching the peace'. Hassan was locked up at Cardiff Bay Police Station overnight where he directly and indirectly encountered 52 officers before being released.[31] According to friends and family, Hassan had bruises over his body. He went to bed not long after leaving the station and was pronounced dead later that evening.[32] At the time of writing (March 2021), the IOPC confirmed that five officers had been served notices to be charged with misconduct.[33]

In February 2021, the parents of Moyied Bashir called the police to their home in Newport. Bashir, who suffered from mental health issues, became unsettled after refusing to take medication to alleviate pain from a recent stab wound.[34] Gwent Police said that nine officers responded to the call,[35] although this number has been disputed by Bashir's brother who claimed 24 officers responded to the call.[36] Gwent Police restrained Bashir initially by handcuffing him and then holding his legs together. When Bashir became increasingly distressed and visibly ill due to the pressure being applied on his stab wound, police called an ambulance, but he died in hospital only a few hours after police responded to the call made by his parents. Gwent Police are currently being investigated by the IOPC.

Welsh police forces have not had a particularly 'welcoming' relationship with people of colour. Black people in SWP policing area are stop-and-searched at seven times the rate of white people.[37] In the Gwent Police area, this statistic is higher with Black people being stopped and searched at over ten times the rate of white people.[38] Asian people in the SWP policing area are stopped at more than two and half times the rate than white people, whilst in Gwent it is over five times the rate. In Wales' other two forces, Dyfed-Powys Police and North Wales Police, people of colour are disproportionately stopped at nearly twice the rate of white people.[39]

Discrimination against the Homeless

Police in Wales have also targeted rough sleepers. In 2018, *FOR Cardiff*, the Business Improvement District (BID) for Cardiff, funded and recruited two SWP constables to specifically tackle claims of aggressive begging by shop proprietors. It became the first BID in Wales to set aside funds to recruit officers to police rough sleepers.[40] It is this type of policing approach that symbolises the complete disdain for vulnerable groups in the neoliberal world. Despite police in Wales and England being able to draw upon the Vagrancy Act 1824, one of the most repressive laws in Europe used to police rough sleepers, the police continue to be supported by local and central government. Dispersal orders, contained under the Anti-Social Behaviour, Crime and Policing Act 2014, can be used by police to exclude, or ban the homeless from certain geographical areas, typically in town or city centres, for 48 hours. It is this type of power that enables the police to remove the visual inequalities that neoliberalism generates and maintain the uninterrupted practice of consumerism in the high streets.

Dispersal orders are cynically used during public specta-cles to metaphorically sweep the problem of homelessness under the carpet. When the UCL final was staged in Cardiff in 2017, SWP threatened rough sleepers that they would use Section 35 of the Anti-Social Behaviour, Crime and Policing Act 2014.[41] This power enables officers to disperse the homeless on the grounds that they are contributing or likely to contribute to behaviour that is deemed as harass-ment or could cause alarm or distress. The elasticity of terms such as *harassment*, *alarm* and *distress* gives officers directive to apply this law in the most minor or trivial cir-cumstances. If the recipient does not adhere to conditions under Section 35, it could result in criminal prosecution where if found guilty the person could spend a maximum three months in prison. According to many rough sleepers in Cardiff, police candidly asked them to leave the city centre before football fans started to arrive. If they did not comply with this request, SWP threatened that they would use Section 35 and emphasised the likelihood that they would spend time in prison.[42]

Additionally, Public Spaces Protection Orders (PSPO) also contained within the Anti-Social Behaviour, Crime and Policing Act 2014 are a common tool used to remove rough sleepers from communal areas. The *raison d'être* of PSPOs concerns 'quality of life': matters that have been explicit in crime policies since the Blair administration. Chapter Two of the Anti-Social Behaviour, Crime and Policing Act 2014 gives guidance for police and local authorities to police behaviour that is causing a 'nuisance' and is 'detrimental to the community'. This legislative language is arbitrary, and conveniently fits into narratives that the homeless are feckless and underserving. Furthermore, it appears to be a quick, easy, and normative method of dealing with an extremely vulnerable group. PSPOs are commonly used in Wales and are celebrated as a victory against the visual blight of homelessness.[43] Such powers are a clear example of how policing policies have naturally drifted to suit the interests of free-market economics over the welfare of vulnerable populations.

Conclusion

Despite the rhetoric around policing the 'Welsh way', there appears to be little difference between Welsh forces and those in the rest of the United Kingdom – or other countries that have been influenced by the neoliberal turn.

Whether it is investment and deployment of technologi-cally enhanced surveillance machinery, the overzealous policing of people of colour, or 'sweeping the streets' of the homeless through the use of dispersal orders, the police in Wales have embedded practices that clearly ac-commodate the needs of neoliberalism. Crime and policing policy under neoliberalism has been rationalised under improving the quality of life. However, it is clear that this is only relevant for those pursing the individualistic and capitalistic goals of neoliberalism.

Increased and enhanced surveillance as well as dispersal orders remove the perceived threats to neoliber-alism to ensure consumerism can continue unabated. The disproportionate use of stop and searches, and discrimi-native policing of people of colour in Wales can be interpreted as policing, not a disadvantaged population, but supposedly an inherently dangerous one that routinely engage in street-level criminality. This criminogenic image of black communities, combined with neoliberal values concerning property rights and quality of life, has led to disproportionate policing.

My research shows that police officers' interpretations of public order policing presented them with an opportu-nity to 'play out' their preconceptions of a 'friendly' Welsh identity and offer a form of policing that is ostensibly an-tithetical towards the incompassionate actions of neoliberalism. However, such approaches were only visible at low-risk events and not at protests, and further analysis revealed that even when officers engaged in this friendly way, they were still preoccupied with controlling the movement of crowds.

Nevertheless, practices of policing built in the mould of a friendly Welsh identity could potentially underpin more progressive or radical forms of policing in Wales. The seeds towards devolving policing and criminal justice have been sown in the recent Thomas Commission, which ardently recommended that these should be devolved.[44] This presents the opportunity for something new, although for real change in Wales, we arguably need a bolder government that takes the initiative on radical social change. This radical change could include adopting the same position as the 'defund the police' movement in the United States,[45] which has called for a reallocation of public funds from traditional policing to where there is a more urgent need for investment in communities: housing, health, and education.

---

[1] Alex S. Vitale, *The End of Policing* (London: Verso, 2017), p. 221.

[2] Jeremy Kaplan-Lyman, 'A Punitive Bind: Policing, Poverty, and Neoliberalism in New York City', *Yale Human Rights & Development Journal* 15:1 (2012).

[3] Ian Bruff, 'The Rise of Authoritarian Neoliberalism', *Rethinking Marxism* 26 (2014), 113–129.

[4] Kaplan-Lyman, 'A Punitive Bind'.

[5] See Malcolm Young, *In the Sticks: Cultural Identity in a Rural Police Force* (Oxford: OUP, 1993); Andrew Faull, 'Police Culture and Personal Identity in South Africa', *Policing: A Journal of Policy and Practice,* 11:3 (2017), 332–345.

[6] Daniel Evans, 'Welshness in "British Wales": negotiating national identity at the margins', *Nations and Nationalism,* 25:1 (2019), 167–190.

[7] Police Sergeant quoted in Mike Harrison, 'A Case Study Analysis of How Public Order Policing is Interpreted and Practised in South Wales' (unpublished PhD Thesis, University of South Wales, 2020), p. 202.

[8] Police Commander quoted ibid, p. 221.

[9] S.D. Reicher, C.J. Stott, P. Cronin and O.M.J. Adang, 'An integrated approach to crowd psychology and public order policing', *Policing,*

27:4 (2004), 558–572. See recent guidelines in College of Policing (2021) 'Public Order' College of Policing https://www.app.college.police.uk/app-content/public-order/

[10] P.A.J. Waddington, *Liberty and Order: Public Order Policing in a Capital City* (London: UCL Press, 1994).

[11] Ibid, p. 69.

[12] G.L. Kelling and J.Q. Wilson, 'Broken Windows – the police and neighbourhood safety', *Atlantic Monthly*, 249:3 (1982), 29–38.

[13] In Wales (and the rest of the UK) this is known as 'stop and search'.

[14] Chapple, K. and Thomas, T. (2020) 'Urban Displacement Project' https://www.urbandisplacement.org/maps/ny

[15] Kaplan-Lyman, 'A Punitive Bind'.

[16] NYCLU (2019) 'Stop and Frisk in the De Blasio Era', The New York Civil Liberties Union [https://www.nyclu.org/sites/default/files/field_documents/20190314_nyclu_stopfrisk_singles.pdf

[17] Center for Constitutional Rights (2014) 'Landmark Decision: Judge Rules NYPD Stop and Frisk Practices Unconstitutional, Racially Discriminatory' https://ccrjustice.org/home/press-center/press-releases/landmark-decision-judge-rules-nypd-stop-and-frisk-practices

[18] C. Stokel-Walker, 'Is police use of face recognition now illegal in the UK?', *New Scientist* (11 August 2020) https://www.newscientist.com/article/2251508-is-police-use-of-face-recognition-now-illegal-in-the-uk/#ixzz6kBrNVSed

[19] P. Lewis and M. Valee, 'Caught on film and stored on database: how police keep tabs on activists', *The Guardian* (6 March 2009) https://www.theguardian.com/uk/2009/mar/06/police-surveillance-database-activists-intelligence

[20] Davies, B, Innes, M., and Dawson, A. (2018), 'An Evaluation of South Wales Police Use of Automated Facial Recognition', Universities' Police Science Institute Crime & Security Research Institute, Cardiff University, https://afr.south-wales.police.uk/wp-content/uploads/2019/10/AFR-EVALUATION-REPORT-FINAL-SEPTEMBER-2018.pdf

[21] L. Dearden, 'UK's largest police force spends over £200,000 on facial recognition trials that resulted in no arrests', *The Independent* (19 January 2019) https://www.independent.co.uk/news/uk/home-news/facial-recognition-uk-police-met-arrests-london-cost-false-positives-accuracy-a8723756.html

[22] South Wales Police, 'Smarter Recognition Safer Community' (2020) https://afr.south-wales.police.uk/

[23] SWP deployed AFR at events that are traditionally low risk. This included rugby games and pop concerts (see South Wales Police, 2020). In London, the MPS used AFR at events that have traditionally been categorised as posing a high-risk although this was probably influenced by racial prejudice (Sharman, 2018).

[24] C. Emsley, *The Great British Bobby: A History of Policing From the 18th Century until the Present* (London: Quercus Publishing, 2009).

[25] J. Sharman, 'Metropolitan Police's facial recognition technology 98% inaccurate, figures show', *The Independent* (13 May 2018) https://www.independent.co.uk/news/uk/home-news/met-police-facial-recognition-success-south-wales-trial-home-office-false-positive-a8345036.html

[26] N. Dermody, 'Facial recognition technology: Ed Bridges appeals human rights ruling', BBC News (21 November 2019) https://www.bbc.co.uk/news/uk-wales-50495575#:~:text=Ed%20Bridges%20appealed%20against%20a,facial%20recognition%20(AFR)%20technology.&text=He%20argued%20the%20AFR%20system,without%20his%20knowledge%20or%20consent

[27] S. Lohr, 'Facial Recognition is Accurate if you're a White Guy', *The New York Times* (9 February 2018) https://www.nytimes.com/2018/02/09/technology/facial-recognition-race-artificial-intelligence.html

[28] D. Sabbagh, 'South Wales Police lose landmark facial recognition case', *The Guardian* (11 August 2020) https://www.theguardian.com/technology/2020/aug/11/south-wales-police-lose-landmark-facial-recognition-case

[29] Kaplan-Lyman, 'A Punitive Bind', p. 207.

[30] Whiteford, M. (2008) 'Street homelessness and the architecture of citizenship', *People, Place and Policy*, 2 (2): 88–100.

[31] IOPC (2021a) 'Update on investigation into death of Mohamud Mohamed Hassan in Cardiff', Independent Office for Police Conduct, https://www.policeconduct.gov.uk/news/update-investigation-death-mohamud-mohamed-hassan-cardiff-0

[32] BBC News (2021a) 'Mohamud Mohammed Hassan: Police misconduct notice served' (15 February 2021) https://www.bbc.co.uk/news/uk-wales-56077386

[33] IOPC (2021a).

[34] BBC News, 'Moyied Bashir death: Gwent Police hand bodycam footage to IOPC', (21 February 2021) https://www.bbc.co.uk/news/uk-wales-56148362

[35] A. Mohdin, 'Watchdog investigates second death after contact with

police in Wales', *The Guardian* (19 February 2021)
https://www.theguardian.com/uk-news/2021/feb/19/watchdog-investigates-second-death-contact-police-wales-moyied-bashir

[36] Cited in White, 'Moyied Bashir: Watchdog Investigates Death Of Man After Being Restrained By Police', *The Huffington Post* (19 February 2021) https://www.huffingtonpost.co.uk/entry/gwent-police-watchdog-death-moyied-bashir_uk_602eb3dbc5b673b19b66f7e6

[37] Stopwatch (2021) 'South Wales Police' https://www.stop-watch.org/your-area/area/south-wales

[38] Stopwatch (2021) 'Gwent Police' https://www.stop-watch.org/your-area/area/gwent

[39] Stopwatch (2021) 'Dyfed-Powys Police' https://www.stop-watch.org/your-area/area/dyfed-powys; Stopwatch (2021) 'North Wales Police' https://www.stop-watch.org/your-area/area/north-wales

[40] A. Lewis, 'The reality of aggressive begging in Cardiff, its impact, its victims and those trapped by its rules', *WalesOnline* (4 September 2018) https://www.walesonline.co.uk/news/wales-news/reality-aggressive-begging-cardiff-impact-15110626

[41] Walford, J. (2017) 'This is the law police can use to move on the homeless', *WalesOnline* (2 June 2017) https://www.walesonline.co.uk/news/wales-news/law-police-can-use-move-13128911

[42] Deacon, T. (2017) 'Homeless people say they have been told by police to leave Cardiff ahead of the Champions League final', *WalesOnline* (2 June 2017) https://www.walesonline.co.uk/news/wales-news/homeless-people-say-been-told-13125908

[43] Griffiths, N. (2018) 'Impact of public spaces protection order on antisocial behaviour 'invaluable' for area of Newport', *South Wales Argus* (23 September) https://www.southwalesargus.co.uk/news/16897723.impact-public-spaces-protection-order-antisocial-behaviour-invaluable-area-newport/

[44] The Commission on Justice in Wales (2019) 'Justice in Wales for the People in Wales', Welsh Government https://gov.wales/sites/default/files/publications/2019-10/Justice%20Commission%20ENG%20DIGITAL_2.pdf

[45] Ray, R. (2020) 'What does 'defund the police' mean and does it have merit?', Brookings https://www.brookings.edu/blog/fixgov/2020/06/19/what-does-defund-the-police-mean-and-does-it-have-merit/

The Prison System in Wales

Polly Manning

Prisons are often perceived as metaphorical islands, untouched by the currents of wider society. According to the age-old protocol of incarceration, an individual commits a crime and is sent to prison, which punishes them by limiting their freedom of movement. However, the prison system in Wales is not as judiciously separate from contemporary trends as one might think. In fact, it couldn't be any more attuned to the demands of free-market capitalism. Despite being governed by an ostensibly 'socialist' Labour Government since 1999, the state of prisons and the criminal justice system in Wales have never been worse. Welsh prisons are more over-crowded than ever, and Wales is continuously proven to have the highest rate of incarceration in western Europe.[1] Does this situation simply represent the failure of Welsh Government ministers to develop progressive solutions to the problem, or is something more sinister at play?

A 'Radical' Vision?

Under neoliberalism, trust is placed in 'the market'. The rich, convinced that their status has nothing to do with the advantages of class and inheritance, claim wealth and success in life is the result of one's personal abilities. By this logic, poverty is the result of the poor not 'enterprising' their way out of deprivation.[2] Yet almost a quarter of people in Wales live in poverty, and that figure has little wavered for a decade.[3] With its key characteristics of privatisation of public services, structural unemployment, unaffordable housing, and austerity, neoliberalism has ensured the creation and maintenance of a colossal *lumpenproletariat* within which criminality becomes a method of material and social survival.[4] In the neoliberal state, the ruling class cites the need to control this criminal *lumpen* population as justification for the expansion of a carceral state in which the security and police services have almost unbridled power. In Wales, as in the US and much of Europe, this power often reveals itself in the form of police brutality, and the racist over-policing of minority populations. In particular, Wacquant argues that African–Americans are subjected to a 'triple exclusion' by the US prison system, removing them from access to cultural capital, social redistribution, and political participation – and that subsequently the prison system creates a separative racial hierarchy which reinforces itself as the police are granted greater power and financial backing.[5] In January 2021, the sudden death of Mohamud Mohammed Hassan following a night in the custody of South Wales Police represents just the latest example of the racist police brutality that is systematic within the force, and subsequently within the prison system itself.[6] A 2020 report found that Black people in Wales were almost 6 times overrepresented in prison in 2019, whilst Asian prisoners were 1.9 times overrepresented and individuals from a mixed ethnic group were 2.7 times overrepresented in the prison system.[7]

When faced with criticism of the high rates of incarceration, appalling prison conditions, and failures in rehabilitation that have accumulated under their watch, the Welsh Government has hit back with their familiar excuse: 'But X isn't devolved!'. Certainly, criminal justice remains under the control of the Westminster Government. It is worth nothing, however, the warm welcome Welsh Labour politicians gave to the announced plans for HMP Berwyn in 2013. The Welsh Labour MP for Wrexham at the time, Ian Lucas, praised the plans – noting that 'a boost to local employment will be welcomed in the town'.[8] The Wrexham Council leader at the time, Welsh Labour's Neil Rogers, celebrated the economic benefits of the prison: 'Not only will the construction phase bring jobs and business opportunities, the running of the prison will offer a whole host of much-needed career opportunities for our young people.'[9] Their celebrations came despite stark warnings at the time from Robert Jones, a leading academic on the Welsh prison system, that HMP Berwyn was destined to sustain high rates of reoffending and prioritise 'importing' prisoners from England rather than enabling Welsh prisoners to remain close to their local area.[10]

Prisons

There are five prisons in Wales: HM Prison Berwyn, HM Prison Usk, HM Prison Cardiff, HM Prison Parc, and HM

Prison Swansea. Construction on the newest, HMP Berwyn, began in 2014. The site, in Wrexham, became partially operational in 2017, and as the largest prison in the UK is regarded by the Prison Service to be their 'flagship'.[11] Rather than decry the construction of what the Welsh Government called a 'super-prison', Wrexham residents were encouraged by the media and by Welsh Labour politicians to celebrate the new jobs Berwyn would bring to the area.[12] The often abhorrent experiences of the prisoners within these institutions was an afterthought.

In 2019, the Wales Governance Centre released a report detailing the inhumane conditions within Berwyn.[13] The prison's population increased by 116% between 2017–19 – and in 2018 the rate of prisoner-on-prisoner assaults rose by 338%. The report also revealed that Berwyn has some of the highest rates of weapon finds, 'use of force incidents' by staff, and prisoner violence in Wales. Assaults on prison staff rose by 405% between 2017 and 2018. Approximately a quarter of all inmates developed a drug problem whilst serving their sentences, and visitors and journalists visiting Berwyn have described the cells as being so low that they can lay their hands flat on the ceiling.[14]

The growing prevalence of so-called 'super-prisons' such as Berwyn indicate that the UK Government is following in the ideological footsteps of its neoliberal cousin, the United States. Primarily touted as low cost and efficient, super-prisons have a proven track-record of worsening – not improving – outcomes for prisoners. It has been reported that larger numbers of inmates are difficult to manage and present a greater threat of violence towards both staff and prisoners; that the frequent location of such prisons far from communities fragments inmates' family ties, and that inmates show higher rates of reoffending than in smaller, more localised prisons.[15]

Berwyn is a symptom of a wider global pattern of hyper-incarceration. Just as Welsh Labour politicians welcomed Berwyn as an opportunity for socio-economic stimulation, prisons in the US – as noted by David Ladipo – have become viewed as opportunities to economically rejuvenate deindustrialised areas.[16] Prisons in the US are typically run for profit, with inmates used as slave labour for numerous global companies – as well as supplying unpaid labour in areas such as municipal works and fire-fighting, amongst others.[17] This is a trend which makes itself apparent in Wales, too: HMP Berwyn, HMP Cardiff, and HMP Swansea all house call centres staffed by inmates paid well below minimum wage.[18] Whilst the call centre scheme is presented by the Prison Service as a chance for prisoners to 'gain employment skills', in 2020 a former Berwyn inmate told the press that call-centre employees were expected to 'cold-call' members of the public – often the elderly and vulnerable – with a survey on behalf of capital entities including Sky and the *Daily Mail*.[19]

Not only does Berwyn represent Wales and the Welsh Government's entanglement in the hyper-incarceration of citizens by western governments, but the neoliberalisation of cultural values. The prison outlines a set of six primary values to be adhered to by its staff; bizarrely, the fifth is to 'embrace Welsh culture and tradition'.[20] Indeed, HMP Berwyn – much like the ill-fated Wylfa B nuclear plant –

has gone out of its way to appear to embrace its Welsh setting. The prison's three houses are named after bodies of water in North Wales: Bala, Alwen, and Ceiriog.[21] It represents a tacky attempt to virtue-signal a connectivity with the community and engineer an image of locality and rehabilitation: something which could not be further removed from the prison's actual ethos of warehouse-optimised incarceration. There is a particular irony, too, in the fact that numerous reports testify to the harassment and separation of first-language Welsh-speaking inmates by prison staff.[22]

Humanely, Decently and Lawfully

HM Prison Service's 'Statement of Purpose' identifies the three major objectives of prison confinement in Wales: to 'hold prisoners securely', to 'reduce the risk of prisoners reoffending', and to 'provide safe and well-ordered establishments in which we treat prisoners humanely, decently and lawfully'.[23]

HM Prison Usk is a 273-inmate capacity prison located in Usk, Monmouthshire, jointly managed with satellite prison HMP Prescoed three miles away. Usk has traditionally been celebrated as the 'best' prison in Wales, lauded for its lack of overcrowding and the positive relationships between staff and inmates. Even in such a 'well-performing' prison, however, structural issues of poor living conditions and drug abuse persist. In 2019, the number of prisoners caught with drugs in HMP Usk increased by 350%.[24] In April 2020, the Ministry of Justice published figures revealing that of the 525 prisoners at HMP Usk/Prescoed between 2018–19, 312 (59%) were living in crowded conditions – all of whom were prisoners doubled up in what were designed to be single-occupancy cells.[25]

Swansea Prison boasts an even worse history. Equipped to hold no more than 250 prisoners, it currently houses approximately 415–450: making it the single most over-crowded prison across Wales and England.[26] In the August of 2017, the watchdog HM Inspectorate of Prisons (HMIP) carried out an unannounced inspection of Swansea prison, and the resulting report revealed shocking findings.[27] In the space of six years (2011–17), eight Swansea Prison inmates took their own lives – all within the first week of their arrival. In the six months prior to the investigation there were 134 reported instances of self-harm amongst prisoners. The report noted that 17% of inmates had become addicted to drugs *after* the start of their sentences in the prison, and the provision of clean bedding and clothing was described as 'unacceptably poor'. The report added that the prison had a 'complacent and inexcusable' attitude towards the safety of the most vulnerable prisoners in its care, and that 'prisoners usually had to eat their meals next to their toilets, which did not always have seats or lids'.

The Prison Industrial Complex

Many people exclusively associate the 'Prison Industrial Complex' with the prison system in the United States.

However, the practice and ethos of governments turning the management of prisons over to private corporations – who run them for profit – is becoming increasingly prevalent in Wales.[28] HMP Parc in Bridgend was one of the first prisons to be built in the UK under the Westminster Government's Private Finance Initiative (PFI) scheme – itself one of the most explicit examples of the neoliberal privatisation of public services in recent history.[29] A PFI was secured for the construction and management of Parc Prison in January 1996, and private sector consortiums entered a bidding war for the contract. The National Audit Office report of the exchange is packed with tables comparing the 'cost-per-prisoner' between various construction options, with little to no mention of inmate welfare, the risk of overcrowding, or safeguarding measures for prisoners in any section of the report.

The prison opened in October 1997, and within eighteen months experienced four suicides and a string of violent disturbances.[30] Operated by Securicor (now absorbed into G4S), an Independent Monitoring Board report published in 2004 revealed that there were seven outstanding inquests into deaths in custody at the prison.[31] These dated back as far as September 2002 and included the inquest into the death of 17-year-old young offender Ian Powell, found dead in his cell on 6 October 2002. In January 2020, Public Health Wales announced an investigation into conditions at the prison following a 'cluster' of tuberculosis cases amongst inmates.[32] In the March of 2020, inspectors noted that, despite 17% of the prison's 1,612 inmates having been convicted for sexual offences, as a remand and resettlement facility, G4S had not resourced the prison to deliver specific rehabilitation for these inmates. Additionally, inspectors voiced concern that despite half of the prisoners having mental health problems, only 23% had received professional help. The inspectors emphasised that 17% of prisoners leave Parc homeless.[33]

Indeed, the homelessness facing newly released prisoners is endemic in Wales. In the November of 2019, the HM Chief Inspector of Prisons revealed that 47% of prisoners released from HMP Cardiff had no accommodation to go to.[34] In their response to this finding, the Welsh Government released a statement claiming that they had 'put a number of measures in place to prevent people becoming homeless, including Housing First …'.[35] However, Housing First schemes in Wales have historically only catered to a proportionally tiny number of homeless cases. Between 2017–2018, Swansea Council secured a £100,000 budget to trial a Housing First scheme which catered for *ten* people – and failed.[36] To put things in perspective, over 200 inmates are released from Cardiff Prison every month.[37] Not only this, but the Housing (Wales) Act of 2014, introduced by the Welsh Government, *removed* automatic priority-need status for homeless prison leavers: that is, the Welsh Government simply decided that it wasn't necessary to provide homeless prison-leavers with accommodation.[38]

Not only this, but much like other housing schemes in Wales, Housing First takes it for granted that social landlords will be instrumental in the provision of housing for vulnerable individuals such as those recently released from prison or on probation.[39] However, with the introduction of the Housing (Wales) Act of 2014, the private rented sector (PRS) will be increasingly used by local authorities to fulfil their homelessness duties. The blind acceptance of landlordism as providing a necessary social service is one of the most significant markers of Wales' descent into a privatised culture defined by the needs of capital, rather than citizens.

'Not in our community'

In Marxist and anarchist theory, prisons represent functions of state control catering to the continued separation of those with and without capital.[40] Unfortunately, Welsh society experiences a deeply entrenched 'false consciousness' when it comes to matters of crime and punishment, which tends to favour the ideological and literal brutalisation of prisoners as 'scum-of-the-earth' types – rather than some of the most vulnerable and let-down people in society.[41] The poor state of the Welsh media certainly plays a role in this, with the country's primary online news outlet – *WalesOnline* – exhibiting a reliably sensationalist and conservative take on the reporting of crime. The website runs a monthly 'Locked Up' feature, gleefully exhibiting the most violent, depraved, or comical crimes. Recent headlines include: 'Locked Up: The killer, drug kingpin, lockdown-breakers, and other criminals sent to prison in August' and 'All of these criminals were given a second chance and they all blew it.'[42] It is no wonder, then, that the familiar response to calls for prison abolition is, 'But what about murderers/paedophiles/rapists?' – who collectively represent a minute percentage of all offenders.[43] This culture of classist distrust and fearmongering has created an environment in which the majority of opposition to the construction of new prisons in Wales – such as the failed plans to construct a 'super-prison' at a Port Talbot site in 2019 – is not concerned with the fact that inmates are subjected to inhumane treatment, but rather nimbyism: that they do not want 'these types' in their communities.[44] It is likely that this response is due, in part, to the failure of any organisation in Wales – charitable, governmental or otherwise – to posit a viable, radical alternative to the prison system as we know it. The left has provided limited dissent towards the prison system as it stands, let alone radical visions of its future. A weak national media, coupled with a sense of apathy generated by Westminster rule, means that there is little discussion of Welsh prisons in the public sphere. Frankly, the rights of prisoners are not seen as a 'sexy' cause capable of wide appeal, and its discussion is regarded as political suicide in the realm of electoral politics. The left appears to have shrunk away from the topic in fear of the sensationalism that surrounds, for example, issues such as prisoners' voting rights.

A Radical Alternative to the Prison System in Wales

In his seminal work on justice systems, *In Russian and French Prisons*, Kropotkin argues that:

> The principle of the lex talionis – of the right of the community to avenge itself on the criminal – is no longer

admissible. We have come to an understanding that society at large is responsible for the vices that grow in it ... and we generally admit, at least in theory, that when we deprive a criminal of his liberty, it is to purify and improve him. But we know how hideously at variance with the ideal the reality is.[45]

Published in 1887, this is an astounding statement: largely because it indicates just how regressive so many contemporary notions of justice have become. Western political thought on prisons seems to have progressed little – if at all – since the end of the nineteenth century. Most mainstream thought on the subject of criminal justice still takes for granted the assertion that prisons have the potential to limit and prevent crime. The Scandinavian 'open prison' system is frequently held up as an ideal of what prisons could be, and its dedication to humanism is of course admirable *within the confines of a capitalist system*.[46] However, whilst they are vastly superior to traditional systems such as those employed in Wales – in terms of low reoffending rates and better conditions for prisoners – Scandinavian prisons are still plagued by issues of underpaid prison labour and a steady recidivism rate of approximately 20%.[47]

The prison system – in any form – must be abolished if any truly just, humane, and effective vision of crime and punishment is to come to fruition in Wales. Naturally, progressive solutions to the prison complex can only be achieved with the devolution of crime and punishment into the remit of the Welsh Government. However, whilst requiring a structural overhaul of justice institutions and the ideologies which drive them, the solutions are fairly simple. Prisons should be abolished, and their funding – approximately £4.56 billion across the UK between 2018–2019 – redirected into schools, community programmes and social services.[48] Abolishing and removing funding from the prison service and funnelling that wealth back into the root causes of crime – unemployment, social neglect, substance abuse and addiction, poverty – could reverse the current cycle of criminalisation and reoffending. This community-based approach is also an ideal environment in which to enact genuine restorative justice. The rehabilitation of those who have committed criminal offences should happen in the community, thus solidifying the crucial practice of social responsibility. Such a method has been proven to reintegrate those who have committed offences back into communities, in a way which de-alienates them from society.[49]

In answer to the sensationalist question of 'But what about murderers/paedophiles/rapists?', Wales could lead the world in rehabilitative justice by establishing specialised units for the most dangerous offenders. Whilst HMP Parc and HMP Cardiff have little to no resources to deal with their sizeable inmate population of sex offenders, for example, in the specialised unit system dangerous offenders would be rehabilitated within a secure environment staffed by specialist and criminal psychologists, medical professionals, and therapists. Individuals charged with offences relating to sexual violence, murder, and paedophilia represent such a proportionally small number of those currently imprisoned that such units could operate at a fraction of the cost of prisons – and produce a reduced rate of reoffending.

Whilst the Welsh Government has been able to evade calls for criminal reform on account of the reserved powers model, there are areas of public life which they can – and should – act on to end cycles of criminalisation. Wales has been slow to consider progressive measures such as the legalisation of drugs – proven in other countries to have decreased criminal offending, drug-related deaths and gang activity.[50] Despite calls, the Welsh Government remain unresponsive to this route, citing the legal control that Westminster has over drugs policy as a reason not to advocate for decriminalisation on the grounds of Health or Social policy – both of which are within their purview.[51] In 2001, Portugal decriminalised the possession of all drugs for personal use, in one of the most high-profile examples of progressive drugs policy in recent history.[52] Between 1999 and 2012, the proportion of drug-related offenders in the Portuguese prison population dropped from 44% to just under 21%, and deaths due to drug use have decreased significantly – from approximately 80 in 2001, to 16 in 2012.[53]

All evidence suggests that, from a progressive standpoint, the prison system in Wales cannot be reformed – and must be abolished and replaced by a truly 'radical', community-*centred* approach to justice, one which takes for granted what the current system cannot: that people convicted of crime are as much members of society as anyone else.

[1] R. Jones, *Imprisonment In Wales: A Factfile* (2018), pp. 5–13 https://www.cardiff.ac.uk/__data/assets/pdf_file/0008/1195577/I mprisonment-in-Wales-A-Factfile.pdf S. Morris, 'Wales has highest incarceration rate in western Europe – study', *The Guardian* (15 January 2019) https://www.theguardian.com/uk-news/2019/jan/ 16/wales-has-highest-incarceration-rate-in-western-europe-prison-population-england

[2] G. Monbiot, 'Neoliberalism – the ideology at the root of all our problems', *The Guardian* (15 April 2015) https://www.theguardian.com/books/2016/apr/15/neoliberalism-ideology-problem-george-monbiot

[3] Oxfam Cymru, *Poverty in Wales* (2020) https://oxfamapps.org/cymru/poverty-in-wales/

[4] J. Welshman, *Underclass: A History of the Excluded Since 1880* (2nd ed.) (London: Bloomsbury, 2013).

[5] L. Wacquant, 'From Slavery to Mass Incarceration', *New Left Review*, 13 (2002) https://newleftreview.org/issues/ii13/articles/loic-wacquant-from-slavery-to-mass-incarceration

[6] BBC News, 'Mohamud Mohammed Hassan's death in Cardiff investigated' (11 January 2021) https://www.bbc.co.uk/news/uk-wales-55611642

[7] R. Jones, *Prison, Probation, and Sentencing in Wales: 2019 Factfile* (2020), p.72. https://www.cardiff.ac.uk/__data/assets/pdf_file/0010/2446129/Pr ison,-Probation-and-Sentencing-in-Wales-2019-Factfile.pdf

[8] BBC News, 'Reaction to £250m super-prison location announcement' (2013) https://www.bbc.co.uk/news/uk-wales-north-east-wales-23961430

[9] Ibid..

[10] IWA, 'Wrexham's super jail will be too big' (2013) https://www .iwa.wales/agenda/2013/11/wrexhams-super-jail-will-be-too-big/

[11] G. Plimmer and H. Warrell, 'Wrexham jail to be run by public sector' (2015) https://www.ft.com/content/ea817594-bc37-11e4-a6d7-00144feab7de

[12] Wrexham Glyndŵr University, 'University helps students pursue career in new multi-million pound super-prison' (2017) https://www.glyndwr.ac.uk/en/AboutGlyndwrUniversity/Newsandme diacentre/Newsarchive/PressReleases2016/Prison/

[13] R. Jones, *Sentencing and imprisonment in Wales* (Wales Governance Centre, 2018)

https://www.cardiff.ac.uk/__data/assets/pdf_file/0004/1547914/W
GC-Report-SentencingandImprisonment04.pdf

[14] O. Wainwright, 'Epic jail: inside the UK's optimised 'super-prison'
warehouses', *The Guardian* (2 September 2019)
https://www.theguardian.com/artanddesign/2019/sep/02/epic-jail-
inside-super-prison-warehouses-architecture

[15] D.P. Mears, *Evaluating the Effectiveness of Supermax Prisons*
(Report no. 211971), U.S. Department of Justice (2006)
https://www.ncjrs.gov/pdffiles1/nij/grants/211971.pdf

[16] D. Ladipo, 'The Rise of America's Prison-Industrial Complex', *New
Left Review* 7 (2001) https://newleftreview.org/issues/ii7

[17] E. Aseltine & K. Wehr, *Beyond the Prison Industrial Complex: Crime
and Incarceration in the 21st Century* (Abingdon: Routledge, 2013).

[18] J. Rees, 'Prison call centres aim to cut reoffending risk', BBC News
(15 October 2019) https://www.bbc.co.uk/news/uk-wales-
50003901

[19] S. Bagnall, 'HMP Berwyn inmates "cold-called elderly" from
"unethical" jail call centre, ex-prisoner claims', *Daily Post* (12 October
2020) https://www.dailypost.co.uk/news/north-wales-news/hmp-
berwyn-inmates-cold-called-19017622

[20] National Offender Management Service in Wales, *Newsletter: HMP
Berwyn* (2016)
http://old.wrexham.gov.uk/assets/pdfs/prison/hmp_berwyn_newslett
er_may2016.pdf

[21] J. Grieve, 'Wrexham's new £212m prison 'can be force for good' as
first inmates arrive', *The Leader* (21 July 2017)
https://www.leaderlive.co.uk/news/15962427.wrexhams-new-212m-
prison-can-be-force-for-good-as-first-inmates-arrive/

[22] BBC News, 'HMP Berwyn: Welsh-speaking inmates "threatened
with sanctions"' (28 September 2020)
https://www.bbc.co.uk/news/uk-wales-54324232

[23] HM Prison Service, *Statement of Purpose* (2010)
https://web.archive.org/web/20100913192642/http://www.hmpris
onservice.gov.uk/abouttheservice/statementofpurpose/

[24] H. Clugston, 'Number of prisoners caught with drugs in HMP Usk
up 350 per cent in 2019', *South Wales Argus* (19 May 2020)
https://www.southwalesargus.co.uk/news/18458679.number-
prisoners-caught-drugs-hmp-usk-350-per-cent-2019/

[25] R. Jones, *COVID-19 and Imprisonment in Wales* (2020) pp. 6–9
https://www.cardiff.ac.uk/__data/assets/pdf_file/0012/2205300/Cov
id-19-and-Imprisonment-in-Wales-April-2020-FINAL.pdf (24/05/2020)

[26] Ibid, p.7.

[27] HM Chief Inspector of Prisons, *Report on an unannounced inspection of HMP Swansea* (2017) https://www.justiceinspectorates.gov.uk/hmiprisons/wp-content/uploads/sites/4/2018/01/Swansea-Web-2017.pdf

[28] J.B. Peterson, *Prison Industrial Complex For Beginners* (Danbury: For Beginners LLC, 2016).

[29] J. Bourn, *The PFI Contracts for Bridgend and Fazakerley Prisons* (London: National Audit Office, 1997).

[30] N. Palit, 'Report: Control is 'fragile' at high-tech prison', BBC News (14 October 1999) http://news.bbc.co.uk/1/hi/wales/474313.stm

[31] BBC News, 'Private jail "worst" says report' (10 August 2004) http://news.bbc.co.uk/1/hi/wales/3549880.stm

[32] Public Health Wales, *Cluster of TB cases in HMP Parc* (2020) https://phw.nhs.wales/news/cluster-of-tb-cases-in-hmp-parc/

[33] HM Chief Inspector of Prisons, *Report on an unannounced inspection of HMP Parc* (2020) https://www.justiceinspectorates.gov.uk/hmiprisons/wp-content/uploads/sites/4/2020/03/Parc-web-2019.pdf

[34] Jones, 2020, *Prison, Probation, and Sentencing in Wales: 2019 Factfile*.

[35] J. Rees, 'HMP Cardiff "bucks trend" on rising violence', BBC News (5 November 2019) https://www.bbc.co.uk/news/uk-wales-50289223

[36] Swansea Council, *Housing First: The Swansea Approach* (2019) https://www.cymorthcymru.org.uk/files/1415/6329/4546/Tales_of _Implementation_Steve_Porter_Swansea_Council_- _Housing_First_Wales_conference_Cymorth_Cymru.pdf (24/09/20)

[37] Rees, 2019.

[38] A. Golten, *Settled: Good practice in homelessness prevention among prison leavers*, Shelter Cymru (2015) https://sheltercymru.org.uk/wp-content/uploads/2015/02/Settled-Good-practice-in-homelessness-pre vention-among-prison-leavers.pdf (01/02/21)

[39] Ibid.

[40] J. Ferrell, 'Against the Law: Anarchist Criminology', in A.J. Nocella II, M. Seis & J. Shantz, eds., *Contemporary Anarchist Criminology: Against Authoritarianism and Punishment* (Bern: Peter Lang Publishing, 2018), pp. 11–21.

[41] G. Lukács, *History and Class Consciousness: Studies in Marxist Dialectics* (London: Merlin Press, 2017 [1923]).

[42] *WalesOnline*, 'Locked Up: The killer, drug kingpin, lockdown-breakers, and other criminals sent to prison in August' (2020) https://www.walesonline.co.uk/news/wales-news/criminals-jailed-locked-up-wales-18831146 *WalesOnline,* 'All of these criminals were given a second chance and they all blew it' (2020) https://www.walesonline.co.uk/news/wales-news/criminals-wales-crime-prison-sentences-18676595

[43] Jones (2020), pp. 10–11.

[44] Nimbyism describes the 'not in my back yard' phenomenon: the opposition of locals to the locating of something 'undesirable' in their community. BBC News, 'Port Talbot super-prison proposals axed' (21 January 2019) https://www.bbc.co.uk/news/uk-wales-46953262

[45] P. Kropotkin, *In Russian and French Prisons* (London: Ward and Downey, 1887), p. 12.

[46] J. Dullum & T. Ugelvik, *Penal Exceptionalism? Nordic Prison Policy and Practice* (Abingdon: Routledge, 2011).

[47] C. Sterbenz, 'Why Norway's prison system is so successful', Business Insider (11 December 2014). https://www.businessinsider.com/why-norways-prison-system-is-so-successful-2014-12?r=US&IR=T

[48] D. Clark, *Public sector expenditure on prisons in the United Kingdom from 2009/10 to 2018/19* (2019) https://www.statista.com/statistics /298654/united-kingdom-uk-public-sector-expenditure-prisons/#:~:text=The%20United%20Kingdom%20spent%20approxi mately,compared%20to%20the%20previous%20year (

[49] Cullen, F. & Lipsey, M. (2007) 'The Effectiveness of Correctional Rehabilitation: A Review of Systematic Reviews', *Annual Review of Law and Social Science*, 3 (1), pp. 24–36. DOI: : 10.1146/annurev.lawsocsci.3.081806.112833

[50] Drug Policy Alliance, *Drug Decriminalization in Portugal: Learning from a Health and Human-Centered Approach* (2018) https://www.drugpolicy.org/sites/default/files/dpa-drug-decriminalization-portugal-health-human-centered-approach_0.pdf

[51] D. Williamson, 'This is how countries are changing their cannabis laws', *WalesOnline* (16 April 2017) https://www.walesonline.co.uk/news/politics/how-countries-changing-cannabis-laws-12892814

[52] Transform: Drug Policy Foundation, *Drug decriminalisation in Portugal: setting the record straight* (2018) https://transformdrugs.org/drug-decriminalisation-in-portugal-setting-the-record-straight/

[53] Ibid.

Cultural Policy and Cultural Crisis

Kieron Smith

Raymond Williams argued that 'culture' is 'one of the two or three most complicated words in the English language'. Somewhat ironically, and as was often the case with Williams, in the process of explaining the concept, he succeeded in complicating matters further:

> in general it is the range and overlap of meanings that is significant. The complex of senses indicates a complex argument about the relations between general human development and a particular way of life, and between both and the works and practices of art and intelligence. Within this complex argument there are fundamentally opposed as well as effectively overlapping positions: there are also, understandably, many unresolved questions and confused answers. But these arguments and questions cannot be resolved by reducing the complexity of actual usage.[1]

If you got to the end of that passage without unconsciously mimicking Limmy's 'steel is heavier than feathers' sketch: kudos to you. For the sake of brevity, I'll take Williams to mean that culture is something irreducibly human and unquantifiably social. It consists not only of what he termed 'signifying practices': the films we watch, the books we read, the music we listen to, games we play, clothes we wear, food we eat. Culture is 'ordinary' – it is bound up with every aspect of social and individual life: our attitudes, our outlook, our ethics, our sense of morality; part of the very fabric of the everyday choices we make as people and as communities. Culture, or more appropriately, cultures, are nebulous, elusive, and always in process: they cannot be straightforwardly defined or pinned down. Cultural activity is complex, plural, and even contradictory; this is part of its significance and value.

Given this elusiveness, where to begin thinking about 'cultural policy', or the state administration of culture? Also – and perhaps more pressingly – why? After all, aren't there other areas of social and political life that are less nebulous, more black-and-white, and more urgent: health, housing, social care, education? While policy decisions on these have their cultural dimensions, they are nevertheless things to which everyone has an inarguable right, and should perhaps be higher on the agenda. In the age of austerity, climate change and, now, pandemic, why worry about the ways the state administrates culture? Isn't that time and energy – not to mention money – better spent elsewhere?

Phrasing the question in terms of economics, productive value, and time, then, probably, yes. However, looked at another way, it is precisely *because* culture is so diffuse, wide-reaching and complex that there is immense value in examining the ways state institutions attempt to handle, make sense of, and administrate it. Culture – the very stuff of the individual and collective soul, the unconscious, whatever you want to call it – eludes straightforward categorisation. It therefore profoundly troubles and disrupts what David Graeber called 'proceduralism': the language in which neoliberal bureaucracies think, talk, write about and administrate their activities. Examining the ways neoliberalised institutions attempt to make sense of something as basically, unquantifiably, elusively human as 'culture' can reveal much about their attitudes, orientations, hidden convictions and unconscious biases.

In a brief lecture delivered in 1984 – the early days of the neoliberalisation of the British state – Raymond Williams made a useful distinction between two forms of cultural policy: cultural policy 'proper', and cultural policy as 'display'.[2] Very broadly, cultural policy 'proper' refers to the state patronage of the arts: the Keynesian ideal of public funding and access to culture as a facet of the welfare state. In Britain, this developed during and after the Second World War, and has since been administrated through 'arms-length' institutions such as the Arts Council(s), the BBC, and the BFI. In contrast, cultural policy as 'display' refers to the ways in which the state constructs symbols and images of itself, and builds these into the national imagination. Williams described this as the performative, aesthetic dimension of the state, the 'public pomp of a particular social order': the signs, symbols and signifiers of state power. Cultural policy as 'display' is a key feature of the way states embed themselves as normalised, accepted features of social life and the public imagination, and manufacture public consent.

What does cultural policy look like in a Welsh context? In Welsh public debate, it is still common to hear talk of a kind of Welsh exceptionalism: the idea that the Welsh have a distinctively socialistic political culture, and that this is upheld in the Senedd by the principle of 'clear red water'. The very image of 'clear red water' is a good example of state 'display': a memorable motif that connotes a kind of paternalistic islandness, evoking the idea that the people of Wales live in a kind of leftist oasis in the midst of barren Tory territory, our needs benevolently quenched by a socialistic, humanistic devolved state.

The language of social progressiveness adorns many areas of Welsh devolved administration, but its usage in the realm of cultural policy 'proper' is particularly revealing. Take one report into the public funding of the arts, produced by the Culture, Welsh Language and Communications Committee (CWLCC) in November 2019: *Count Me In! Tackling poverty and social exclusion through culture, heritage and the arts*.[3] This is, in some respects, a well-meaning document, and indeed it makes some undeniably laudable recommendations. It advocates the extension of the 'Fusion' programme, which currently employs community co-ordinators to create links between cultural and community groups. It also recommends an initiative to subsidise public transport to and from cultural venues and events. Such initiatives could make a substantial difference to grassroots venues and their audiences across Wales, and they appear to work against the neoliberal grain.

However, one of the substantive features of neoliberalism is its ability to cloak its demands in the heart-warming language of liberal – even socialist – humanism. Neoliberalism doesn't outwardly impose authoritarianism:

in fact, on the surface, it celebrates and condones human-istic principles: difference, diversity, social inclusion, and so on. Rather, it imposes its authority by, firstly, tighten-ing the purse strings, and then, crucially, narrowing the limits of public debate around state expenditure: what can be thought, said, and achieved by state apparatuses. Naturally, *Count me in!* speaks the argot of social awareness, seeking as it does to 'tackl[e] poverty and social exclusion through culture, heritage and the arts'. It would be churlish, even reactionary, to disagree with the idea that we should 'tackle' such things. However, this is the way neoliberalism makes its demands. Dissent becomes not only disagreeable, but unconscionable. In this way, limits are surreptitiously imposed. Note Recommendation 5 of *Count me in!*:

> The Welsh Government, via the Arts Council for Wales [*sic*], should require all arts and cultural bodies in receipt of public funding to set out their objectives for tackling poverty and social exclusion in their strategic plans. Those in receipt of funding should also set out how they intend to co-design creative activities and content with these target audiences.

Here arts organisations – already strenuously run by low-paid and precariously employed workers – are not only expected to produce high-quality art, but to shape their practice to pick up the slack of a state that has failed to look after its most vulnerable. In fact, there is little con-sideration of what is meant by the term 'culture' in this report. Artists and cultural organisations are invoked – as

Williams foresaw – as agents of state display: 'cultural flag bearers', to borrow the language of the report. No space or time is made for culture for its own sake, as an unquantifiable variable, or as a medium for social critique and dissent. Art must be functional, and already cash-strapped cultural organisations, if they are to receive public money, must set themselves to the task of ameliorating any and all of the social ills imposed by austerity.

The Arts Council of Wales (ACW) currently receives substantial sums of public money, and naturally its expenditure and decision-making processes should be – and are – transparent and accountable. But grassroots artists, writers and musicians are increasingly being forced to justify the limited funds they receive in ever more bureaucratic terms. ACW has issued new guidance for funding recipients in response to Covid-19, offering advance payments of grants, but also halting new funding applications. As the situation develops over the coming months, this may be an opportunity to rethink the kinds of projects that are possible, and to relieve pressures imposed upon artists and organisations to perform and produce work within a rigid agenda.

Meanwhile, developments elsewhere suggest a different set of rules to those governing ACW funding. Early in 2020, Welsh Government announced 'Creative Wales', a 'new agency set up within Welsh Government' whose 'mission is to drive growth across the creative industries [...] positioning Wales as one of the best places for creative businesses to thrive'. According to its website, the agency is positioned to support many areas of the creative industries, including publishing and music venues. However, discussions within the CWLCC strongly suggest that the vast majority of the budget – £7.7m of public funding in the first year, with a somewhat vague sum of £30m being touted to be made up from 'a range of sources, from local authority, private equity, other things'[4] over the next five years – will be directed at the film and TV industry, which is now supposed to be one of Wales' fastest growing 'creative' sectors.

Should such vast sums of public money earmarked for culture be entrusted to an internal government agency? Dafydd Elis-Thomas, then Minister for Culture, Tourism and Sport, states in the agency's introductory statement, 'Priorities for the Creative Sector in Wales', that he is 'not convinced that an arms-length body is required', and that Creative Wales is structured as an 'internal agency with similar outlook, values and flexibility as other internal government agencies, such as Cadw and Visit Wales'. Naturally, given the neoliberal mindset within which Welsh Government currently operates, in which competition for foreign investment is deemed to be the panacea to all of Wales' social and economic problems, a central pillar of the remit of Creative Wales is to invest in culture as state 'display'. 'Priorities for the Creative Sector in Wales' makes several nauseating references to 'the national brand'; 'the Wales brand'. Yet there is a worrying lack of imagination for a supposedly 'creative' agency. Their slogan – 'This is Creative. This is Wales. This is Creative Wales.' – bears a notable resemblance to that scene from *The Simpsons* in which a roomful of hack TV executives try to come up with a name for a new TV show: 'Police. Cops. *Police Cops.*' It's also worth recalling the last time Welsh Government attempted to invest a large sum of money in the creative industries: the 'Media Investment Fund' and the infamous deal with Pinewood Studios, which resulted in a catalogue of ineptitude, including forgetting to calculate VAT on a management fee (amounting to an additional expenditure of £438,000), and throwing £6m at a dilapidated building without conducting a full survey.[5]

Welsh Government investment in film and TV continues to haemorrhage money on box office flops such as the action film *Take Down*.[6] In the face of criticism, the Director of Culture, Sport and Tourism replied that 'profit' was 'never really the prime objective'.[7] While I would agree that profit should not be the measure of success of spending on cultural activity, surely, if such enormous pots of funding are available, these would be better spent on new, exciting, imaginative initiatives that are harder to cultivate within the commercial economy. Perhaps we could prioritise emerging and grassroots artists, writers, musicians, and the institutions and spaces they need to thrive – venues, studios, rehearsal spaces, galleries, magazines – rather than bolstering a mediocre 'creative industries' sector that produces film and TV that few watch and makes no money. This is all the more vital at a time when further coronavirus lockdowns threaten the future of so many Welsh cultural organisations and the livelihoods of those who work for them. It is also worth mentioning that, of the success stories gloried by Creative Wales, *Doctor Who* is a long-established brand produced by the BBC, and *His Dark Materials* is a collaboration between the BBC and HBO – both global media heavyweights who, like Amazon, Aston Martin, Ineos, and all those other companies rubbing their hands together at the sight of the Minister for Economy, certainly don't need more Welsh public money. Moreover, if the rationale for directing public money at Welsh productions is 'jobs', then surely this would be money better invested in a sector that doesn't exploit precarious workers quite so ruthlessly as the creative industries.

Commercial considerations aside, we should be suspicious of cultural initiatives too closely wedded to the state. Raymond Williams warned of the dangers of cultural policies that distort the boundaries between state culture 'proper' and state culture as 'display'. Blur the two, and you dilute the potential for culture to offer anything truly new, distinctive, and relevant, and sell the arts out to purely market-driven considerations. As Williams wrote, the arts then become mere

> business entertainment; [and] in this sense an arts policy of a certain kind turns out when examined to be not a policy for the arts but a policy for embellishing, representing, making more effective a particular social order or certain preferred features in it.[8]

In the midst of the current crisis, we must remember that, besides its more obvious biological and material manifestations, Covid-19 is radically reshaping the collective imagination. We will need a radical imaginative response to cope with and make sense of the repercussions of this. It would be foolish to prescribe a vision for the ways culture or the arts should do this, but at the very least, it seems to me uncomplicated for the state to help safeguard cultural and intellectual freedom, for its own sake – and ours.

This essay previously appeared in *Planet* 238.

---

[1] Raymond Williams, *Keywords* (Fontana, 1976) p. 80–81.

[2] Raymond Williams, 'State Culture and Beyond (1984)', in Jim McGuigan, ed., *Raymond Williams on Culture and Society: Essential Writings* (Sage, 2014).

[3] http://senedd.assembly.wales/documents/s95457/Report.pdf

[4] https://record.assembly.wales/Committee/5935#C253946

[5] https://www.assembly.wales/laid%20documents/cr-ld12165/cr-ld12165-e.pdf

[6] https://www.bbc.co.uk/news/uk-wales-politics-51207094?intlink_from_url=https://www.bbc.co.uk/news/topics/ce zd30x8443t/pinewood-studios&link_location=live-reporting-story

[7] https://record.assembly.wales/Committee/5935#C253946

[8] Williams, 'State Culture and Beyond'.

NEOLIBERALISM IN FOCUS

Popular Culture is Ordinary: Welsh Devolution, Pop Culture and Identity

Rhian E. Jones

Past

Popular culture in Wales may have changed over the past hundred years, but its social and political significance has not. Welsh social and leisure patterns from the nineteenth century onwards were shaped not only by the tensions between pub and chapel, but by a surrounding civic culture of choirs, brass bands, amateur dramatics and operatics, miners' galas and Eisteddfodau. Although this culture was driven by a sense of locality, national and international achievements by Welsh teams and competitors caused collective celebration. The importance of books, newspapers, music and sport was inculcated through grassroots educational and civic infrastructure like libraries and miners' halls, trade unions and mutual aid societies. The attempts at 'high culture' which followed the 1946 formation of the Welsh Arts Council were only supplementary to an already flourishing working-class cultural life which existed across Wales as an offshoot of the country's material conditions.

Welsh cultural success has played a fundamental part in bolstering a sense of social and political enthusiasm and optimism: from the victory of a working-class Welsh rugby team against England in 1897 to Welsh rugby's second golden era in the 1970s and the concomitant success of Bassey, Jones and the Treorchy Male Choir, to the Manic Street Preachers' millennial homecoming gig, to the grass-roots galvanising around Euro 2016. But culture can only go so far in solving problems enmeshed in the economy and social fabric. This was made obvious when the cultural glory years of the 60s and 70s, following a surge of post-war optimism centring on economic recovery and the welfare state, were followed by the neoliberal onslaught of the 1980s and the post-industrial shadow it still casts.

Wales' identity can look especially uncertain in the twenty-first century, with economic changes having levelled its supporting pillars of industry and agriculture.[1] But the idea of 'Welshness' has always been a disputed one with no definitive answer, and popular culture can reflect and perpetuate these disputes as much as it can shape and express more coherent and familiar identities. Popular culture can offer the opportunity to create new, inclusive and tolerant accounts of Welsh identity that stretch beyond the unhelpfully bleak or sentimental. Indeed, the hope expressed by Welsh creatives like Russell T. Davies was that devolution would allow not only the creation of a state but the space to create new and inclusive ways of being Welsh. Popular culture can also help to reconcile historical tensions within the construction of Welshness – notably those based around class and language – and to revitalise the country's radical political heritage.

Representation and Identity

After the 1990s' consolidation of neoliberalism, the post-devolution period has seen it become further entrenched in both politics and culture. This is an impasse which, if no political alternative is offered to solve economic problems, instead attaches to culture a weight of political responsibility that it is often ill-equipped to bear. This criticism could certainly be made of the 90s cultural phenomenon 'Cool Cymru'. The Welsh Assembly was established amidst a flowering of Welsh popular culture, as musicians, actors and sports teams took the national and international stage. The sudden mainstream popularity of the Manic Street Preachers after their 1996 hit 'Design for Life' foreshadowed the emergence of a nebulous 'New Welsh Cool', containing bands of varying quality and longevity – several of whom, notably Catatonia and the Super Furry Animals, gave prominence to the Welsh language in their art and interviews. This was combined with iconic moments of triumph – along with heartbreak – for Welsh rugby and football, the building of the Millennium Stadium and the securing of the 1999 Rugby World Cup. The re-branding of Wales enabled by this success also facilitated a certain shift away from pre-existing ideas and stereotypes – even if the presentation of 90s Welsh pop culture could sometimes itself hinge on dated and lazy tropes, overly reliant on the inherent hilarity of regional accents and vernacular.

Like devolution itself, however, Cool Cymru was accompanied by significant hyperbole. As with the politicised pop culture of 90s Britain as a whole, cultural boosterism took priority over attention to structural and economic problems. The buoyant sanguinity of Cool Cymru's cheer-leaders stood in stark contrast to the material conditions which prevailed in much of 90s Wales, as the stubbornly post-industrial economy and Old Labour politics of much of the country made it an awkward fit with the twin tri-umphalisms of Britpop and Blairism.

In addition to the dispiriting micro-machinations sur-rounding the attempt to impose Alun Michael as London's man in Cardiff, New Labour's post-socialist direction and the Assembly's initial lack of significant powers under-mined the possibility of any commitment to concrete economic improvement.[2] Furthermore, less fashionable aspects of Welsh identity, like the adherence to a socialist tradition, were made to feel in New Labour's discourse like throwbacks or weaknesses instead of the strengths they can still be both culturally and politically. Devolution has seen little improvement in the quality or prospects of life in areas beyond Cardiff: even before the Covid-19 pandemic, almost a quarter of people in Wales were in poverty, including 3 in 10 children.[3] Welsh cultural life has not been immune to the economic damage caused by a decade of austerity and unchallenged cuts to jobs and public services: by 2018, austerity had cost over 28,000 local authority jobs and seen the closure of 193 youth centres and 1 in 6 of Wales' libraries.[4] No longer condemned to an industrial past, much of the country now seems condemned to a post-industrial future.

Both language and class have historically fractured attempts to understand and explain what it means to be Welsh, and this is played out as much in popular culture as in high politics. Welsh nationalism gained mainstream prominence in the UK with Gwynfor Evans's election for Plaid Cymru in 1966, in addition to public reaction against the drowning of Tryweryn and the investiture of Prince Charles. Over the next decades, many nationalists and Welsh-language activists directed their politics into nascent rock, folk, drama and comedy, and into broadcasting with the establishment of both BBC Wales and S4C – the latter achieved after an unprecedented level of direct action including the threatened hunger strike by Gwynfor Evans MP. This harnessing of cultural impetus and energy at a time of crisis and opportunity contrasted with the industrial decline of much of anglophone Wales, which received from Welsh Labour a political direction that had, since Bevan at least, rejected Welsh nationalist identity as narrow and reactionary, less amenable to socialism than to a Unionist and capitalist status quo. This political rejection of Welsh identity left the country's anglophone majority less capable of confidently articulating new or distinct cultural forms to replace or nuance previous industrial identities when the materialist basis for this identity collapsed.

Welsh Labour's prioritising of a London-led reworking of the state economy was valid and commendable, but, after deindustrialisation, the lack of any distinctly Welsh perspective which could have sharpened regional identity left the party's Old Labour heartlands uncertain as to how to define ourselves. There is a residual but strongly felt cultural identity attached to the former Welsh coalfield – as illustrated by its (often dubious) prominence in the 'origin stories' of several contemporary Welsh politicians

– but it's one that often eludes a precise definition. Its absence certainly feeds into the current handwringing over 'white working-class' identity, but it also disproves the presumption that a class-based cultural identity can be smoothly replaced by one based on national affiliation.[5] This tension is apparent throughout the history of Welsh Labour politicians: Bevan himself, although a product of a very specific community and mode of life which made not just South Wales but South Welsh Labourism cultur-ally and politically distinct, consistently disavowed any Welsh particularism to his politics, at times in the name of internationalism and at other times in an admirable attempt to universalise the politics of his particular origin – for instance stating, on adapting the Tredegar Medical Aid Society as a country-wide blueprint for the NHS, that 'We are going to Tredegarise you'.

In 2015, research by Dan Evans in Porthcawl found re-sistance, alienation or indifference in relation to ideas of Welshness which are narrowly tied to being either Welsh speaking or working class – ideas which could exclude from 'proper Welshness' not only the community's English-born population but also women and ethnic mi-norities.[6] Evans's subjects saw images of working-class Welshness as unappealingly linked with vulgarity and stupidity, as notably expressed in MTV's 2012 *The Valleys*. Less grimly sensationalist shows, like *Gavin and Stacey* or *Stella*, despite their success in establishing non-traditional images of Welshness on a British stage and beyond, have also been critiqued for their sentimental or one-dimensional portrayal of Welsh life, demonstrating that identities well-received outside the country are often viewed from within as stereotypical or simplistic. This situation is hardly helped by Wales' lack of an independent national broadcaster. In contrast to what was hoped for during devolution, little if anything has emerged to complicate or challenge traditional ways of understanding or being Welsh. And again, cultural representation, however heart-warming, is no salve for a material lack of economic prospects and financial security, and no substitute for effective democratic representation.

Following devolution, the growth in Welsh-language learning, extended offering of Welsh at GCSE level, and public sector requirements for bilingual skills, provided a marked contrast to historical trajectories tending toward official abandoning of the language. The recent increase in numbers of Welsh speakers after decades of decline, particularly in south-east Wales, has challenged fixed – and frequently inaccurate – conceptions of the language's use and value as a middle-class preserve. But, within nationalist conceptions, there has also been a shift away from Gwynfor Evans's adherence to the Welsh language as a unifying salvific force, a style which unhelpfully posited 'complete' Welshness as something the mass of the industrialised and Anglicised country did not and could not hope to possess. The 1980s saw more of a political convergence between Plaid Cymru and Welsh Labour, partly in response to Thatcherism, while later under Leanne Wood's leadership the party emphasised socialist republican tendencies rather than language, broadening its appeal to anglophone Old Labour constituencies. By contrast, Welsh Labour's post-devolution attempts to articulate a distinctively 'Welsh' brand of civic identity has been undermined by a reluctance to interrogate ideas about what 'Welshness' is.

Institutional vs. Grassroots Representation

The principle of public subsidy for arts and culture in Wales has been established since the founding of the Welsh Arts Council. Cultural policy gained greater prominence after devolution with the opening of the Wales Millennium Centre, the establishment of the Artes Mundi Prize, and the inclusion of Welsh art at the Venice Biennale. Wales also hosts a number of international highbrow music and literary events, not least the National Eisteddfod, the Brecon Jazz Festival and the Hay Literary Festival. But under neoliberalism, with culture increasingly pitched in terms of instrumental value rather than intrinsic worth, the development of arts and culture within Wales has had to contend with a top-down cultural policy that concentrates on 'promoting' the country, prioritising the commodification of Wales for a global audience, rather than platforming more complex or disruptive grassroots understandings of it. This approach risks tethering Welsh artists to a mission of providing a positive promotional image of Wales rather than exploring or critiquing it more deeply – and ironically therefore militates against anything new emerging.

If devolution rests on greater local democracy, how might this translate to opportunities for popular arts and culture? Section 61 of the Government of Wales Act 2006 granted the Assembly extensive powers to act in support of cultural development in Wales. Two years later, a main plank of the Assembly's 'One Wales' strategy was that 'high-quality cultural experiences' should be 'available to all people, irrespective of where they live or their background'.[7] Setting aside the obvious question of who decides what 'high-quality' culture looks or sounds like, it is debatable how well this commitment has been honoured: cultural development is still more often directed by top-down quangocracies than by grassroots projects, and viable conditions for vibrant cultural production are increasingly few. Even Cardiff – despite the millions spent there on redevelopment – has faced closures, cuts and downgrading of its libraries and other cultural facilities, while the independent music venues of Womanby Street would have been sacrificed to gentrification and rising rents were it not for public protest.[8] Meanwhile, the Valleys continue to contend with the social and cultural impact of economic devastation, and austerity forces councils across Wales to cut spending on essential services, with cultural amenities often the first to go.

In 2011, an Assembly report listed 'theatre, a sports event, or a concert in [your] local pub' as examples of cultural events, which commendably recognises the ordinariness of culture and the extent to which it is embedded in Welsh social life.[9] But beyond this, social and economic opportunities for participation in and production of culture by ordinary people matter as much, if not more, than opportunities for its passive consumption.

Amateur, grassroots and DIY culture are hardly alien to Wales: small presses, newsletters and zines still flourish today, as do local and national networks of poets, musicians, dramatists and other performers. The 70s and 80s saw the formation of grassroots theatre companies like Theatr Bara Cws, taking drama directly to local communities to challenge what they saw as the cultural elitism of traditional productions, while in Cardiff, punk and post-punk artists, promoters and fans built up a network of alternative venues, bars and coffee shops. Whereas previous Welsh singers and actors achieved success in industries centred on London and New York, the present era of DIY recording, distribution and audience engagement makes it possible to reach the world from a provincial bedroom.

However, the erosion of the welfare state since the 80s has made it far more difficult to subsist as an artist on the dole, as has the restriction of access to the cultural industries to those with independent wealth or pre-existing connections.[10] The Assembly's 2009 inquiry 'Promoting Welsh Arts and Culture on the World Stage' recommended that attention be paid to the financial constraints faced by artists, and to equality of opportunity, but the report itself notes that the latter was given little consideration by its respondents. Furthermore, the Welsh Government explicitly rejected the implementation of the 2011 Localism Act which would allow local communities to buy back community assets like playing fields, libraries and welfare halls. While on the one hand they recognise that culture is ordinary and exists and is sustained by community institutions, on the other they refuse to take the political steps necessary to allow these spaces to remain in the hands of communities.

Rather than a cultural policy shaped by the bureaucratic distribution of funding in accordance with top-down designs of what Welsh culture should look like, or with a view to maximising the proceeds of the tourism industry, funding could also – or indeed instead – be directed at nurturing local talent through the provision of community arts spaces and facilities for recording, rehearsal and exhibition. Given the barriers to access formed by the cultural sector's tendency towards low-paid and precarious work, the provision of living grants would also encourage equality of opportunity or at least its greater distribution, as well as enabling arts and culture to flourish outside the mainstream, funding artists and performers themselves rather than – or at least as well as – project managers.

Culture in Wales can, and does, exist beyond Cardiff. In 2018, Plaid Cymru called for a permanent base for both the National Eisteddfod and Urdd Eisteddfod in Powys, both to boost the area's economy and to establish the region as a 'unifying bridge' between the country's north and south.[11] In addition to publicly funded projects and institutions, there already exists a host of local cultural centres, mutual aid networks, welfare halls and social clubs, often run by communities and volunteers, all of which continue Wales' rich tradition of an autonomous civic and cultural life. 2018 saw the launch of the Rhondda Arts Festival, based in Treorchy with support from local arts venues, schools and pubs, which follows the similar local-led success of the Merthyr Rising festival and Blackwood's Velvet Coalmine. Along with Brynmawr's volunteer-run Market Hall Cinema or

Treorchy's High Street Social arts café, these projects challenge the perspective that arts and cultural experiences are for an elite few, or that they must be funded, directed or staffed from the top down.

In 2012, the widespread backlash against MTV's sensationalist showcase *The Valleys* included an evening of short plays from Valleys-based writers in response to the show, assembled by the alternative theatre group Dirty Protest.[12] This artistic reclaiming of the Valleys had a necessarily limited audience, but such counterblows against cultural exploitation could be struck more effectively with institutional support – not least a dedicated country-wide broadcaster.

In Wales as in the rest of the UK, the concentration of press ownership which followed the 1996 Broadcasting Act has seen the loss of local ownership of local media and a decline in anti-establishment reporting, with editorial priorities decided largely outside Wales. Concurrently, despite the situating of BBC Drama Studios in Roath Lock and the filming of some iconic BBC programmes in Wales, representations of Welsh people on British TV are vanishingly few – which in itself contributes to the unfair responsibility placed on those few presentations which do exist.

An independent or devolved broadcaster could broaden and deepen cultural representation, including greater opportunities for the Welsh language, and extend its arts coverage from the current 30 minutes which BBC Radio Wales devotes to it. In addition, it would lessen the widely recognised information deficit caused by Wales' reliance on British media outlets, and fill the gap in provision between English-speaking Welsh audiences and Wales-focused Welsh-language broadcasting – much of the latter already good quality, like S4C's *Newyddion* or the sub-sidised news website Golwg360. This in turn would hopefully invigorate the Welsh public sphere, increasing public awareness of and engagement with political and social issues, including scrutiny of the Senedd and trans-parency and accountability in local politics.

Future

Under neoliberalism, financial imperatives and the basic problem of survival will, of necessity, take precedence over the capacity for social and cultural engagement, con-straining the ability of ordinary people to participate in or contribute to creative pursuits or civic life, and thereby diminishing the potential for a full and optimal represen-tation of Wales and the Welsh. Solutions to this will require economic as well as artistic effort and investment, and an end to the attitude among both policymakers and commentators that 'any work is good work' which, with in-work poverty and precarious labour at a peak, is often as destructive as long-term unemployment.

If culture can do little structurally to combat economic malaise, that does not mean it can do nothing. Popular culture has always been a powerful force in Wales, whether shaping and representing a variety of identities or galvanising political causes. Wales' distinctive politics and class-conscious heritage is reflected in the radicalism inherent to much of Welsh arts and culture, from the poems of Idris Davies to the speeches of Michael Sheen and the anti-establishment interventions of latter-day Charlotte Church. A popular culture which draws on this left-populist instinct could do a great deal to combat the resurgent racism, antisemitism and xenophobia of the far-right in Wales and beyond – including threats to the devolution settlement from both the Welsh Conservatives and more fringe elements like the Abolish the Welsh Assembly Party.[13] It could also work to bring together the country's Welsh-language, socialist and environmentalist traditions.

Given neoliberalism's tendency towards homogenising, atomization and individualism, a radical Welsh popular culture should both focus on collectivism, solidarity and structural power, and acknowledge the disparate, often overlooked or forgotten, identities which make up the nation. If the word *neoliberal* has finally become acknowledged as a legitimate descriptor, perhaps the word *Welsh* needs to be broadened on the one hand, and broken down on the other. Even beyond the country's linguistic, geographic and political divisions, there exist multiple fractured identities, frequently defining themselves by the local not the national.

There is no single Welsh experience. The Wales of swords and stone circles, drowned lands, dragons and druids exists in romance alongside the reality of GLC's Newport, *Gavin and Stacey*'s Barry Island, the Valleys' anti-romances of Rachel Trezise, and a multitude of others. Exclusionary ideas of the only 'real' Wales as one which is variously Welsh-speaking, hill-farming, chapel-going, Labour-voting, vomiting glitter into Cardiff gutters

or indelibly stained with coal dust, obscure not only linguistic and class identities but also such lesser-known
facets of the country as the diverse ethnic communities
which shaped Cardiff or the internationalist tradition
which sent Welsh socialists, anarchists and communists
to the Spanish Civil War – part of a Welsh anti-fascist
heritage that stretches from 1930s Spain to Swansea in
2013. It's also possible to find this complexity presented
in popular culture, whether Merthyr's Kizzy Crawford's
blend of English, Welsh and Bajan musical traditions or
the post-industrial realism that fuels Tredegar's Stay
Voiceless. Any worthwhile cultural policy will recognise
this multiplicity of identities, while also recognising the
economic effects of the recent past and their capacity to
stifle social and cultural life, making it a political and
cultural priority to alleviate them.

---

[1] R. Merfyn Jones, 'Beyond Identity? The Reconstruction of the
Welsh', *Journal of British Studies*, vol. 31, no. 4 (1992), 330–357.

[2] See D. Ceri Evans, *Whispers of a Forgotten Nation*
https://valleysunderground.files.wordpress.com/2020/04/whispers_
of_a_forgotten_nation_-_the_wri-2.pdf

[3] https://www.jrf.org.uk/report/poverty-wales-2020

[4] https://cymru-wales.unison.org.uk/news/2019/12/shocking-
picture-austerity-cuts-services-wales-revealed-unison/

[5] See https://gov.wales/sites/default/files/statistics-and-
research/2018-12/090923-impact-migration-central-eastern-europea
n-countries-labour-market-en.pdf

[6] http://orca.cf.ac.uk/75609/

[7] http://bankssolutions.co.uk/powys/wp-
content/uploads/2013/05/Tab-2.doc

[8] http://gwallter.com/libraries/cardiff-libraries-a-council-dispossesses-
its-people.html
https://www.walesonline.co.uk/news/local-news/victory-save-
womanby-street-campaigners-13690072

[9] http://www.assembly.wales/Laid%20Documents/CR-LD8392%20-%20Communities%20and%20Culture%20Committee%20Report%20-%20The%20Accessibility%20of%20Arts%20and%20Cultural%20Activities%20in%20Wal-03022011-209211/cr-ld8392-e-English.pdf

[10] See e.g. Dave O'Brien et al., 'Producing and Consuming Inequality: A Cultural Sociology of the Cultural Industries', *Cultural Sociology* Vol 11, Issue 3 (2017).

[11] https://nation.cymru/culture/plaid-cymru-call-for-permanent-eisteddfod-base-in-powys/

[12] http://www.iwa.wales/click/2012/11/a-welsh-reality-tv-car-crash/

[13] https://nation.cymru/news/fears-about-the-rise-of-right-wing-extremism-in-wales/

Nation of Sanctuary?

The Plight of Asylum Seekers and Refugees in Wales and the Future of the Welsh and UK Asylum System

Faith Clarke

At the end of 2019, the UN Refugee Agency estimated there were 79.5 million displaced people around the world.[1] 26 million of these people were refugees, and 4.2 million were asylum seekers. There are also millions of people declared 'stateless', lacking basic access to health care, education, employment, and freedom of movement.

Reasons for fleeing their homes vary. Many attempt to leave due to war and conflict, political or religious perse-cution, or hunger – all of which are increasingly being exacerbated by climate change, with drought, flooding, and irregular precipitation patterns disrupting agriculture, inflating food prices, and triggering conflicts over land and resources. The World Economic Forum estimates that by 2050, between 150 to 200 million people are at risk of being forced from their homes as a result of 'desertifica-tion, rising sea levels and extreme weather conditions'.[2]

As millions flee to northern regions of Europe, the irony is that so much of the conflict and devastation they run from can be traced back to western imperialism and colonial and postcolonial involvement in the Middle East and Africa. The pillaging of natural resources and the ex-ploitation of the land for oil has driven climate change:

from the swelling tides of Bangladesh to the arid flatlands of Sudan – where food, water and fuel is scarce, and conflict over these resources rife. Previously, the western world has been largely removed from the effects of climate change that we played such a significant role in causing. Only recently have we seen the impacts emerge in the shape of wildfires in Australia, drought in California, and even flooding in Wales.

Still, it can be difficult to link climate change and the global refugee crisis back to the small, powerless country of Wales, but it is important to do so, because the two are inherently linked. Talking about asylum seekers means talking about these issues, and our role in them – historically and presently – as a country.

Wales as a Tolerant Nation

When Williams et al. published an updated version of *A Tolerant Nation? Exploring Ethnic Diversity in Wales* in 2015, Alida Payson noted in her chapter 'Changes in Sanctuary Seeking in Wales' that 'the story of contemporary sanctuary in Wales is not one of fleeing persecution elsewhere for free, full exercise of rights and citizenship in "a tolerant nation"'. Instead, she explains, the story of asylum seeking in Wales is 'marked out by entrenched racism and discrimination in immigration law.'[3] This is just as true in 2020, with crowded accommodation, widespread destitution, and a lack of support services the reality for many asylum seekers in Wales and the wider UK.

During the 2020–2021 coronavirus pandemic, Wales saw 250 asylum seekers temporarily housed in Wales in the MOD camp on the outskirts of the village of Penally, Pembrokeshire. The conditions of the camp have proven to be appalling with insufficient sanitation and over-crowded rooms posing an increased risk of the virus. Months after moving in, residents of the camp were forced to take matters into their own hands, with around 40 of the men protesting against the poor living standards which they described as a 'jail', where six men were crammed into a room, limiting their opportunities to self-isolate.[4] It has also been reported that men inside the camp created their own union, Camp Residents Of Penally (CROP), with the aim of improving their well-being and educational resources, as well as taking issues up with politicians.[5]

The reality of seeking sanctuary in Wales is little different to seeking it elsewhere in the UK, as immigration policy is not devolved in Wales. That said, the reality of life in the Penally camp is a far cry from the idyllic image set out by the Welsh Government's latest Refugee and Asylum Seeker plan, published in January 2019, and entitled 'Nation of Sanctuary'. Jane Hutt, Wales' Deputy Minister and Chief Whip, describes the plan as 'a major milestone on a longer journey which will drive [Wales] towards becoming a true nation of sanctuary'. Yet in the same paper, she acknowledges that many of the challenges faced by those seeking asylum 'cannot be fully resolved without policy changes by the UK Government'.[6]

Similarly, when First Minister of Wales Mark Drakeford expressed concern over the living conditions in the Penally camp, calling for it to be closed 'as quickly as possible', he swiftly pointed the blame at the UK Home Office, describing their 'failure to act' as 'unacceptable'.[7] In the 2019 Nation of Sanctuary plan, the Welsh Government state that they believe accommodation and financial assistance for asylum seekers needs to be improved, however they also note that '[they] will continue to work with the UK Government on these matters as far as possible, [but they] have to accept that [Wales] cannot control [Westminster's] decisions'. So, how far can this plan go without immigration being devolved to Wales – particularly as we head towards a far more aggressive and austere points-based immigration system in the wider UK?

The 'hostile environment' currently faced by some 35,000[8] asylum seekers in the UK was born out of Theresa May's cabinet but this was not something which simply emerged from nowhere. Instead, its overt racism was the logical outcome of a narrative initiated years earlier by New Labour's approach to immigration, with home secretary at the time John Reid, promising to make life 'constrained and uncomfortable' for asylum seekers in Britain.[9] Since Brexit, things are set to worsen for those seeking sanctuary, with UK Home Secretary Priti Patel promising the 'biggest overhaul' of the UK's asylum system in 'decades.'[10]

Westminster's new immigration model, which came into force from 1 January 2021, will see the UK nations transition to a points-based system based on those of countries such as Australia, renowned for their tougher immigration laws which let in a restricted, highly skilled minority. According to the UK Government, this new system will cater 'for the most highly skilled [and] skilled workers, students and a range of other specialist work routes including routes for global leaders and innovators'. There will be no route for 'low-skilled' or 'temporary' workers, despite the UK currently being heavily reliant on cleaners, factory workers, and agency staff, many of whom are originally from outside of the UK, and who have proven to be the backbone of the country during the pandemic.[11]

These new laws which promise a 'crackdown' on UK immigration come at a time when the country has witnessed a rise in migrant channel crossings, which have peaked since Covid-19 slowed lorry traffic into the UK. It is estimated that in 2020, more than 7,400 migrants crossed the English Channel in attempt to reach the UK, in contrast to the 1,800 in all of 2019.[12] However, it is important to place these figures into context. Due to coronavirus lockdowns at the time of writing, legal routes into the UK, such as the government's resettlement scheme, have failed to resume since being paused in March 2020,[13] meaning asylum applications received between April and June 2020 nearly halved compared with the first three months of the year. As a result, asylum seekers have been forced to find other ways to enter the country, which partly explains the increase in channel crossings.

It should also be pointed out that the UK takes in far fewer asylum seekers than other European nations. The Refugee Council indicates that in 2018, the European average for the number of asylum seekers per 1,000 population was 1.21, whilst the corresponding figure for the UK was 0.57. Not only this, but countries such as

Sweden, which has a smaller population than the UK, had 'proportionally more applications'.[14] The idea of an asylum seeker 'crisis' in the UK is more a government ploy for shifting the blame onto anyone but themselves when it comes to facing the effects of austerity, a broken welfare system, and an overstretched NHS.

The current environment for asylum seekers in the UK nations is anything but easy. According to the Wales Strategic Migration Partnership, as of last October, there were 2,626 asylum seekers in Wales. This year, things have arguably been tougher than ever before for those awaiting their applications to be processed. Due to Covid-19, many have been left in 'limbo': unable to work, having their face-to-face meetings cancelled, and living off just £37.75 a week to cover food, toiletries, and other essential items, not to mention the general delay in the asylum process and the poor living standards of the privatised accommodation they are placed in.[15] The effects of this process are enough to wear anybody down. One woman who was seeking asylum in Wales described to the BBC how the coronavirus lockdown 'destroyed' her 'mentally and physically'[16] after she went without food for a week to ensure her children were fed.

While the Welsh Government may be paying lip service to the plight of refugees and asylum seekers – painting Wales as a 'nation of sanctuary' – the reality of seeking asylum here differs little to that of seeking asylum in England. The image conjured by a title such as 'Nation of Sanctuary' is very much in line with the 'tolerant Wales' myth favoured by many in Welsh civic society, but how tolerant can a nation be when Westminster has the final say on immigration and foreign policy? What does it say about Wales when we are, in theory, a part of the government who dropped bombs on Syria and then afterwards opened its doors to 20,000 Syrian refugees via a 'resettlement scheme'?[17] Or when Welsh airspace and land is used to train Saudi Arabian pilots, at a time when Saudi forces are dropping bombs on famine-stricken Yemen?[18]

This contradiction is a theme which seems to run throughout Welsh Labour and their policies. In theory, it is a separate government to the Conservatives of Westminster, yet in reality, the devolved Welsh Labour Government is perhaps a slightly lighter, more palatable, 'Diet Coke' version of the full-sugar, Tory alternative. There is currently a gaping hole between what the Welsh Government says it wants Wales to look like (a nation of sanctuary), and the reality that it is still very much chained to Westminster when it comes to some of the most pressing issues such as the asylum system. There is also the looming threat of climate change, which is driving the global refugee crisis, with forecasts predicting this is only the beginning of widespread climate devastation.

Wales and the Global Climate Emergency

In April 2019, amidst climate protests and Extinction Rebellion 'uprisings', the Welsh Government declared a 'Climate Emergency'. Part of the Welsh Government's plan to address climate change is their commitment to achieving a carbon-neutral public sector by 2030.[19] But, as Asylum Justice lawyer Hussein Said pointed out when

I interviewed him the same summer, 'what are [we] doing about climate refugees?'

A commitment to a cleaner and greener Welsh public sector is one thing, but how does this help a Sudanese farmer who can't grow his crops, or a Bangladeshi family whose home will soon be under water? It *doesn't*.

Wales' Energy and Rural Affairs Minister Lesley Griffiths, speaking on the day of the announcement, said she hoped the declaration 'can help to trigger a wave of action at home and internationally'. Not only has this announcement been proven to be mostly empty rhetoric, it also simplifies the climate emergency by ignoring the western world's role in *creating* these conditions in the first place. The devastation of climate change is rooted in colonialism, western imperialism, and capitalism. It is not a matter of humanity versus nature, nor of having a collective 'responsibility'. Different countries have played different roles in the climate crisis, and the consequences of climate change are just as inequal. A report by Oxfam in September 2020 stated that the per capita consumption footprints of the richest 1% are approximately '35 times higher than the target for 2030', and 'more than 100 times higher than the poorest 50%'.[20]

Wales' Future Generations Report, released in 2020, rightly mentions how a 'globally responsible' Wales can only be achieved in the coming years if we 'identify how what we do here in Wales, impacts the rest of the world'. In order for Wales to become a welcoming, safe nation for all, the report states that Wales 'will [or rather, must] take action to mitigate against negative global issues, and through actions of solidarity, welcome our fair share of refugees who may have been displaced due to climate change or conflict'.[21]

We often do not make the link between climate and conflict (it is largely omitted from the mainstream media), but these two issues are intricately entwined, and both are significant reasons why many flee their homes for Europe. Sudan is a prime example of this: back in 2014, researchers found that abnormal temperatures and sporadic precipitation patterns 'systematically increase the risk of conflict, often substantially'.[22] Around a quarter of Sudan's population are thought to rely on humanitarian aid due to continual cycles of food insecurity, water shortages and conflict, all made worse by the current coronavirus pandemic and price inflation.

This is why the Welsh Government's commitment to both national and international action on climate change needs to consider the intersecting issues of *who* is most impacted by climate change, and *why*. Welsh Government's declaring of a climate emergency, much like their Nation of Sanctuary plan, is merely a rhetorical tool that is not accompanied by the substantive policies required to take progressive action on climate breakdown. Wales' plans for addressing both climate change and welcoming refugees and asylum seekers cannot be successfully met without recognising the link between these two issues. As the Future Generations report points out, immigration policy may currently lie in the hands of the UK Government, but plans for integration lie firmly in the hands of the Welsh Government. The 'Nation of Sanctuary' plan acknowledges this, but as the Future Generations report notes, Wales now needs to follow through on these plans to successfully integrate refugees and asylum seekers into Welsh society, and to ensure they have access to the health, education, and support services they need, in order to meet the goals of the Future Generations Act 2015.

Asylum seekers are some of the poorest people in Wales, yet families relying on asylum support of £37.75 a week or those with No Recourse to Public Funds (NRPF) can only access free school meals (FSM) and education grants such as the Public Development Grant if their local authority permits it. Around 6,000[23] children in Wales are not eligible for FSM because their family has no recourse to public funds. At the beginning of the pandemic, the Department of Education in England expanded FSM to families with NRPF, but instead, Welsh Government only issued 'guidance' to local authorities to 'encourage'[24] them to 'exercise their discretion' to these families while schools are closed.

Similarly, the 'hostile environment' is perpetuated in Wales through a lack of accessible free healthcare for non-UK citizens. Although those who have been refused asylum in Wales are not charged for healthcare here as they are in England, NHS Wales charges some non-UK citizens for secondary healthcare services. Docs Not Cops Swansea[25] published research in 2019 highlighting that migrants are being left in thousands of pounds of debt for accessing necessary healthcare, despite the fact that their care accounts for just 0.016% of the Welsh NHS budget.

Moreover, Section 39 of the Immigration Act 2016 includes 'Right to Rent' checks which makes it an offence to lease accommodation to 'disqualified migrants'. While this is currently only applicable in England, the UK Secretary of State has the power to apply this in Wales too. Right to Rent checks are another example of hostile environment and could see an increase in destitution, homelessness, and the number of NRPF cases. In order to uphold the aims set out by the Nation of Sanctuary plan Welsh Government needs to take a firm stance in saying such checks *won't* be introduced in Wales.[26]

Wales and the Far-Right

Wales is often renowned for its warm, friendly locals, and it is true that Wales has a history of being a 'welcoming' nation.[27] However, we cannot ignore the fact that a prominent far-right presence lurks here, one which mirrors a far-right populism spreading across Europe and the globe, which heavily capitalises off opposition to asylum seekers and refugees.

Aside from the previous successes of UKIP and the Brexit Party in Wales, there has since been the emergence of several other groups which also suggest Wales is vulnerable to the threat of the far-right. Towards the end of 2020, UKIP acting leader and MS Neil Hamilton tweeted his support for a group called Voice of Wales (VoW), an organisation with links to various far-right and fascist figures across Britain. The group went as far as demonstrating outside of the Penally camp where asylum seekers were housed. One woman told media platform *voice.wales* of how she was asked by a VoW demonstrator: 'Do you want your kids to be raped? That's what they [refugees] do in their country.'[28] A neo-Nazi group known as Patriotic Alternative (PA) were also reported to have been leafleting in Welsh neighbourhoods in Swansea and Porthcawl last year, distributing flyers which claimed, 'White Britons' would become a 'minority by the 2060s – or SOONER'.[29] In mainstream politics, anti-immigrant rhetoric was at its most flagrant during the run-up to the 2016 Brexit referendum, with Nigel Farage using images of refugees on his campaign bus. These photographs used immigrants as scapegoats, and were accompanied by slogans such as 'breaking point', implying that it is the fault of a small inflow of refugees and asylum seekers that jobs are scarce, the NHS stretched, and social services overrun – rather than these issues being the reality of decades of austerity. Moreover, the Abolish the Assembly party, a single-issue party aimed at abolishing the Senedd Cymru (Welsh Parliament), holds two seats in the Senedd and is led by former UKIP leadership candidate Richard Suchorzewski. Members of the party also include Gareth Bennett, the former leader of the UKIP Senedd group and Independent MS, and Mark Reckless, previous Leader of the Brexit Party in Wales. While far-right, anti-immigrant rhetoric is not at all a Welsh-specific issue, it has certainly permeated Wales, and one reason for this is that it has been allowed to, with political parties such as these being normalised – and largely accepted – by a meek political class and to some extent, embraced, by a public who are fed up with a stagnated Welsh Labour.

Ideas of nationality fuel the immigration 'debate'. Far-right, anti-immigration protesters and politicians often proclaim that our jobs, culture, resources, and national identity are under threat due to immigrants and asylum seekers, and this is incited by an equally vicious tabloid media which leads voters to believe that the UK is a soft, easy target where outsiders can simply waltz in and claim a free hand-out of benefits and a council house.

At the time of writing, anti-immigration protests are rife, despite frequent lockdowns due to the coronavirus pandemic. While hundreds of asylum seekers in the Penally camp have continually faced issues on the inside of the camp, they have also had to deal with the chants of protesters on the outside. According to media reports, up to 70 police officers have been needed every day due to a continual stream of protests, with far-right protesters travelling from other parts of the UK to protest the camp. There's also concern that certain regions of Wales – such as Swansea – have been scouted out by far-right recruiters such as the likes of Voice of Wales and Patriotic Alternative who increasingly use a stagnant Welsh Labour and opposition to asylum seekers to propel their campaigns.[30]

Mark Drakeford and other Welsh politicians condemned these far-right protesters, however the persistence of these protests – which are not isolated to Penally alone, nor to Wales – once again indicates a need for the issue to be addressed at a far deeper level. These ideas stem from systemic, structural racism within Welsh society, and can only truly be addressed through education and ameliorative social policies.

The Future of Asylum in Wales

Debates around immigration and the asylum system are all too often simplified into a 'for and against': on one hand, those who believe we have a moral duty to embrace those seeking sanctuary with open arms, and on the other hand, those who have been convinced that asylum seekers and immigrants are an enemy and threat to Wales and the UK. However, as is the case with all political issues, the vital context, and the nuances of the reality of the situation are often left out of the conversation.

If Wales is to truly become a nation of sanctuary, it must acknowledge that the refugee crisis is intrinsically linked to climate change and conflict, which is the direct result of western imperialism and colonialism. Wales is not exempt in this role, and if it is to fulfil the goals set by the Future Generations Act, the Welsh Government needs to do far more than pay lip service to the hardships of asylum seekers, claiming their hands are tied due to Westminster whilst simultaneously not advocating for immigration to be devolved.

Currently, there is no clear way in which Wales can become a 'Nation of Sanctuary' whilst it operates under the UK immigration system, which determines a person's worth based on the number of 'points' they are able to offer. However, if Wales is to become a nation of sanctuary, not only must it break free from Westminster, but it must also break free of the neoliberal constraints of its own centrist Labour government. This would mean taking a clear stance on policies that impede the quality of life of those trying to seek asylum in Wales – for example, ensuring asylum seekers and refugees have access to free healthcare and support services, that children of families with NRPF have free school dinners, and that all asylum seekers have the right to clean, secure accommodation.

In addition to this, Welsh Government must look at how it can not only integrate asylum seekers and refugees into society (through developing bilingual language skills, offering support services, etc.) but also needs to address how it can better educate the rest of the public on the reality of the plight of asylum seekers, and our role in causing these people to leave their homes in the first place. This would also mean making Black and People of Colour histories an essential part of the Welsh curriculum, in order to embed anti-racism into Welsh education from a young age. It would also involve highlighting the many benefits of embracing different cultures in Wales and to illustrate the ways in which welcoming asylum seekers can further enrich the country.

Ultimately, this would also involve taking a firm stance on racism – systemic and otherwise – austerity, the horrors of war, and Wales' direct and indirect role in foreign conflicts and climate breakdown. This would require more than just lip service, and, under the current administration, this feels far from likely, though the size and momentum of recent Black Lives Matter protests across Wales over the past year instil some hope that younger generations can pave the way to a more tolerant, safe, and multicultural Wales. One thing is certain: there is no room, nor time, for a government that is passive, neutral, and laissez-faire in the face of injustice.

[1] UN Refugee Agency (18 June 2020) https://www.unhcr.org/figures-at-a-glance.html

[2] M. Ahmed, 'How climate change exacerbates the refugee crisis – and what can be done about it', *World Economic Forum*
https://www.weforum.org/agenda/2019/06/how-climate-change-exacerbates-the-refugee-crisis-and-what-can-be-done-about-it/

[3] Alida Payson, '"This is the place we are calling home": Changes in Sanctuary Seeking in Wales' in Williams, Evans & O'Leary, eds., *A Tolerant Nation?: Revisiting Ethnic Diversity in a Devolved Wales* (Cardiff: UWP, 2015), p. 279.

[4] BBC News, '"Human rights ignored" at asylum seeker camp' (11 November 2020) https://www.bbc.co.uk/news/uk-wales-54907333

[5] S.C. Cook, 'Penally Asylum Seekers form their own union to help themselves & the community', *voice.wales* (30 October 2020)
https://www.voice.wales/penally-asylum-seekers-form-their-own-union-to-help-themselves-the-community/

[6] Welsh Government, *Nation of Sanctuary – Refugee and Asylum Seeker Plan* (2019)
https://gov.wales/sites/default/files/publications/2019-03/nation-of-sanctuary-refugee-and-asylum-seeker-plan_0.pdf

[7] ITV Wales News, 'First Minister calls for Penally asylum seeker camp to close "as quickly as possible"' (23 October 2020)
https://www.itv.com/news/wales/2020-10-23/first-minister-calls-for-penally-asylum-seeker-camp-to-close-as-quickly-as-possible_

[8] UK Home Office, 'How many people do we grant asylum or protection to?' (21 May 2020)
https://www.gov.uk/government/publications/immigration-statistics-year-ending-march-2020/how-many-people-do-we-grant-asylum-or-protection-to

[9] BBC News, 'Reid targets illegal immigrants' (7 March 2007)
http://news.bbc.co.uk/1/hi/uk_politics/6424377.stm

[10] BBC News, 'Priti Patel promises 'firm and fair' asylum system' (4 November 2020) https://www.bbc.co.uk/news/av/uk-politics-54408228

[11] Home Office, 'The UK's points-based immigration system: policy statement', UK Government (19 February 2020)
https://www.gov.uk/government/publications/the-uks-points-based-immigration-system-policy-statement/the-uks-points-based-immigration-system-policy-statement

[12] Press Association News and *The Independent*, '4 dead, 15 rescued in English Channel migrant boat sinking' (27 October 2020)

https://www.independent.co.uk/news/4-dead-15-rescued-in-english-channel-migrant-boat-sinking-britain-french-boat-migrants-people-b1374919.html

[13] A. Bulman, 'Refugee services face permanent cuts as Home Office fails to reopen resettlement scheme', *The Independent* (6 November 2020) https://www.independent.co.uk/news/uk/home-news/refugee-resettlement-home-office-vprs-b1050485.html

[14] The Refugee Council, 'Asylum Seekers in Europe' (May 2019) https://www.refugeecouncil.org.uk/wp-content/uploads/2019/06/Asylum-in-Europe-May-2019.pdf

[15] J. Rees, 'Asylum seekers in Wales "in limbo and unable to work"', BBC News (24 August 2020) https://www.bbc.co.uk/news/uk-wales-53820877

[16] BBC News, 'Coronavirus: Asylum seeker "went without food" in lockdown' (28 July 2020) https://www.bbc.co.uk/news/uk-wales-53568465

[17] Home Office, 'Syrian Vulnerable Persons Resettlement Scheme (VPRS) – Guidance for local authorities and partners', UK Government (July 2017) https://assets.publishing.service.gov.uk/government/uploads/system/uploads/attachment_data/file/631369/170711_Syrian_Resettlement_Updated_Fact_Sheet_final.pdf

[18] B. Wray, 'Revealed: Saudi pilots trained by the RAF in Wales', *Source News* (30 October 2018) https://sourcenews.scot/revealed-saudi-pilots-trained-by-the-raf-in-wales/#:~:text=A%20WRITTEN%20question%20to%20the%20UK%20Government%20has,with%2014%20million%20on%20the%20verge%20of%20starvation.

[19] Welsh Government, 'Welsh Government makes climate emergency declaration' (29 April 2019) https://gov.wales/welsh-government-makes-climate-emergency-declaration

[20] Oxfam, 'Confronting Carbon Inequality' (21 September 2020) https://oxfamilibrary.openrepository.com/bitstream/handle/10546/621052/mb-confronting-carbon-inequality-210920-en.pdf

[21] Future Generations Report, 2020, pp. 400–401 https://www.futuregenerations.wales/wp-content/uploads/2020/05/FGC-Report-English.pdf

[22] Burke et al., 'Climate and Conflict' in *National Bureau of Economic Research* (2014) https://www.nber.org/system/files/working_papers/w20598/w20598.pdf

[23] Child Poverty Action Group, 'Wales: over half of children in poverty

missing out on free school meals' (16 October 2020)
https://cpag.org.uk/news-blogs/news-listings/wales-over-half-
children-poverty-missing-out-free-school-meals

[24] Welsh Government, 'Revised guidance for schools in Wales:
supporting children eligible for free school meals' (20 March 2020)
https://gov.wales/free-school-meals-coronavirus-guidance-schools

[25] Docs Not Cops, 'New research exposes extent of Hostile
Environment in Welsh NHS' (23 October 2019)
http://www.docsnotcops.co.uk/newresearch-hostileenvironment-
wales/

[26] Equality, Local Government and Communities Committee, National
Assembly for Wales, '"I used to be someone" Refugees and asylum
seekers in Wales' (April 2017), p. 25. https://senedd.wales/laid%
20documents/cr-ld11012/cr-ld11012-e.pdf

[27] Payson, "This is the place we are calling home", p. 282.

[28] M. Redfern, 'Exposed: Neil Hamilton's links to far right group
where members call for race war', *voice.wales* (15 October 2020)
https://www.voice.wales/exposed-neil-hamiltons-links-to-far-right-
group-where-members-call-for-race-war/

[29] M. Redfern, 'New fascist threat to South Wales: the neo-nazi anti-
semites behind patriotic alternative', *Voice.Wales* (11 December 2020)
https://www.voice.wales/new-fascist-threat-to-south-wales-the-neo-
nazi-anti-semites-behind-patriotic-alternative/

[30] ITV News, 'Penally camp in Pembrokeshire used to house asylum
seekers putting huge strain on west Wales police' (5 November 2020)
https://www.itv.com/news/wales/2020-11-05/penally-camp-in-
pembrokeshire-which-is-being-used-to-house-asylum-seekers-is-putting-
a-huge-strain-on-west-wales-police

Building on History: A Forward-Orientated Curriculum for Wales

Savanna Jones

The social awakening to racism in its many forms that took place in the western world during 2020 – including here in Wales – has brought to the fore plentiful challenges that long lay dormant in the fabric of Welsh society. A living, breathing Wales – at once colonised and coloniser – has provided an opportunity to consider what we learn from this crisis/awakening, and how we move forward from it. This has recently become even more important as we become an increasingly diverse nation, allowing the effectiveness of equality, diversity and inclusion policies in addition to supporting legislation to form part of everyday discussions. As we become more receptive to such notions, it is not enough to identify certain policies and practices in a tokenistic manner. We need to consider critically what this means in practice: diverse to whom; inclusive to what? It is no longer good enough to copy and paste models from our nation's dominant White community's standpoint. Rather, we need to better understand our locality here in Wales. For example, what, in practice, do equality and diversity mean in a Welsh context? What do they look like, and how can they live? Are these concepts and ideas radical enough to facilitate change and challenge the institutional racism that remains within our education system? Ultimately, we must ask whether we are ready as a society to move beyond a racist neoliberalism. This chapter explores why we must think of decolonising our curriculum in these terms, and what this might entail.

Education and Race

The new curriculum has set out the importance of 'cynefin' as part of its vision; a concept aligned to developing individuals that are 'ethical, [and] informed citizens of Wales and the world'. To fulfil this sentiment, our education cannot continue to deliver a disjointed version of historical truth, or only one version of it shaped by a White Welsh perspective. We need to remember that education is not detached from the rest of society – it is both a product and producer of it. Education also holds the ability to open our eyes to the wider world of which we are a part, and to make us look at that world in alternative ways. With this in mind, it is rather taken for granted within common-sense discourse that change must start at the top, with the decision-makers who have been invited (or invited themselves) to take a seat at the decision-making 'table'. But when we live in a society whose invitations are limited in scope – that is, limited to individuals from similar class and/or ethnic backgrounds – it begs the question whether our desire and abilities to deliver meaningful change are genuine.

When considering racial discourses in education, they can appear to have represented a rather detached approach. Although we have progressed from ideas of as-similation and total integration prevalent in the 1960s and 1970s to multiculturalism and pluralistic tolerance, such a shift, despite the best of intentions, has led to a parallel existence for minority ethnic communities[1]. By the time we reached the 1990s, we had turned a corner and had begun to celebrate ethnic diversity and difference, recognising value in a plurality of opinions. We were beginning, possibly, to see the benefits of our differences as a catalyst for change.

At the start of the millennium, we embraced the coming together of various equalities and human rights legislation. Once the novel ideas in Ted Cantle's *Community Cohesion: A New Framework for Race and Diversity* were published, the conversation was broadened to consider the impact of segregation and how a 'fear of difference' had infiltrated mindsets.[2] This arguably was when a par-ticular Pandora's box was opened, and palpable differences in terms of ways of thinking about race (re)emerged. In the late 2010s, we moved into a suppos-edly 'post-racial' society, a myth of sorts. It appears to have been a false dawn, or to be more accurate, another false dawn!

This brings us to where we find ourselves today, having moved along a continuum into the territory of 'decoloni-sation'. This is an opportunity to free our minds from the 'colonial ideology' that has shaped our knowledge, as identified in societal discourse. This new buzzword has been offered by some as a silver bullet; a panacea to cure all related ills. However, the question of whether we are ready to challenge our shared assumptions about Wales and the world, including what and how we believe, is still unresolved. In the field of education, we must enable and support learners to critically question racial hierarchies within and beyond societal silos, in order for decolonisation not to be co-opted and enervated by the forces of the status quo. Moving beyond the assumptions of neoliberalism is central to this.

Where Are We Today

Today, when it comes to race, the majority unconsciously view Wales and the world through a White racial frame. Because of the 2020 learning journey, including the uprising of Black Lives Matter, we have arrived at a tipping point in shifting discussions about race in education. We have begun to collectively understand that making no changes to the way we educate ourselves about race will be profoundly detrimental to our society. The new curriculum provides us with a unique opportunity to develop a new racial perspective in Wales, to review our normative ways of thinking and lead us to a space that facilitates inclusive dialogue. No doubt, to achieve a society of inclusion and harmony, we need to decolonise education. However, how might such an intention be reflected in a more radical, inclusive curriculum in Wales?

What decolonising the curriculum means in practice is yet to be fully articulated. Where do we start with such a mammoth task? Perhaps the first step is to identify the problems which are rarely articulated. The education system in Wales is embedded in institutional class inequality, of which race is an undeniable factor; the teaching profession in Wales is generally White, and governors, as a rule, are not as diverse as the schools they serve. Similarly, the pedagogy employed is driven from a perspective of White-ness, while higher education continues to be similarly grounded in White perspectives, and a curriculum built upon a White middle-class foundation. Given the extent of these issues and the way race is enmeshed with class inequality, we need structural changes to the education system that will benefit all and, in doing so, remove the in-built, often unconscious advantages which only benefit those already in power. This is where it becomes tricky. To really develop a decolonised education system, we must focus on coalition building between us all, including enabling marginalised and minority ethnic groups' voices to be heard. Doing so, we can collectively enforce long-term meaningful change. To do this, an element of self-education must be inherent in what we do, and this starts with our educators.

Beyond Neoliberalism: The New Curriculum

In Wales, it is welcoming that change is being considered at an institutional level. Professor Charlotte Williams, commissioned by the Welsh Government, is leading the working group to advise on and improve the teaching of themes related to Black, Asian and minority ethnic communities and experiences. Here in Wales, there is an argument that we possess a 'rich history based on diversity and difference' (Welsh Government, 2020)[3].

Consequently, the new curriculum must offer an opportunity to resist deficit narratives based on old stereotypes around the ability and aspirations of minority ethnic individuals. It is important we do not lose sight of the purpose of education, notably for the public good, and that we all, both as individuals and a collective, invest in this. It is welcoming that the new curriculum provides an opportunity to ensure that the rhetoric in use recognises race as more than just a single issue, thus becoming more than a tick-box exercise. It must be authentic change.

The conventional thinking underpinning neoliberalism is that of celebrating diversity and respecting differences in the hope that doing so will somehow morph into a more inclusive Welsh society, one that naturally fosters and safeguards individualism and increases opportunities. By this reasoning, the best, no matter what their point of difference, will rise to the top as part of a meritocracy. This chimes with Nancy Fraser's description of the hegemonic 'progressive neoliberalism'[4] built during the Clinton and New Labour era that entrenched class hierarchies whilst securing longevity by encouraging a little more diversity amongst its beneficiaries. It is a view that ignores power dynamics and the issue of class, and as a result, racial disparities perpetuate despite society now being saturated with the progressive rhetoric of inclusivity and diversity. Revisiting education, in all its practical and theoretical messiness, is an ideal place to start in addressing this gap between rhetoric and reality. Here then, we need to understand the causes of social inequality and rebuild better knowledge structures to inform the creation of a more just society.

To inform a decolonised Welsh society we need to acknowledge that 'progressive neoliberalism' enables some
members of society to exercise privilege and be rewarded
without requiring systemic change; notably those who
reflect White middle-class perspectives. In this sense, it is
particularly important that 'schools do not just reproduce
culture, but that they shape the new society that is coming
into existence all around us'[5]. It is incumbent on us as a
society that we deliver an inclusive curriculum that takes
us forward as an inclusive nation. We cannot view
children as empty vessels; we must enable them to
become critical lifelong learners who challenge life's hier-
archical structures and ask more of Wales and the world.
The sentiment here is for collective social reform to come
to fruition, and that we must question what it means to
be Welsh.

An alternative argument is one that begins with
Margaret Thatcher's claim that 'there is no such thing as
society'.[6] Her Conservative government ushered in a
political change that we in Wales have, rhetorically at
least, resisted. Having said that, as this book makes clear,
'Labour Wales' has also increasingly lost ground as a
political tradition. This has been somewhat reflected in
policies that have not facilitated meaningful diversion
from the norm or recognised our diverse communities in
Wales. This tendency has contributed, albeit indirectly, to
the narrow-minded approach that has stunted progress
and our understanding of what actually constitutes decolonisation given its many interpretations.

Separate or Equal? What do we want to see in Wales?

From the start of the millennium, we have seen the in-creasing representation of seperate groups, as brought about by the UK Equality Act 2010. We now see that minority groups are increasingly establishing their respec-tive voices within a more general empowerment agenda, thus claiming, in some instances, a 'seat at the decision-making table'.[7] Small steps are thus being taken that benefit diversity and difference in the Welsh population. This recognition of differences has been positive in facili-tating self-respect, efficacy, recognition of diverse voices and, more importantly, making clear that you can't be what you can't see.

However, the question still stands: can separate ever equate to equal? The debate between anti-racist and mul-ticultural education is a good example for considering this dilemma. The ongoing discussion has accused multicul-tural education of being inadequate and naïve in its failure to recognise the institutional domination of the White majority and its requirement for conforming with the pre-dominant normative culture. In a nutshell, multicultural education '... ignores the fact that racial differences and discrimination must be challenged by changing the total organisational structures of the institutions' rather than mere tokenism.[8] In comparison, anti-racist education teaches the economic, structural, and historical roots of inequality. It stems from the mantra that race and racial discrimination are systemic: that is, socially and institu-tionally produced and reproduced. If we then return to how this argument impacts us in Wales, we can see that only a fully inclusive curriculum, one that acknowledges our differences and how society views us as individuals, no matter how uncomfortable this learning might be, can enable us to make some advances around eradicating racism and the basis of inequality.

It can be said then that discrete structures and practices magnifying differences in Welsh identity can only really then be viewed as staging posts on the way to a form of genuine integration. From this perspective, convergence and not divergence would appear to be the key to a collective Welsh identity. That is not to say we can develop an argument for total assimilation in any form, but it encourages us to recognise the limitations of placing our differences in silos that we draw attention to separately for a particular day, week, or month during each year. Paying lip service to diversity will only dilute the richness and coherence of our collective, lived Welsh identities that are themselves constitutive of a more equal, living society.

All of us have our unique identities made up of intersectional characteristics and experiences. We are all many pieces of a jigsaw because our identities are constantly shifting, and the new curriculum should offer a safe opportunity to explore this. The complexity and ambiguity of boundaries imposed on the curriculum has resulted in individuals from minority ethnic communities being denied a strong emotional connection to Wales despite the fact that we don't have to be one set of characteristics. The current curriculum merely reflects society, shaped by those in dominant positions within society. This means many learners do not feel Welsh – not because of the narrow curriculum per se, but because Welsh society and culture is institutionally racist. To progress the inclusive Welsh narrative and to develop our social identity we need ensure there is no erasure in terms of our collective history. We must facilitate the agency to reclaim memory that speaks to our collective Welsh identities.

In some ways, this is also a paradoxical argument as it argues that individual responsibility requires we put the collective first. In turn, we should not aim for the segregation of individualist multiculturalism in its past form. We need our future leaders to be truly inclusive and make a real difference, not woke comments. It is this latter step – the collective first – that we should consider as intrinsic to Wales and Welshness; a collective, social identity that militates against the 'me first' neoliberal agenda. So far, multicultural education has not enabled a view of the wider landscape, but rather has encouraged individual exceptionalism. This distorted view of the world is far from honest and is alienating to us all, especially if we want to understand how we arrived at this position in the first place.

The late American politician Shirley Chisholm (2010) identified the importance of coming together to address greater collective needs despite her own challenges as an individual:

> I am not the candidate of Black America, although I am Black and proud; I am not the candidate of the women's movement of this country, although I am a woman and I am equally proud of that. I am the candidate of the people of America.[9]

The sentiment here is to educate beyond social characteristics and constructions of a person, and towards how that person can contribute to make a greater whole. The curriculum should therefore welcome positive contributions from different types of people, so that it becomes rich in diversity and raises the aspirations of all children, whilst striving to smash the glass ceiling that has limited the aspirations of marginalised groups in the past. We should strive to deliver a dialogic approach that supports both teachers and children to require a decolonised education, one that works to eradicate agonistic otherness.

Conclusion

In Wales we are fortunate to have an opportunity to revisit the purpose of education in the form of the new curriculum. For those teachers who in the past took it upon themselves to challenge bureaucracy and widen their individual classroom curriculums, there is now an opportunity to re-envisage how education can develop each and every child from a supportive, whole system approach. This is an opportunity to reclaim the joy of learning and turn away from the unhealthy focus on examinations, which has failed children who do not conform with normative expectations within our society.

The dismantling of the current system should provide us with an opportunity to look beyond the 'right type' of education that has shielded us from uncomfortable truths. We need to turn to another way of critical thinking, recognising that our place shapes us and our experiences, which results in our actions and how we respond to others. As people, we are uncomfortable with certain truths, but this does not mean we cannot learn from these. A collaborative approach that recognises legacies of the past in post-imperial societies, and the fundamental links between race and class, is the only place to start.

As it stands, we are not collectively in control of our stories in and about Wales. Using the new curriculum to reset the narrative as much as possible will enable us to tell stories that align to all of our different perspectives and experiences. The new curriculum provides an opportunity for us to stand in solidarity and to develop a freshly egalitarian consciousness in our Welsh communities and collective Welsh identity.

The range of factors and experiences that inform our diverse features do not advocate that we become immune to our differences: we cannot and should never become colour blind. But what we should strive to see goes further than the value of the person to something more than him – or herself – the Welsh collective. This is what I believe the curriculum should aim for: not just inclusive content that is no longer Whitewashed, but a way of engaging with a dynamic civic responsibility for all.

---

[1] Walter Benn Michaels, *The Trouble with Diversity: How we Learned to Love Identity and Ignore Inequality* (Metropolitan Books: New York, 2006) p. 49.

[2] Ted Cantle, Community Cohesion: A New Framework for Race and Diversity, (Palgrave Macmillan UK, 2008),101- 126.

[3] Charlotte Williams, Professor Charlotte Williams to lead work on teaching Wales' "rich history built on difference and diversity". Available at: https://gov.wales/professor-charlotte-williams-to-lead-

work-on-teaching-wales-richhistory-built-on-difference-and-diversity [Accessed: 7 February 2021]

[4] Nancy Fraser, The Old is Dying and the New Cannot be Born, (Verso: London, 2019).

[5] R. Connell, 'What would a socially just education system look like?' *Journal of Education Policy*, 27(2), 2012, 681-683.

[6] Margaret Thatcher (1987). Interview for Woman's Own ("no such thing as society"). Margaret Thatcher Foundation. Available at: https://www.margaretthatcher.org/document/106689 [Accessed: 25 October 2020].

[7] Shirley Chisholm, *Unbought & Unbossed*, (Washington, D.C: Take Root Media, 2010).

[8] Carol Tator, and Frances Henry, *Multicultural Education: Translating Policy into Practice*, (Ottawa: Multiculturalism and Citizenship Canada, 1991) p.122.

[9] Shirley Chisholm, *Unbought & Unbossed*, (Washington, D.C: Take Root Media, 2010).

All Mothers Are Working Mothers

Catrin Ashton

This is the farm road. It leads from the mountain and its wild moorland, back to the village of Bedlinog that sits hacked into the slopes of the Taf Bargod valley. After running on the open windy terrain of Cefn Gelligaer, the farm road feels like the home straight. The landscape is tamer here, sheep are brought to its lower slopes during lambing season; in the hedgerows nettles grow and cowslips, with bluebells in the shaded spots. Families have long walked here; children ride alongside their parents or grandparents on bikes and scooters.

I walk here with my own children, pushing my little boy in his pushchair mid-morning, lulling him to sleep while my little girl runs beside me. *We're running!* she exclaims full of amazement. *We are!* I answer; it's true. The breeze dances, playing in our hair and my little boy falls asleep to the sound of our voices and the warm song of the world around him.

A path leads to the woods below and to the spot where Pit Number 2 stood, in the days when the village was one big coal mine. We stop here, it is our cafe. *Oh thank you for coming to see me!* my little girl says to me, in Welsh. *What would you like today, chips and beans?* She serves me chips of grass, beans of stones or woodland sorrel in the spring. It is around this time that my little boy wakes and we wend our way home, the three of us and the buggy. In the springtime we stop to watch the lambs or newborn calves teetering on spindly legs. *They're feeding!* My children call out in wonder – still young enough to know the pleasure it brings.

When I run here on my own, I hear their voices. I see their chubby little hands fumbling for moss, or stones or a cwtch. Their laughter mixes with the sound of the stream and I am tricked for a second, turning my head to look, knowing they are not there really, yet catching myself looking still. Just here the road rises, the gradient a little steeper, and I'm surprised at how easy it is to run it without the struggle and negotiation of carrying a little boy who's just woken up, cajoling his by-now-sleepy (and sometimes crying) sister, while pushing the buggy and sometimes a scooter too. But this daily ritual of walking with and carrying my children is something I hold onto tightly, knowing it will inevitably end.

This period of having children has felt like one long pause (of sorts). A moment of stepping out of life as I knew it and seeing the world from a completely different angle. I watch it whirr by with all its drama as I slow down: allowing my pockets to be filled with twigs and feathers; turning over rocks, watching spiders and woodlice going about their day as we slowly, slowly, go about ours.

With the birth of my children came many beautiful presents; but one gift stood out from all those others. It arrived a few months later and it made me stand up a little straighter, not feel so vulnerable. It was sent by a friend from Australia and it was a well-read, slightly battered copy of an out-of-print booklet from 1972. The pamphlet, by Mariarosa Dalla Costa from Italy and Selma James from the USA, is called *The Power of Women and the Subversion of the Community*. It uses a feminist reading of Marx to analyse the situation of mothers staying home to care for their children.

What I found astonishing was that the circumstances of a mother who stays at home to look after her children has hardly changed in over forty years, and of course, much longer before that. I was also shocked at myself: I had not taken into account, or thought seriously about, the history of the role I was stepping into. I was excited too that this pamphlet, originally written in Italian, had been translated into many languages and had started an international movement demanding rights for housewives. In Padua the 'Wages for Housework' campaign was launched by Selma James, Brigitte Galtier, Mariarosa Dalla Costa and Silvia Federici, but by the end of the 1970s groups belonging to the movement had sprung up in the USA, Britain and many other countries around Europe.

The pamphlet insists that reproductive labour is fundamental to waged work: it generates the workers of the future; it cares for the children of those in waged work as well as, in the sense of domestic work more generally, taking care of the waged-labourers themselves through household chores – all integral aspects of a capitalist society. Engels states that:

> the determining factor in history is, in the final instance, the production and reproduction of the immediate essentials of life ... On the one side, the production of the means

of existence, ... on the other side, the production of human beings themselves, the propagation of the species.[1]

Yet, despite its centrality to capitalist accumulation, it is not considered productive enough to deserve a wage. In fact, a mother caring full time for her children is not considered to be working at all. We depend on the wages of a partner (if there is one) and if that wage is too small we are dependent upon supplementary government benefits that fluctuate in relation to our partner's income. This does not only affect the 'traditional' working class. Many workers in our society do not receive a fair living wage – even at the cultural and national institutions that we are so proud of here in Wales.

A single full-time mother on benefits is not considered to be working either, and on top of having to fulfil this role alone, the stigma of financial dependence is more obvious. The fact that these benefits are decidedly *not* a wage but are considered 'handouts' that are means-tested further disrespects the work that these women accomplish under extremely difficult circumstances.

Returning to waged work would give us autonomy, but it would not allow us to care for our children. And there lies the crux of the issue. Where is the freedom of choice? At six months, nine months or one year our babies are utterly dependent on us but not yet eligible for government-funded childcare, or school nursery places. So what are we to do? We are expected to pay for childcare, though many of us can't afford it.

In areas of Wales deemed deprived, it is possible to receive 30 hours free childcare from the age of two years via the Flying Start scheme. In areas of Wales not deemed deprived the Welsh Government introduced the Childcare for 3 and 4- year-olds scheme.[2] The guidelines state, amongst other criteria, that in order to be eligible to apply, parents of lone-parent families need to be working and parents of two-parent families must both be working.

This offer does not help parents who do not work but would like to return to work. Nor does it attempt to help those who do not wish to return to work as they want to care for their own children but consequently have to live in low income or zero income households.

Even in families where both parents manage to work through a mix of full-time and part-time jobs, depending on extended family for childcare, the household income of many of these families still does not raise them out of poverty. They are the working poor who depend on government schemes such as Child Tax Credits and Universal Credit in order to survive. The limitations of these schemes mean that it is almost impossible for families to prosper, and for children to flourish, on so little money. There has been much research and many surveys highlighting the debilitating restrictions of these schemes.

One such report is the Child and Family Poverty Survey Report published in July 2020 by the charity and national umbrella body Children in Wales, which states that 'Poverty happens when a family's resources fall below what they need, including taking part in their local community or society more generally.' The Welsh Government defines poverty as 'A long-term state of not having sufficient resources to afford food, reasonable living conditions or amenities or to participate in activities (such as access to attractive neighbourhoods and open spaces) that are taken for granted by others in their society.'[3] In the 'Low Wages' chapter of that same report it states that 'Low wages are one of the major causes of child poverty in Wales. Many respondents to the survey, as well as participants at regional child poverty events held across Wales, spoke of the paucity of decent paid work in some parts of Wales.'[4] Paying parents a good wage to look after their children would pull families, and therefore children, out of the poverty trap.

Our culture tends to stereotype women, splitting them into opposing categories. This trend continues in the way that motherhood is superficially constructed within our society: the flip side of the single mother on benefits is the phenomenon of the 'yummy mummy' of affluent communities who lives on via Instagram and wellness blogs. We are used to hearing about the 'juggling act' facing middle-class working mothers (but we are all working mothers!). What we don't tend to hear so much about is the situation of the stay-at-home mother who has no other choice: her economic situation allows her none, as childcare is too expensive to make having a job viable. Nor do we hear so much about those who choose this role despite knowing it will consign her to economic struggle and dependency. This situation is complicated by the fact that watching your children grow, helping them to negotiate the world is also a privilege. It is special, fleeting and poignant. And this is another reason why it's inconceivable to some that what we do *is work*.

We are not doing anything remotely revolutionary: we are not chief executives of successful companies, we are not scientists or engineers, we are not monetising our lifestyle projects from our bespoke kitchens. We are just at home, covered in splodges of food and snot and felt-tip pen ... It is often felt that we are not really doing our part for the feminist cause at all: we are not being dazzling or interesting, not pushing any boundaries.

Finding this pamphlet showed me the possibilities of groups of women uniting to demand better working conditions through wages and, consequently, the recognition that what we do as mothers *is labour*: moreover, it is productive labour, and it is essential. By confronting the irrationality of the fact that a stay-at-home mother (for want of a better term) does not get paid for her labour, the infrastructure of the whole system underpinning this begins to fall apart – as does neoliberal feminism. Because regardless of how many CEOs or directors are women, as long as this system of organising our society is upheld, we will always need a body of workers to look after our children until they are old enough to be sent to school. This body of workers consists of parents, family members, child minders, nannies and nursery staff – the overwhelming majority of whom are women.

The dominant neoliberal model of feminism – where we try to enter the workforce demanding the same positions, opportunities and wages as men – is a capitalist take on what it means to be a woman. Capitalism offers only the illusion of choice by ignoring – and in turn forcing us to ignore – our own biology. We go back to work despite the sadness that we feel at leaving our babies; if we were still breastfeeding at the time we also often end up dealing with mastitis or engorged breasts as we cannot feed our babies during those hours that we spend at work. If we do not return to waged work we also find ourselves in the difficult situation of having no real community in which to raise our children in any manageable way. Capitalism has disbanded the community – which is absolutely necessary to women if we are to recover from childbirth properly and raise children happily – by forcing everybody that it possibly can into waged labour, leaving hardly anyone around to help us.

Although the feminist struggle has allowed women to go out to work it has not yet freed us as mothers. The movement granted us access to those roles traditionally handed out to men and gained further ground in recent years with the campaign for freedom of information relating to pay, with demands for equal wages. Although necessary, this is still an example of women trying to be equal in a society that is organised around the high-earning capitalist class and the male worker, rather than an alternative version of society, organised considering the needs of children and their mothers.

As Mariarosa Dalla Costa pointed out, all of these demands – access to workspaces, equal pay, free childcare – are reactionary, defensive responses to our situation. The only revolutionary response is the demanding of a wage because it is the demanding of a wage that forces us to ask questions about the nature of care in our society and to ask what kind of futures are possible for our children: what kind of life can they hope for? In her 1975 essay 'Counterplanning from the Kitchen' Silvia Federici (of the Wages for Housework Campaign) writes:

Our Power as women *begins* with the social struggle for the wage, not to be let into the wage relation (for we were never out of it) but to be let out of it, for every sector of the working class to be let out.[5]

It echoes Selma James, who insists that the working class is always anti-capitalist, always revolutionary and is constantly fighting to be a self-governing power outside of capital so that it can eventually get rid of itself as a class. The working class is always looking for that power that will allow it to rid itself of its own slavery:

The women's movement is an expression of that power. So is the black movement. So are the movements of schoolchildren and students who are resisting their capitalist present and future as workers, as labour power ...[6]

In her 2004 book *Caliban and the Witch*, Silvia Federici traces the low wages of women in the workplace back to the transition to capitalism. Across Europe, starting in the late fifteenth century, women were expelled from workshops by craftsmen (assisted by the urban authorities), and also banned from other waged work before being banished to the home where they were not paid for their labour (now named 'housekeeping'). This normalised the practice of not paying women a wage at all or simply paying them a much lower rate than men.

From this perspective it seems illogical that we demand equal wages for women in the workplace without also demanding an actual wage for mothers – or for any parent – whose work it is to look after their children full time.

296

Neither does it help if middle to high-earning parents are still willing to pay nursery staff or their cleaner (all usually female) the minimum wage. Yet what is the alternative? Most families are unable to cope financially on just one income and, other than resorting to economic precarity or state benefits, going back to work is the only option. This is only made possible if, as a society, we pay our child-minders very badly – or not at all.

Denying women a wage for their reproductive labour, or paying them as little as possible for their care work, is a means of repressing the female population and, consequently, the working class in general. In *Caliban and the Witch* Federici considers the concept of primitive accumulation (also discussed by Marx):

> primitive accumulation was not simply an accumulation and concentration of exploitable workers and capital. It was *also an accumulation of differences and divisions within the working class* whereby hierarchies built upon gender as well as 'race' and age became constitutive of class rule and the formation of the modern proletariat.[7]

One of the most significant differences within the proletariat is that division between the waged and the unwaged worker but also, just as critically, the difference between the amount of wage earned by individuals each year. This difference in wage is played upon by the ruling class, pitting the 'benefit scroungers' and the working-poor against other, 'successful' and 'hard-working' citizens. This system rewards the champions with good homes, holidays abroad and nice cars while the rest are left struggling to hold it all together.

Along with considerably longer maternity and paternity leave, paying parents a decent wage for raising their children would be a step towards allowing women a real choice when it came to working or being at home with their children. The Welsh Government has recently anounced its plan to trial Universal Basic Income. This could work alongside UBI. The revolutionary element lies in the political significance of paying mothers/parents a wage for caring for their children: something that is missing if we discuss only UBI. If a mother's reproductive labour was taken seriously and paid seriously, the repercussions would allow for *all* care work to be taken seriously: it would set a precedent for nursery staff to earn better wages along with cleaners and those working in care homes or helping the vulnerable members of our communities. In short, it would not just be mothers or parents: many of the working poor and the unwaged poor would be brought out of poverty if their labour was fully acknowledged and if their wage reflected the essential nature of what they do.

It is difficult to discuss childcare without also discussing the care that we will need at the end of our lives. When women care for their children without a wage they are placing themselves in a vulnerable position when they are older. In Wales, as in the rest of the UK, if you are receiving benefits you do not automatically pay your National Insurance and are not necessarily reminded to do so either: this is significant as our pensions are based on our National Insurance contributions. Women (because the majority are overwhelmingly women) who have cared for their own children without a wage, often go on, in later life, to care for elderly parents and sick spouses and many do not even receive the full state pension for doing so.

In Bedlinog, the village in the South Wales valleys where I live, a common sight around teatime is plates of food under foil being taken to family members who need assistance. But looking after parents in their old age often involves much more than this. These women are bathing their parents or elderly family members at night, washing them when they have been ill. Many times a day they wash clothes and bedclothes soiled with diarrhoea and sick, they give emotional support – and it is hard to watch the giants of your life begin to fail. Time and time over, in those hours between official care visits, they pick up bloodied parents from the floor after a fall, always dreading what they will find as they turn the key in the lock. Cuts to services in Wales mean that there is not enough support for the elderly and their families – mainly the women – who are helping them to cope. Although health is a devolved matter in Wales, the Welsh Government has privatised care work and has repeatedly refused to countenance the idea of nationalised care. Compare this to Scotland where Nicola Sturgeon has resolved to build a National Care Service as a lasting legacy of the Covid-19 crisis.[8]

What does this say about our politics in Wales and the way that we are governed? We seem to subscribe to the myth that we are an inherently socialist country without truly questioning what that would actually mean and what socialist policies would look like. We are run by an overwhelmingly neoliberal government but as a nation we seem to have swallowed its policies almost without question, as though it were the politics of common sense, when all along we could have been aiming for something so much bigger.

In her 2009 essay 'On Elder Care Work and the Limits of Marxism' Silvia Federici writes:

> As feminist economists have argued, the crisis of elder care, whether considered from the viewpoint of the elders or their care providers, is essentially a gender question. Although increasingly commodified, most care work is still done by women and in the form of unpaid labour ... Thus, paradoxically, the more women care for others the less care they can receive in return, because they devote less time to waged labour than men.[9]

Insisting on a decent wage to raise children also, by extension, insists on a decent pension in old age. It would allow working-class women who have spent a lifetime caring for others the dignity of a financially secure, eco-nomically stress-free old age.

Where capitalism succeeded in making women's work invisible, socialism – despite its unions, political education and workmen's halls – failed to make our labour visible again. The very term 'workmen's halls' – part of my up-bringing in the valleys – irritates me now. How could men ever have imagined the struggle was theirs alone? One of the ways in which capitalism divided the proletariat was through its war on women. By not recognising the repro-ductive labour of women as equal to all other work, socialism is failing the working class as a whole. Women have, fundamentally, been left out of the struggle for equality, so that even as basic a concept as demanding a wage for a mother's labour seems radical.

In Wales, however, a new campaign is forming, inspired by Wages for Housework, working towards securing a wage for mothers/parents and consequently securing a pension, too, for their labour. The choice to look after our children in a financially secure setting should be available to all – not just the wealthy. We hope that this campaign will help place the question of care at the forefront of Welsh Government policies, because one day our children will be the older generation and they will need comprehensive care all over again. When my own children reach the end of their lives I will no longer be around to help them – but I want them to be safe when I am not here. That will require a good pension and a transformation of the way we organise ourselves as a society by placing children and care work at the heart of everything that we do. As the domestic workers' movement based in Madrid, the Territorio Domestico, insists 'Sin nosotros no se mueve el mundo' – without us the world does not move. We have a lot of work to do, but as Silvia Federici and others have shown, this is not a utopian vision. Through a combination of direct action and protest, all over the world communities of people are defying what is expected of them and organising themselves according to their own needs and values. They show us that these changes are possible: especially, I hope, in Wales.

Parts of this essay have appeared in *Planet* issue 231 and in *O'r Pedwar Gwynt* issue 15.

1 Friedrich Engels, The Origin of the Family, Private Property and the State, p. 4.
https://www.marxists.org/archive/marx/works/download/pdf/origin_family.pdf

2 Welsh Government, 'Childcare for 3 and 4-year-olds: guidance for providers' (2019) https://gov.wales/childcare-3-and-4-year-olds-guidance-providers

3 Welsh Government, *Child Poverty Strategy for Wales* (March 2015) https://gov.wales/sites/default/files/publications/2019-06/child-poverty-strategy-for-wales-report.pdf

4 Child and Family Poverty Survey by Children in Wales, (July 2020), p. 17

5 Silvia Federici, *Revolution at Point Zero: Housework, Reproduction and Feminist Struggle* (Oakland: PM Press, 2020), p. 33.

6 Selma James, *Sex, Race and Class: The Perspective of Winning* (Oakland: PM Press, 2012), p. 77.

7 Silvia Federici, *Caliban and the Witch: Women, the Body and Primitive Accumulation* (Brooklyn: Autonomedia, 2014), p. 63.

8 https://www.thenational.scot/news/uk-news/18690018.sturgeon-announces-plan-national-care-service/

9 Silvia Federici, *Revolution at Point Zero,* p. 141.

First as Comedy, then as Tragedy:

How the High Ideals of The Well-being of Future Generations Act Have Fallen Short

Frances Williams

The Well-being of Future Generations Act (WFG) was welcomed as a ground-breaking piece of legislation when it was passed by the Welsh Assembly in 2015. The moment was celebrated as auspicious by the Head of Sustainable Development at the United Nations, no less: 'We hope that what Wales is doing today, the world will do tomorrow.'[1] Six years on, how have the high hopes for the WFG Act panned out? And what can we learn about Welsh Government by way of this distinction?

Here I explore the WFG Act through the focus of lived experience, noting feelings of disillusionment and frustration. I look at how the participation of local authorities was enlisted, speculating if 'unchecked hypocrisies' might lie behind negative effects (Quaintance, 2017). Whilst citing policy understandings of 'well-being',[2] I draw primarily on my PhD research, where I became a participant observer within community groups at 'the receiving end' of policy, (as one volunteer phrased the dynamic at play).

People living in Wales suffer worse health relative to people living in England. But during the pandemic we died in greater per capita number too.[3] Underlying conditions of poverty in areas of deindustrialisation have exacerbated high mortality rates inflicted by Covid-19, but other more recent political histories have also proven harmful. These include histories of devolved government and its promise of enabling policy differences that can make a difference to being able to lead healthy lives as part of living in a healthy society.

Similarities and Differences

The WFG Act was premised on the belief that a guiding framework for policy makers in Wales could forge progressive 'different' ways of working, leading to better, sustainable outcomes. Opportunities for quick financial return would have to be held in check with longer-term consideration of individual and collective health and well-being. The seven Well-being goals of the act include not only 'a prosperous Wales', but 'a resilient Wales', 'a healthier Wales', 'a more equal Wales', 'a Wales of cohesive communities', 'a Wales of vibrant culture and thriving Welsh language' and 'a globally responsible Wales'. Five ways of working were further set out which, alongside 'longer-term' thinking, asked public bodies to adopt principles of 'collaboration', 'integration', 'prevention' and lastly, 'involvement'. Mark Drakeford noted in 2014 how the 'Future Generations Bill makes a positive contribution to this (health) agenda, as such an approach will recognise that improving health will require collective effort across the devolved public service'.[4]

I held a privileged position to witness these aspirations unfurl. During my PhD, I observed how arts, health and well-being policies were jointly implemented across regions of the UK.[5] Between 2016–2019, I spent time with people involved in Arts in Health projects in North Wales, as well as the North of England, observing how policy difference made itself felt amongst people living in differently devolved regions. This made for an intriguing comparative analysis, given that Greater Manchester was embarking upon its own experiment in English regional devolution, claiming by many there as 'future-facing'.[6]

Agreed in the same year as the WFG Act, 'Devo-Manc' allowed Mancunians to elect a City Mayor, granting combined local authorities more freedom to run their own affairs. But the deal was conditional on working to reduced budgets. Unlike Welsh devolution in the 1990s, this 'devo-deal' was not born out of any referendum but struck in secret.[7] Former Chancellor, George Osbourne, flattered local political elites in their belief that 'what Manchester does today, the world does tomorrow'. This phrase first originated at the time of the industrial revolution but was now sorely felt by many in the 'left behind' north. Believing this mythology, Welsh precedent was ignored: many GM representatives proclaiming competitive advantage in being 'further ahead' than other parts of the UK. But beyond the scrutiny of academics, few representations of these two types of 'devolution' – so near and yet so far – made it into the news, let alone popular imagination.

An exception to this rule was a film made by artist Bedwyr Williams.[8] It appeared to tie together these two differently devolved Welsh and English regions through dystopian imagery. Tyrrau Mawr (Large Towers) portrays a future megacity atop of Cadair Idris, an urban conurbation tall enough to look down on 'Manchatten' (as Manchester's high-rise city centre has been dubbed). Williams presents an alternate Northern Powerhouse where Welsh skyscrapers wink with the fulfilment of great wealth. His computer-generated film is, of course, an absurd fiction. The voice-over adopts a sardonic tone, especially when making reference to 'wellness'. The narrator solemnly informs that the city's founder was killed when struck by 'a jet of wet concrete, bursting out of badly constructed wooden shuttering, at the base of what was going to be a spa and wellness centre'. Poor health and safety then. But much dry humour.

One art critic pointed out that Tyrrau Mawr was one of the few works in the Artes Mundi exhibition in 2017 to critically reflect on the conditions of cultural production in Wales. We can only wonder if there was any irony, then, in Arts Council Wales' (ACW) decision to use a still from this film for the cover of their 2017 financial report. In this annual audit of cultural activity, lost income and 'continuing pressure on public funds' is emphasised in order to show how efficiencies have been won. 'We've cut our costs and reduced staff numbers by around 25 per cent. It's been a challenging process for our hard working and committed staff,' ACW's Chair acknowledged. 'But it's been the right thing to do.'[9] Phil George rearranged blame and responsibility from a snug 'arm's length' distance through his words, which strike a note of virtue, not vice.

Visions

The use of this artwork to enhance a leaner ACW, on such slippery moral ground, gave early warning of how visionary futures – even dystopias – could quickly become co-opted by those seeking to use art for their own ends. In the same year, I invited 'Lead Change-Maker' (as she was unusually titled) from the newly created WFG Commission to speak at an event I organised with other researchers at Cardiff University. I invited Cathy Madge to engage with the findings of a recent All Party Parliamentary report, *Creative Health: the Arts, Health and Wellbeing*, which advocated arts and culture as an 'essential vaccine' that could 'mitigate' the negative effects of 'adverse environments' and 'health inequalities'.[10] Might this report's findings dove-tail, I speculated, with the emphasis on the different way of integrated working enabled through the WFG Act?

Madge introduced the WFG Act by first pointing to the most pressing issues: climate crisis, poverty and inequality. But for the most part, her PowerPoint was peppered with upbeat illustrations. One image, produced by Cardiff and Vale Health Board, envisioned future Welsh communities participating in a diagrammatic vision of preventative public health. Colourful figurines moved around a model town to visit a library, community centre and carrot-filled allotments, with the local hospital tucked away in a far corner. She presented the piece of legislation as one which placed Wales at the forefront of global sustainable development. But her job spec, Madge openly stated, set her on a collision course with those perpetuating 'business as usual'. She called for a 'completely different thinking about how we design services' and cited the recent creation of Public Service Boards (or PSBs) as the 'mechanism for collaboration at local level'. While admitting these local forums were 'not perfect', they offered a place to 'start somewhere'.

My research sought to find out to what extent this vision was beginning to be realised. The community groups I studied in North Wales made all too real the weakened state apparatus and social fabric into which the WFG Act's frame was imposed. One project, based in Prestatyn, saw locals weave a network of mutual aid. The Artisan Collective comprised many retired people at risk of social isolation. Based in the town's old library, a range of voluntary activities were housed under this roof, including coffee mornings for the bereaved; family treasure hunts; dementia support; food bank collection point and art club. They also held close links with occupational health specialists based at the GP practice sited opposite.

But the Artisan Collective did not receive the support they would have liked from the local council working through the freshly created PSBs. This was the case despite the Artisan's willingness to translate 'institutional talk' into citizen action: 'It's all very well talking about it like that, but the patients have to buy into it too...'. Despite the success of the project, they were not able to secure access to the building beyond rolling two-month contracts. After threatening to sell the place 'from under us', the fate of the former library was put to further public consultation by the council, eventually seeing this group displaced and disbanded.

Measuring Up

The promises of sustainability held out by WFG arrived too late for the Artisan Collective, with council decisions continuing to be dictated by short-term revenue gain over longer-term social and health benefit. Other councils in Wales made similar choices and offered reasons for failure. One Swansea council leader wrote to the Commissioner for WGA in 2019 to explain lack of progress, stating how austerity had created 'a vicious circle'.[11] Lack of resource 'put pressure' on staff which 'limited their capacity' for collaboration and 'joint working through PSBs'. No extra funds had enabled them to deliver WFG.

Alongside austerity's disabling effects, target culture also played its part in thwarting AFG. Other community organisers in North Wales, I discovered, felt hampered by the wrong kind of local government attention, made through New Public Management. Many in the third sector experienced negative repercussions from insistence on 'benchmarks' and formal 'certification' for their work. 'They are more interested in measuring us than supporting us', one quipped. One Welsh academic, who made a study of Social Prescribing, used the word 'kidnap' to characterise the process of disempowerment set in motion by those in local government claiming to enact WFG principles. Community health initiatives were being 'appropriated into a medicalised health model'. Or as one project leader made the point: 'we did this long before they came along and started calling it social prescribing!'

The author of a book examining the policy concept of 'well-being' also cites a sense of stolen agency. Jennifer

Wallace observes that 'much of what makes life worth living' lies beyond 'the scope of government and cannot be subjected to the reductive rigour of performance measures'. 'If governments were to be truly transformative in their approach,' she suggests, 'they would also recognise the contribution of the people.'[12] Government could adopt a different role as an elected power that 'contributes to social progress, rather than owning it'. Damningly, Wallace notes how, in Wales in particular, 'a strong culture of performance management has arisen which detracts from the original aim' of the Act. 'There is a sense that the transformation has not been as far-reaching as its architects would have hoped.'[13]

One critic interprets the relation between government and public bodies as evidence of a more calculated deception based on neoliberal consensus rather than any difference forged by way of devolution. 'The new conservatism' Morgan Quaintance believes, 'advances its agenda surreptitiously by presenting itself as forward-thinking, inclusive and socially conscious'. Such deceptions cover up the 'exploitative logics that many arts professionals, and a large proportion of the general public are either fighting against, or oppressed by'.[14]

'Well-being'

This radical rhetoric – a camouflage whereby regressive economic policy can pass as socially progressive – might be understood by looking back at the decade in which the WFG Act arose. For as much as it is unique to Wales, the

Act can be placed in a broader progressive movement to challenge the idea that economic growth is a prize that must be won at all (human) cost. Critiques of Gross Domestic Product (GDP) as the primary indicator of governmental success had been championed at the beginning of the decade by influential author, Richard Laylard.

Laylard's research seeks to address the puzzle that 'as our societies become richer, people get no happier' through capturing the 'evidence' that subjective feelings provide (not just material circumstance alone).[15] While his ideas informed new understandings of governance, any implicit critique of capitalism's profligacy was quickly co-opted by the Right. Acting on this 'new science' of happiness, David Cameron set up The National Well-being Index alongside his 'Nudge unit'. The latter deploying behavioural economics to prompt individuals into making 'good' choices. Cameron himself suggested that there are limits to what markets can deliver: 'Well-being can't be measured by money or traded in markets. It's about the beauty of our surroundings, the quality of our culture and, above all, the strength of our relationships.'[16]

This definition of 'well-being' went hand in hand with his proposal of a 'big society' and was cleverly judged to re-brand the negative perception of the Tory party as the 'nasty party' of old.[17] Such as task would be difficult to pull off in Wales, though, which suffered the catastrophic social effect of monetarist policy under Thatcher. Mark Fisher credits Thatcher as the originator of the phrase 'there is no alternative' characterising this ethos as a 'self-fulfilling prophesy'. In devolved Wales, it was in the muddy depths Rhodri Morgan's 'clear red waters' – party political divide upheld through devolution – that the struggle to establish Welsh policy 'difference' has been fought.

Public health policy is a case in point. Researchers have shown how successive Welsh administrations have adopted 'fluctuating' policies over time.[18] This is especially so of policies which purposefully address the 'social determinants of health' – i.e., the social conditions we are born into that inform our health, such as housing and education. The early years of Welsh devolution displayed early impetus to integrate 'health in all policies', albeit an aim hampered by devolution's limited scope and leverage.[19] However, as devolution wore on there was a 'complete overshadowing of the health inequalities agenda' in subsequent decades when more emphasis was laid on individual lifestyle choices.[20] The social determinants of health were downplayed to enable emphasis shift toward individual responsibility. Public Health Wales brought individual and collective health together through their championing of an 'asset-based approach' for example, one of many terms which deploy economic languages in public health contents (with others including David Putnam's influential concept of 'social capital').

Early advocates of Arts for Health used these descriptors in order to affirm ineffable human values – the 'emotional transaction which makes for genuine empowerment' held above any 'balance sheet deduction'.[21] But other critical writers on public health have warned against the risk of intangible human resources being valued above material goods if they are used to downplay socioeconomic inequality. As Lynne Friedli argues,

'Psycho-social factors are abstracted from the material realities of people's lives and function as an alternative to addressing questions of economic power and privilege.'[22] Friedli identifies the flipping of Laylard's logic within public health policy, whereby poverty can be cast as an attitudinal disposition, with the remedy of 'positive thinking' punitively applied (through cruel welfare sanctions).

Dying for Change

Public Health has come unexpectedly to the fore with the shock – and 'shock doctrine' – of the current global pandemic.[23] Every Welsh citizen can now understand the kinds of 'differences' enabled by the Welsh Government. Drawing heavily on focus groups, a PR war was waged between English and Welsh governments along party political lines.[24] Fighting the pandemic's ill-effect on his own political future, Johnson's administration is in 'permanent campaign mode', some now argue.[25] Competitive advantage during the pandemic rests on who can blame the other for 'playing politics' with people's lives (and hide their own complicity in doing so). Alan Finlayson argues that the production of affect has become the goal, rather than by-product, of policy: 'not to change the situations people find themselves in, but to change people's feelings about their situations'. Under this new populist paradigm, governments do not 'require your participation, just to know how you might respond to the things it might do to you'.[26]

During the first lockdown in March 2020, Sophie Howe, the WFG Commissioner, published her first progress report. The experience of pandemic led Howe to believe that the WFG Act was now more important than ever. An illustrative 'map of the future of Wales' is deployed throughout, using computer-generated images of a generic non-place populated by square-headed people. In relation to Welsh publics, Howe seamlessly positions herself between the people and the government, close adviser, but also a conduit for public opposition.[27] 'I get my hope from this growing number of frustrated champions out there agitating, ruffling feathers, speaking truth to power and challenging leaders.'[28]

In casting herself as the leader of a social 'movement', she echoes the sentiments of the Mayor of Manchester. Andy Burnham has also spoken of regional devolution in similarly apolitical terms, as being 'about providing services, working from the bottom-up, with community and voluntary organisations ... It's a grassroot movement. A different way of doing politics'.[29] Questions that would complicate such assertions – 'Different to where, to whom, to what' – are avoided in favour of sounding radical notes. This is a common trait amongst establishment Labour party figures in Cardiff and Manchester alike, keen to claim small differences as large.

Devolved government in Wales – in common with the devolved city of Manchester – exhibits an unhealthy consensus amongst politicians of all political stripes whose normative values represent orthodoxy, not radical difference. This has enabled populist actors to demand not merely the abandonment of the WFG Act, but Welsh devolution in its entirety. It is the (far) Right who have exploited the anger of 'frustrated' citizens, acknowledged as such by Howe, late in the day. In summoning up such a brittle better future, the acknowledgment of legitimate complaint – expressions of social suffering – has been stifled. The sense of hope promised through the WFG Act now threatens to become a sideshow that compliments, all too well, Johnson's disparagement of 'doom-mongers'. It is a further sad development that constructive critique is now cast as 'right wing' in a climate of extreme polarisation, where positions of nuance are no longer permitted.

The WFG Act reveals much about the neoliberal flavour of Welsh Labour and the successive administrations it has led. Noble ideals have been knocked into the cocked hat of Welsh devolved government, with policy intention subject not just to latitude, but constraint. Thus its fate can be placed within accounts of the 'slow cancellation of the future' that pose advanced capitalist societies as those which continue to foreclose the needs of future generations rather than protect them.[30]

Mark Fisher articulates the 'widespread sense that not only is capitalism the only viable political and economic system, but also that it is now impossible even to imagine a coherent alternative to it'.[31] 'Once, dystopian films and novels were exercises in acts of imagination – the disasters they depicted acting as narrative pretext for the emergence of different ways of living,' Fisher notes. But now such depictions seem 'more like an extrapolation or exacerbation, than an alternative'. His words are apt for Tyrrau Mawr, a nightmare vision of a future Wales that deployed a dark humour, never taken seriously enough.

[1] Nikhil Seth was speaking in 2018 to endorse the United Nation's Global Guardians for Future Generations programme. https://www.futuregenerations.wales/news/a-voice-for-future-generations-across-the-world-is-crucial-says-future-generations-commiss ioner-for-wales-at-un-summit-new-york/

[2] Jennifer Wallace, Wellbeing and Devolution (London: Palgrave, 2019).

[3] https://www.theguardian.com/world/2021/feb/08/inequality-high-covid-toll-south-wales-valleys

[4] https://business.senedd.wales/documents/s23819/PtN%203%20-%20Additional%20information%20from%20the%20Minister%20for%20Health%20and%20Social%20Servcies.pdf

[5] Frances Williams, In a creative healthy place? Situating arts and health within the discourse of 'the devolution revolution', (Doctoral thesis, Manchester Metropolitan University, 2019).

[6] I quote Alison Clarke, Director of Arts in Greater Manchester, here, as one example amongst many other local authority figures I heard use this phrase (Williams, 2019: 226).

[7] Philip Blond and Mark Morrin, Devo Max – Devo Manc: Place-based public services (Respublica, 2014).

[8] See the work here [video]: https://www.youtube.com/watch?v=9SVJ91Mq5g0

[9] https://arts.wales/sites/default/files/2019-02/Report_and_Financial_Statements_2016-17_Web.pdf

[10] All-Parliamentary Group on Arts, Health and Wellbeing, Creative Health: The Arts for Health and Wellbeing (2017) https://issuu.com/alexandracoulter5/docs/creative_health_inquiry_re port_2017_bd5edea9d662b7

[11] Councillor Mary Jones, Swansea Council's Public Services Board Performance Panel.

[12] Wallace, Wellbeing and Devolution, p. 90.

[13] Ibid, p. 74.

[14] Morgan Quaintance, 'The New Conservatism: Complicity and the UK Art World's Performance of Progression', e-flux conversations (2017) https://conversations.e-flux.com/t/the-new-conservatism-complicity-and-the-uk-art-worlds-performance-of-progression/7200

[15] Richard Laylard, Happiness: Lessons from a New Science (London: Penguin, 2006).

[16] David Cameron, quoted in Jacob Goldstein, 'Well Being Can't Be Measured By Money Or Traded In Markets', NPR (15 November

2010)
https://www.npr.org/sections/money/2010/11/15/131338770/-well-being-can-t-be-measured-by-money-or-traded-in-markets?t=1623342251127

[17] As Teresa May recalled in 2011
https://www.newstatesman.com/uk-politics/2010/06/david-cameron-party-budget

[18] Katherine E. Smith et al., 'Divergence or convergence? Health inequalities and policy in devolved Britain', Critical Social Policy 29 (2009).

[19] 'Health in all Policies' proposed by WHO
https://www.who.int/cardiovascular_diseases/140120HPRHiAPFramework.pdf

[20] Ibid.

[21] Michael White, Arts Development in Community Health: A social tonic (Oxford: Radcliffe, 2009).

[22] Lynne Freidli, '"What we've tried, hasn't worked": the politics of assets based public health', Critical Public Health 23:2 (2012).

[23] Naomi Klein, The Shock Doctrine (London: Penguin, 2008).

[24] Frances Williams, 'Laggers or Leaders? The Politics of Lockdown', Institute of Welsh Affairs (2020)
https://www.iwa.wales/agenda/2020/05/laggers-and-leaders-the-politics-of-lockdown/

[25] Alan Finlayson, 'Britain doesn't have a government, it has a permanent campaigning machine', The Guardian (10 August 2020)
https://www.theguardian.com/commentisfree/2020/aug/10/britain-government-permanent-campaigning-machine-johnson-cummings

[26] Ibid.

[27] Some claim she is an 'insider'. https://www.bbc.co.uk/news/uk-wales-politics-34709434

[28] Sophie Howe, The Future Generations Report 2020
https://www.futuregenerations.wales/wp-content/uploads/2020/06/Intro-Chap-1.pdf

[29] Burnham, A. (2019), speaking on Radio 4's Today programme in 2019.

[30] Franco Berardi, After The Future, ed. by Gary Genosko and Nicholas Thoburn (Oakland: AK Press, 2011).

[31] Mark Fisher, Capitalist Realism (London: Zero Books, 2009).

317

News Black Holes in Wales, and What We Can Do About Them

Rae Howells

We often hear that the loss of newspapers is bad for democracy. Even that a 'news black hole' might open up when a newspaper shuts. But hard evidence is not always easy to find. As a journalist, former hyperlocal news editor, trade union activist and media academic, I've been (un)lucky enough to have a front row seat to the precipitous decline of local journalism in Wales over the last dozen or so years. Unfortunately, the news, both for journalism and democracy, is not good.

My tale starts in 2008, when I was made redundant from my job as editor of a current-affairs publication in Wales. I joined a co-operative of other newly redundant Swansea-based journalists from my local National Union of Journalists branch, looking to create new jobs in the industry against what felt like an overwhelming tide of closures and cuts. When a neighbouring weekly newspaper, the *Port Talbot Guardian*, closed in late 2009, we were able to move quickly to establish a local news service online. This became the *Port Talbot Magnet*, a website and, from 2013, a free quarterly tabloid newspaper delivered to 20,000 local homes.

The closure of the *Guardian* provided not just a news gap for the *Magnet* to try to fill. It also provided an opportunity to research how a newspaper closure might impact on a community. With no salary from the *Magnet*, I applied for a funded PhD at Cardiff University, and for the next five years Port Talbot was my case study as I set about researching the nature and effects of a news black hole.

A newspaper closure doesn't come out of nowhere. The story of the *Port Talbot Guardian*'s demise was tied up with the economic fortunes of industrial and post-industrial Port Talbot itself, while also being symptomatic of much wider trends in the global newspaper industry.

News and How We Fund It

A fundamental idea to grasp in understanding the problems faced by the news industry today is that public interest journalism is not economically viable as a product on its own. It therefore must be subsidised – by the state, private interests, philanthropy, or – the model we have relied upon for the last century or so – advertising. Through the latter half of the twentieth century in the UK, advertising accounted for between 50 and 80 per cent of most paid-for newspapers' income, much of it based on classified ads, as well as lucrative jobs pages and property supplements, and significant income from government in the shape of statutory public notices.

Advertising's prevalence means that rather than selling newspapers to readers, in reality, most publishers are in the business of selling their readers' attention to advertisers. However, our attention was a commodity for which many industries began to compete, and from the 1950s, with the rise of commercial radio and television, newspaper circulation figures showed a gradual, sustained decline. By the 1990s, cruel cuts began in order to preserve profit margins. Newspaper acquisitions by increasingly remote corporations led to a culture of editorial redundancies, district office closures and convergence into centralised hubs, as well as an increasing trend towards automation of the newsroom.

The arrival of the internet expedited this trend. Both display and classified advertising were rapidly filleted: classified advertising was usurped by websites such as eBay and Gumtree; once-lucrative property pages and recruitment sections were outgunned by internet search. As circulations fell and readers began to fragment into smaller, niche audiences (who became quickly accustomed to reading news online for free), spending on display advertising – traditionally linked to audited circulation figures – was chipped away.

The virtual collapse of advertising revenue has meant their own survival has become the most urgent priority for newspaper businesses today. Companies such as *WalesOnline*, *Western Mail* and *Daily Post* publisher, Reach Plc, have demonstrated this by restructuring their company and refocusing their editorial output to maximise clicks in a digital-first strategy that aims to appeal to as many people as possible. An unfortunate side effect, however, is that public interest journalism and local reporting that serves comparatively smaller communities have become unsustainable. *WalesOnline* has become Wales' most-read news outlet, but (in spite of some improvement through the introduction of the BBC Local Democracy reporter scheme) as a reader living in, for example, Port Talbot, it has become much more difficult to find out what's happening in council meetings, magistrates' courts, schools, hospitals and local politics. This has real-world implications for citizens.

Port Talbot – Case Study of a News Black Hole

The *Port Talbot Guardian* offers a case in point. Launched in 1925 by a group of local businessmen, the *Guardian* was established to provide news coverage for the town and its surrounding villages. In its 84-year history the title was acquired four times by successively larger companies, finally ending up in the hands of the Trinity Mirror Group in 1999. Around that time, the Port Talbot office of the *Guardian* was shut, and its journalists were relocated first to Neath, and later to Bridgend. Circulation halved between 2000 and 2009, and it was finally closed by Trinity Mirror (now Reach Plc), who cited financial unsustainability as the reason for its closure. Meanwhile, that year, the Trinity Mirror group posted a pre-tax profit of £42m.

Port Talbot had once been an economic 'treasure island' built on the wealth of its steel industry. From the late 1960s into the early 90s, no less than five different newspaper offices were located in the town centre. As many as 11 journalists worked there, competing with each other for the scoop and covering courts, council meetings, public meetings, protests, conferences, accidents, sports matches and more: the whole gamut of events and developments that make up community life.

I interviewed a dozen reporters who had worked as journalists in Port Talbot between 1960 and 2015. Those who had worked in the 1960s to 1980s gave me examples of competing with other newspaper reporters for stories, leaving the office to follow or find leads, and attending courts and council meetings as a matter of routine.

By the mid-2000s, reporters told me they were not allowed to leave the office unless by express permission, that their primary focus was on sourcing large numbers of stories and filling boxes in page templates – as many as 17 in a day, or 35 across a weekend – and that completing large volumes of work was the main focus, a kind of sausage factory approach that prioritised quantity. As a result, they leaned increasingly on public relations and social media to source their stories. Meanwhile, their workload increased. Newspaper paginations went up and the advent of the internet meant that there was a new pressure to write breaking news, to fill the ever-hungry mouth of the newspaper's website, and compete for the attention of readers and their clicks on advert-heavy pages.

Jobs were cut, printing presses were closed, and the race to a (much less lucrative) digital world began to take hold. By 2015, there were no permanent journalists based in Port Talbot. Our small news service, the *Port Talbot Magnet* operated a hot-desking and part-time service and struggled to make ends meet, while the daily newspaper based in nearby Swansea, the *South Wales Evening Post*, employed two reporters (down from the four it had employed since the 1960s) to cover all of Neath and Port Talbot, based in an office 10 miles away. This represented a 90 per cent drop in the number of dedicated Port Talbot reporters between 1970 and 2015. Similar reductions in reporter numbers are to be found across Wales – we lost between 60 and 90 per cent of our journalists in four decades, everything from junior reporters to news editors, photographers to subeditors, feature writers and specialist journalists to patch reporters. Many titles became zombie newspapers – ghosts of their former selves that continued to roll off the printing presses every week, but which now operated with a skeleton staff of perhaps one, or half a reporter responsible for everything from sourcing photographs to writing the front-page story.

It is perhaps no surprise that I found a tangible decline in the quantity, quality and localness of news articles about Port Talbot across this time. Between 1970 and 2015 the number of stories about Port Talbot fell significantly, by 66.3 per cent. I measured the quality of news coverage by examining how many sources were quoted, how local the story was, whether the reporter had used press releases or attended meetings in person, and several other quality indicators. Over time, stories became less local, journalists less likely to attend meetings and more likely to use press releases. Higher status sources such as politicians or government officials were more likely to be quoted in the news than members of the public.

Do We Need Journalism in the Information Age?

An argument I hear frequently is that the loss of local newspapers doesn't matter. We have the internet now, they say. Online news is free and plentiful. Information is easily available. We need only pick up our phones and search for what we want to know.

However, online platforms are only as good as their content, and there is evidence that the news and information available to residents is not adequate to furnish them with the knowledge, representation and scrutiny they need. The people of Port Talbot have lived without a journalist in their community since the turn of the millennium and without their own dedicated weekly newspaper since 2009.

In 2015 I surveyed 364 residents about their news consumption habits and their knowledge of local affairs. I also carried out four focus groups. I found many concerning trends. The level of local knowledge about important issues was low. Many people reported that they found out about important, life-affecting stories too late to act on them or protest against them. They had lost trust in the news media as they often saw it did not represent their views or contained factual inaccuracies. Their sources of information were varied and unsatisfactory, and often came through word of mouth or posts on social media. Many reported discovering information by stumbling across it in public spaces (one man told me he had discovered news of a mooted permanent closure of the town's motorway junction by reading it on protest graffiti). There was a prevalence of rumour and speculation, and a lack of certainty about facts.

Leading from this, people also reported it was difficult to get information they needed from public bodies, and that they felt government agencies were not transparent or open in communicating with them, and it was not always clear which level of government was responsible for decisions. On one issue, local government pointed protesters to Welsh Government. Welsh Government pointed them to UK-led agencies, who pointed them back to local government.

Activists and campaigners who had taken on the challenge of keeping up with Council decisions (or similar) said they struggled to find the information they needed and often failed to obtain answers from officials. This was labour-intensive, time-consuming work. Even when they did find accurate information on a particular point, they lacked the ability to convey it to a wider audience.

Most seriously, I found high levels of anger and frustration, particularly among younger groups, who were also much more negative about Port Talbot than older groups, reporting that they felt a lack of opportunity and a dissatisfaction with the town and what it offered them. Some of the younger group suggested rioting could give them a voice and force those in authority to listen to their concerns.

Democratic Engagement in a News Black Hole

Through the research, I found plentiful evidence for the existence of a news black hole, and what seemed to be a serious impact on citizens' knowledge and representation.

But had the closure of their last newspaper impacted their engagement with the democratic process?

I examined election turnout data for local, Assembly and Parliamentary elections for Port Talbot's Aberavon constituency, looking for average turnout figures and comparing them with national averages. Between the 1970 and 1999 local elections, turnout for the seats within the Aberavon constituency was consistently high – an average of 2.45 percentage points above the UK average. For general elections, this figure was an average of 1.17 percentage points above the UK average until 2001, while figures in the first Welsh Assembly election in 1999 were 0.5 per cent above the Welsh average. I expected to find this trend would continue until the closure of the *Port Talbot Guardian* in 2009. I was in for a surprise.

I did in fact find a drop in turnout, but it was not in 2009. Instead, I found that turnout in the Aberavon constituency for general, local and Welsh Assembly elections began to fall consistently below the national average for the first time from around the year 2000. For example, in the local elections from 2004 onwards, turnout fell to 0.72 percentage points below the UK average. General election figures fell to 2.91 percentage points below the UK average, and Welsh Assembly elections to an average of 2.89 per cent below the rest of Wales.

In spite of evidence in other countries of newspaper closures affecting election turnouts, and new evidence in 2020 that newspaper closures are linked with falls in election turnout, I did not find this in association with the closure of the *Guardian*. But these earlier declines did seem to tally with some of my other data around the quantity and quality of news. What happened at the turn of the millennium that might account for the change? As you may remember, one significant occurrence was the closure of the *Port Talbot Guardian* district office and the removal of its editorial staff to neighbouring Neath.

The closure meant journalists were distanced from local people and communities, becoming more remote and less easy to access: 'I think people were losing touch with the paper because we weren't there to keep touch,' said one reporter. Local people told me they found it harder to get the ear of a reporter for stories that mattered to them, while journalists told me they found it harder to get out and see news stories unfolding, often relying instead on press officers to confirm reports of accidents or emergencies, or on meeting minutes or agendas for their coverage of council meetings rather than attending the meeting in person. I found the trend repeated in my news analysis, too. Both the quantity and quality of news declined more rapidly after the district office shut.

The significance of this is enormous. It suggests a link between democratic engagement and the presence of good quality local news, produced by reporters embedded within communities. If this is the case, we have much cause to worry in Wales. Our local news media have been hollowed out and converged to the point where properly local reporters have become almost as rare as unicorns. If news black holes are linked to a lack of local journalists, they are likely to be very widespread indeed. But there is some hope.

Hyperlocals and Independent News Publishers

The withdrawal of mainstream media has opened a vacuum in many towns and cities across the UK in which independent news organisations have sprung up to fill the gap. In Wales 12 independents are now accredited by the Independent Community News Network (ICNN), a representative body run out of Cardiff University's Centre for Community Journalism. There are many different business models being employed in the sector: co-operatives, social enterprises, limited companies, franchise models and sole traders, online, in print, or with hybrid web/print offerings. Some are run by paid staff members, others by dedicated volunteers or people subsidising their reporting by working in other jobs.

The *Caerphilly Observer*, *Wrexham.com*, *Deeside.com*, *Llanelli Online*, *Inksplott*, *My Cardiff North*, *My Welshpool*, *My Newtown*, *Cwmbran Life*, *Oggy Bloggy Ogwr*, *Tongwynlais.com* and *Senedd Home* have all gone through ICNN's application process, committing to a strict code of conduct and satisfying a range of editorial criteria including political independence and producing regular, genuinely local news. Though each is different in company structure, publishing format and financing, they are all run by people who live and work in the communities on which they report.

Funders have recognised the potential of these digital-first businesses to fill the gap left by legacy media, and many of them have received modest funding, some through specialist grants tailored to the sector, others through general funding from more traditional philan-

NEOLIBERALISM IN FOCUS

thropic or business funders. Welsh Government, too, has, to its credit, recognised their potential for filling the gap in the Welsh public sphere, providing a £200k fund to help the Welsh hyperlocal sector between 2018–20, some of which, following lobbying from the sector, was appropriated into a Covid rescue fund for ICNN members in Wales in 2020.

Sadly, funding such as this came too late for the *Port Talbot Magnet*. In 2017, the steel crisis made it obvious that Port Talbot's already weakened local economy, tied as it was to the fate of the vulnerable steelworks, would never be able to sustain journalism through advertising alone. Though we saw the same model working in Bristol and Caerphilly and many other places, we couldn't achieve the same success in such an economically deprived community.

It's obvious, however, that there are other Welsh towns and areas similarly economically deprived and abandoned by traditional media. My current work is focused on finding a new model for these places, something different and, hopefully, radical.

Potential Business Models

There are several potential funding models that have not yet been tried in Wales, but which might offer a way forward. I set out five of them here. First, membership models, such as the *Bristol Cable*'s members' co-operative, *The Ferret*'s subscribers-only investigative news service in Scotland, or the Dutch slow news website

De Correspondent, have all found commercial success and been rewarded with grant funding. In Bristol and Scotland, a mix of crowdfunding, subscriptions, grant funding and advertising has helped them provide investigative or alternative news. In the Netherlands, *De Correspondent* says their approach is less a business model than a reimagining of journalism. They have consciously placed readers on a more even footing with reporters, engaging them in investigations and stories early in the process and calling on their expertise to expand stories, inform reporting and engage in comments. Members can only participate using their own names, and their areas of expertise are verified by the company. This transparency ensures comments sections are less toxic, while journalists also participate and keep discussions productive, allowing for a meaningful style of journalism that asks deeper questions and addresses wider, structural issues.

Second, subsidy from grant funding is worth considering. As it stands, most grant funding is organised around start-up funding for new companies or roles, or discrete projects with measurable outcomes. It is therefore not ideally placed to support the local news sector where the key issue is ongoing sustainability. Of course, start-up funding can be helpful, but digital solutions are relatively cheap for new enterprises, and these agile digital businesses do not necessarily require expensive offices or equipment since much of their work can be done remotely. Ongoing costs, in particular human resources, are usually the biggest outlay and the hardest cost to underwrite.

It is unlikely philanthropic grant funding could step into

this breach. Government funding could be a solution, but there are no indications that the UK Government will step into the arena of funding news publishers any time soon, in spite of a recommendation by the 2018 Cairncross Review that a Journalism Foundation should be set up for this purpose. The Welsh Government has not announced any further funding plans since their one-off £200k pot was made available for start-up hyperlocals in 2018. An obvious solution would be a tax on tech giants such as Facebook and Google, who have benefited from the migration of advertising to digital platforms and make use of news content to populate their platforms while keeping ad revenue for themselves. Taxation of corporations is not a power devolved to Wales and so not within the gift of Welsh Government, but there is nothing to stop Welsh Government lobbying the billionaires of Silicon Valley for a philanthropic fund to dispense a fair distribution of their profits.

Third, another kind of subsidy is cross-subsidy from a commercially successful enterprise to a less-sustainable one. This is not unheard of in news publishing. For example, Rupert Murdoch's highly profitable television and multimedia company BSkyB allows him to continue publishing his less profitable UK newspapers, *The Sun* and *The Times*. Reimagined within a social enterprise model, this funding method might be employed success-fully in Wales by fostering social enterprise networks or towns where businesses work together for the good of the community, while ensuring news is one of the services funded by other enterprises.

A fourth model to consider is the provision of news

through education. A 'learning by doing' approach, along the lines of a teaching hospital, has already been successfully tried in Missouri in the United States. Alongside lectures and formal lessons, students have opportunities to work on a suite of real publications which serve, and are read by, the local community. The department also provides an advertising agency, where marketing and advertising students work on genuine campaigns for businesses and on advertising sales. The method could include a community element, where the community itself fundraises or pays sponsorship for training places and opportunities for local young people, rather than paying for news itself.

One final model is already staring us in the face. This is to foster existing local independent news publishers, to help them to become financially sustainable and to strengthen their existing network. These publishers may not yet be wealthy, but they own an invaluable asset that has largely been lost by traditional news publishers – the trust of their communities. Trust is likely to become a hugely valuable commodity in the information age. Cardiff's Centre for Community Journalism has already spotted this potential and has been working in the sector for ten years, with a remit of supporting existing community news projects and encouraging new ones. Their ambition now is to level the playing field for independents, to help them access government advertising budgets or to pool their output to enable them to licence and monetise their content. These initiatives provide a more fertile landscape for new publishers to set up. The hope is that a new kind of grassroots journalism will emerge in many more places, owned by and answerable to local people, without the pockets of distant shareholders to satisfy.

These models will require a sea change in thinking – in policy, social structures, the way we think about business, the way we think about grant funding and the way we think about journalism. Any of them could work, with political innovation, ambition, imagination, financial backing and/or the right people to take them forward. Each of them has its problems and potential pitfalls. None of them is an easy answer.

But I am optimistic. Eleven years ago, we set up the *Port Talbot Magnet* and applied for grant funding. We found a funding world that was almost universally geared around capital projects such as building new community centres. The idea of journalism as a public good that was deserving of funding was entirely alien. And yet, in the intervening decade, we have seen several funds set up specifically for public interest or investigative journalism, including NESTA's news innovation fund and Carnegie UK Trust's Neighbourhood News project. The Welsh Government is perhaps the first government in the world to set up a fund specifically for hyperlocal journalism. These changes give me hope that more change is possible.

Conclusion

Good quality trustworthy local news journalism is vital. It is a critical requirement of the well-being of both citizens and wider society. Without it we are ignorant of what's happening in our localities and beyond, of what's planned in the future, of how our money is being spent. Misinformation is poison in the reservoir, as we have seen with the spate of fake news – something the World Health Organisation has called an 'infodemic' – during the global pandemic of 2020–21. Well-resourced, independent, trust-worthy journalism is perhaps the only way to clean it up. We're not starting from zero. Thankfully we already have a network of successful independent community news outlets in Wales, and there are moves afoot to help strengthen them financially and improve links between them with a view to a new, pan-Wales approach to news in the future. Working with the talent we already have available is a great place to begin. In Wales, our communities are strong. We should play to our strengths. A grassroots approach, led by communities, serving communities, and with trust at its heart – this is where I hope the next phase in the evolution of Welsh media will spring from.

VIEWS OF A NEOLIBERAL WALES

Lost Utopias: the Failure of Imagination in Welsh Politics and Fiction

Jamie Harris

As a Labour First Minister I'm here to say to the left in Scotland that the promise of a socialist utopia post-separation is a siren call from the Yes camp that must be resisted.[1]

(Carwyn Jones,
speaking on Scottish Independence, 2014)

Prior to the Scottish independence referendum in 2014, Carwyn Jones urged left-leaning voters of Scotland to resist the 'siren call' of a 'socialist utopia', apparently promised by the Scottish National Party in the event of a 'yes' vote.[2] A year later, in the midst of campaigning for the 2015 UK General Election, Jones criticised Plaid Cymru's manifesto – and its markedly socialist direction under its then leader Leanne Woods – in similar fashion: 'big unaffordable plans, and wild utopian visions'.[3]

The anti-utopian rhetoric of contemporary Welsh politics, encapsulated in Jones' imagined 'siren call' and 'wild visions', has yet to be countered effectively. There is, of course, a clear irony in the leader of Wales' (then) most electorally powerful (nominally) leftist party urging voters to reject socialism by deriding it as an unachievable utopia. However, Jones' anti-utopian politics is reflective of a wider political malaise since the successful devolution referendum in 1997. That malaise might have its origins in devolution itself, which was summed up in the often-quoted Ron Davies plea for patience: 'devolution is a process, not an event'. Or, to give that mantra some much-needed context: 'Devolution is a process. It is not an event and neither is it a journey with a fixed end point.'[4] For Davies, the idea of devolution was '[to enable] us to make our own decisions and set our own priorities'.[5] This is emblematic of the processual utopianism of the devolution campaign, the kind that Fredric Jameson might place in the realms of the 'utopian impulse'. Jameson identifies two lines of utopianism (descending from Thomas More's original). The first, the 'utopian program', includes 'revolutionary praxis'. The second, the utopian impulse, is more 'equivocal', and involves 'reform' rather than revolution.[6] Welsh devolutionary discourse most closely resembles the latter. The implementation of devolution (beyond the rhetoric of the Yes campaign) was procedural and resistant to closure. It provided neither a clean break with the past, nor any clear indication that it was going *anywhere*.

Such trepidation is understandable and should be read in the context of the narrow margin of the referendum itself (50.3%–49.7%). Nonetheless pro-devolution discourse was, at least aesthetically, utopian. Writing in 2015, Sir Paul Silk reflected on the utopian aura of devolution:

> When the National Assembly for Wales first came into being in 1998, there was enormous expectation that something new and different was about to transform the

lives of the people of Wales. There was rhetoric about a new sort of politics – a sort of *Welsh Utopia*. It is good to have high goals, but transforming politics is rarely realised. The balance between realism and idealism needs to be maintained if public disillusionment is to be avoided.[7] [my emphasis]

While Silk recognises the desire for a new politics in Wales post-devolution, there is also a distinct anti-utopian logic in his analysis. The creation of a post-devolutionary 'Welsh Utopia', is prevented by a political realism that doesn't allow for utopian politics (here 'high goals' and 'idealism' are synonymous with Jones' 'wild visions' remark).

Such anti-utopianism, and the inability to imagine Wales as a utopia, might be accounted for by its current political reality. Raymond Williams suggests that:

When *utopia* is no longer an island or a newly discovered place, but our familiar country transformed by specific historical change, the mode of imagined transformation has fundamentally changed.[8]

The 'mode of imagined transformation' – how Wales might become a utopian nation in theory if not in actuality – is rendered as severely limited by both historical and geographical reality. Any imagined utopian Wales must reckon with Wales' relationship with the UK, or so it goes. Lamentably, any post-devolutionary Welsh utopia was destined to be 'no place' in the original sense of Thomas More's neologism (a pun on *eutopos/outopos*, good place/no place).[9] The 'new politics' promised by devolution have found *no place* in the Senedd. A Wales that cannot build renewable power stations without UK government approval, and that cannot, for example, decide unilaterally how it might combat climate change (which will be discussed shortly), can hardly be thought capable of creating any utopia worthy of the name.[10]

Jones is not an outlier in his sceptical use of the term utopia. He finds a perhaps unlikely ally in Karl Marx, who coined the term utopian socialism in his criticisms of the ideas advanced by Henri Saint-Simon, Charles Fourier, and – to this day Wales' most prominent utopian thinker – Robert Owen (whose seminal *Book of the New Moral World* is the closest Wales has come to producing a canonical utopian text). Roger Paden summarises Marx and Engels's critique of Owen and utopian socialism as follows:

> Like the communists, the utopian socialists were progressives who wrote in opposition to the bourgeois order, however, writing too early in the modern period to understand the nature and role of the proletariat, they could only criticize the emerging bourgeois society on what Marx and Engels took to be highly questionable moral grounds.[11]

Owen's brand of utopianism might thus be thought of as a *moral* rather than *revolutionary* response to the ills of capitalism, correct in its targets (the emergent bourgeoisie), but suggesting that solutions could be found solely in co-operatives. Ruth Levitas suggests that '[Owenite groups] were not outside the dominant society

[...] Owen and his followers believed that their example would lead to the replacement of capitalism by the co-operative commonwealth.'[12] That such a change has yet to materialise in the country of Owen's birth is obvious. Instead, the political stasis resulting from almost uninterrupted one party (Labour) rule since devolution has clearly not created the conditions to inspire Owenite co-operatives to emerge *en masse*.

An example of the problems of modern Welsh utopianism (and devolution itself) is the recent Swansea Bay Tidal Lagoon project. Posited as a futuristic vision of a greener Wales, the lagoon was a privately funded energy project, backed with substantial investment from the Welsh Government.[13] Its marketing rhetoric, exemplified in its slogan 'Ours to Own', was unashamedly utopian (with echoes of Owen), as were the publicity images that were reproduced in national media outlets.[14] Its 'cultural partner', the 'think/do tank' Cape Farewell, commissioned submissions for sculptures and 'local interventions' to gather ideas for the area surrounding the lagoon, as part of the 'Utopia 2016' festival.[15] The images that appeared on the lagoon's website (as well as on several media reports on the lagoon) looked like covers of pulp science fiction paperbacks. One study quoted bay locals remarking that such images 'presented a desirable destination and an almost utopian landscape'.[16] The utopian vision offered by the lagoon was in stark contrast with reality. The artistic renderings of idyllic walking paths along the proposed barrier had hardly taken into account the strength of the winds and waves that would likely make such routes unwalkable.[17]

Such regenerated coastal utopias are a common trope in modern society, as Levitas also notes the preponderance of 'the degenerate utopia[s] of urban spectacle especially around the regenerated waterside'.[18] The seductive prospect of the tidal lagoon, and Wales becoming a world leader in green energy, was a technocratic solution to reducing carbon emissions in Wales (and securing its future energy supply). Perhaps such visions cannot become reality, in Wales or elsewhere. Etienne Balibar argues that '[t]here are no more utopias, then, because we have in reality gone beyond the conditions for their realization [...] they have survived intellectually only in the most degraded, mutually opposed forms: technocratic programs and messianic preaching'.[19]

The marketing of such renewable energy generation projects as a plausible route to a green Welsh utopia must be seen in the context of the increasing neoliberalisation of Wales' energy sector. David Harvey suggests that we can 'interpret neoliberalization [sic] either as a *utopian* project to realize a theoretical design for the reorganization of international capitalism or as a *political* project to re-establish the conditions for capital accumulation or to restore the power of economic elites'.[20] The former, Harvey contends, has 'primarily worked as a system of justification' to achieve the latter. That is, utopianism in the era of neoliberalism is no more than a rhetorical device that, in effect, obscures the political reality of 'neoliberalization'. The recognition of this process is crucial in protecting against further private sector incursions. 'The more neoliberalism is recognized as a failed utopian rhetoric masking a successful project for the restoration of ruling-class power,' writes Harvey, 'the more the basis is laid for a resurgence of mass movements voicing egalitarian political demands and seeking economic justice, fair trade, and greater economic security.' (Harvey, p. 204).

The failure of such white elephants as the tidal lagoon to materialise might suggest that contemporary Wales isn't ready for such projects. However, the current crisis of utopianism in Wales can be seen as part of a broader crisis of the imagination. Russell Jacoby suggests that the success of liberal anti-utopianism in the twentieth century is not the only reason for the demise of utopia, and that the 'dwindling force of the modern imagination' is also to blame. The consequence of this crisis is a kind of unimaginative 'blueprint' utopianism, in which its boldest ideas (like 'free higher education', 'ecological vehicles', and 'clean parks') could be 'realized [sic] by a comprehensive welfare state'.[21]

A preponderance of creative visions of utopia might prepare the ground for actual utopian politics to emerge in Wales. Utopian fiction offers writers a way in which to overcome their existing political reality without having to offer detail as to how such a society might occur. While Levitas's contention that '[u]topianism is too important to be consigned to the realm of art and literature' is understandable, a reading of Welsh utopias might provide a lens through which the current post-devolution malaise might be viewed.[22] The two authors with perhaps the clearest vision for what Wales could look like as a utopia, Jan Morris (in *A Machynlleth Triad/Triawd Machynlleth*, 1993) and Islwyn Ffowc Elis (in *Wythnos yng Nghymru*

Fydd, 1957), provide detailed visions of a future Wales, and both texts imagine Wales as a distinct nation outside of the United Kingdom.[23]

Jan Morris's *Machynlleth* imagines Wales' route to independence as being achieved by democratic means, via 'the Grand Referendum, and by the common sense of the Westminster Parliament'.[24] Morris's Wales projects an outwardly utopian image: 'the relieved diplomat lately posted here from Burundi or El Salvador, may feel Wales to be a kind of Utopia' (*Machynlleth*, p. 72). It is also 'a pacifist Republic', but one that nonetheless maintains an armed forces on the grounds of maintaining jobs (p. 75). There are 'Green politicians everywhere' (p. 70), and in place of the Alternative Energy Centre [sic] is 'the massed windmill cluster of Welsh Energy, Ynni Cymru' (p. 64). There are distinctly Owenite ideas, such as Wales' 'cooperatively owned steel and coal industries' (p. 74), and new houses have been erected to the town's east, designed to 'complement the Garden Village, [which is] now listed as a historical monument' (p. 66). Fortunately, Morris's Wales does not have to reckon with climate change, which has not changed 'despite wild claims to the contrary by overzealous propagandists' (p. 82).

Machynlleth also depicts a distinctly conservative utopian Wales (an image of dystopia to those on the left). Economically, it is modelled on a 'gently retrained capitalism' (p. 73). It also has a radical immigration policy, stipulating 'strict entry quotas – numerical, professional, ethnic, and of age' (p. 76). In a section that contains a both resounding and prescient – Morris's book was published more than two years prior to the 1997 referendum – critique of devolution as a consolidation of power in Cardiff, Morris writes:

> In the days of the United Kingdom the pseudo-capital of Wales was Cardiff, Caerdydd, supplied under British auspices with an ornate formal centre of government. After independence the Welsh determined that their new capital, like the republic itself, would contain nothing so grandiose. (p. 65)

Morris's utopian vision thus recentres Welsh power in the place of Glyndŵr's apocryphal parliament. It demonstrates some of the possibilities of utopian thought, although it doesn't explain Wales' route to becoming an independent utopia in detail. While *Machynlleth* contains some undoubtedly problematic ideas such as ethnic nationalism and climate change denial, and an unwaveringly conservative ideology ('retrained capitalism', armed forces), it points towards a 'kind of' Owenite moral utopia – emblematised in Westminster voluntarily ceding control of Wales – full of publicly owned co-operatives, green politics, and clean energy.

Elis's *Wythnos yng Nghymru Fydd* (A Week in Future Wales) is the most significant and substantial example of a modern Welsh literary utopia. In the novel, the protagonist Ifan Powel is transported (by time-machine) to two future versions of Wales. The first is an archetypal literary utopia; a fully bilingual, progressive Wales 'built', argues Robin Chapman, 'in the image of Plaid's ten policy points of 1933'.[25] The second version is a dystopia in which Wales is now known as 'Western England', 'a nightmare of urban decay, mob rule and bureaucracy' (Chapman, p. 45). *Wythnos* was essentially written as propaganda, and Elis himself considered it 'a story not fit to be treated as literature', while Chapman echoes the criticism of Elis's strict adherence to Plaid policy, writing that 'the utopian section [...] is so worthy and dull. Who would really want to live there?'[26]

Elis's utopian Wales was overtly politically motivated, unsurprising given that it was published by Plaid Cymru.[27] The novel, writes Craig Owen Jones, incorporated 'elements of nationalist policy, [...] especially Plaid Cymru's eagerness to consider Wales as a discrete entity in relation to international affairs'.[28] Jones argues that the credibility of Elis's, and thus Plaid's, vision of a Welsh utopia is dependent upon 'the conceptualisation of Wales as an entity distinct from England'.[29] Although Elis was somewhat embarrassed by *Wythnos*, it nonetheless provides a fascinating vision of a Welsh 'blueprint' utopia. As with Morris's *Machynlleth,* coal mines and farms are run by co-operatives (and miners work for three months a year on farms).[30] Because of co-operative models of ownership, striking is a thing of the past ('Streico yn ein herbyn ein hunain? Nid ffyliaid ydyn ni, cofiwch.'/'Strike against ourselves? We're not fools, you know', p. 73). There are even electric, driverless cars running on automated 'radiofagnetig' (radiomagnetic) roads (p. 171).

While both Morris's and Elis's literary utopias imagine a Wales that is, for the most part, co-operatively owned and run, neither are particularly radical. The technological innovations of Elis's novel render it a more traditional twentieth-century literary utopia, while Morris's emphasis on nostalgia for the age of Glyndŵr enshrines the anti-modern 'Principle of Simplicity, Egwyddor Symlrwydd' in its constitution (*Machynlleth*, p. 64). Of course, visions of utopia are necessarily subjective. Both Elis's technologically advanced Wales and Morris's nostalgic simplicity contain elements that some would consider problematic at the very least. In political and fictional discourse, Morris's vision is hampered by a pragmatic, but nonetheless selective commitment to realism. Ethno-nationalist immigration policies are enshrined in law, suggesting racism is a prominent feature of *Machynlleth*'s future Wales. Climate change, on the other hand, is not.[31] That it is of greater expedience to write climate change out of existence than to imagine even a small decline in racist political rhetoric is striking.

It is not enough, then, to simply imagine an independent Wales, no more than it is to think of devolution as anything more than a 'process'. Capitalism, 'gently retrained' or not, is still capitalism. The failure of Welsh fiction to imagine a radical utopian Wales, combined with the anti-utopian rhetoric of Welsh politics, presents a major barrier for the emergence of utopian politics. A utopian project such as the tidal lagoon might thus be thought of as a truly representative piece of contemporary utopianism, yet there are lessons to be taken from the flaws in its design, and in its failure. First, that the left abandoning utopian thinking altogether risks ceding further ground to the (ab)use of utopian imagery as a cover for neoliberalism. This is a kind of modern utopianism that attempts to (re)package neoliberalism as being in the interest of the people of Wales. Second, that the absence of radical fictional utopianism in Wales leaves the left increasingly vulnerable to accusations of unrealistic utopianism when suggesting even modest reform.[32] Both Elis's and Morris's utopias posited nationalised energy generation (*Ynni Cymru*, to use Morris's term), the very thing that would have enabled the building of a tidal lagoon. A truly iconoclastic Welsh utopian vision would 'resist the modern seduction of images' (Jacoby, p. 16) such as those of the tidal lagoon. So, rather than political 'blueprint' utopianism, there is room for a more creative, iconoclastic utopianism to emerge in Wales, one that imagines something beyond neoliberal white elephants, and perhaps even beyond independence as a route in itself to achieving a better Wales.[33]

[1] 'Scottish independence referendum: Carwyn Jones tells Scots to vote No for "solidarity and justice"... and hails Welsh NHS as a reason to stay', *WalesOnline* (9 September 2014)

http://www.walesonline.co.uk/news/wales-news/scottish-independence-referendum-carwyn-jones-7741897

[2] 'Scottish independence: Carwyn Jones backs "No"', *The Scotsman* (10 September 2014)
https://www.scotsman.com/news/politics/scottish-independence-carwyn-jones-backs-no-1526737

[3] Carwyn Jones, 'Welsh Labour - The Real Voice of Wales' [blog], *Huffington Post* (1 June 2015)

https://www.huffingtonpost.co.uk/carwyn-jones/welsh-labour-the-real-voice_b_6986742.html

[4] Ron Davies, *Devolution: A Process Not an Event* (Cardiff: Institute of Welsh Affairs, 1998), p. 15.

[5] Ron Davies, *Devolution: A Process Not an Event*, p. 15.

[6] Fredric Jameson, *Archaeologies of the Future: The Desire Called Utopia and Other Science Fiction* (London: Verso, 2005), p. 3.

[7] Sir Paul Silk, *Devolution and Decentralisation: Lessons from the*

United Kingdom and Wales, (London: Global Partners Governance, 2015), p. 5.

[8] Raymond Williams, 'Utopia and Science Fiction', *Science Fiction Studies*, 16:5, Part 3 (November, 1978) https://www.depauw.edu/sfs/backissues/16/williams16art.htm

[9] Thomas More, *Utopia*, eds. George M. Logan, Robert M. Adams, trans. Robert M. Adams (Cambridge: Cambridge University Press, 2003).

[10] While the Climate Change Committee recommended that the UK aimed for net-zero emissions by 2050, it granted Wales a lower target of 95% reduction https://www.theccc.org.uk/publication/net-zero-the-uks-contribution-to-stopping-global-warming/

[11] Roger Paden, 'Marx's Critique of the Utopian Socialists', *Utopian Studies*, 13:2 (2002), 67–91, pp. 67–8.

[12] Levitas, 'On dialectical utopianism', *History of the Human Sciences*, 16:1, 137–150, p. 145.

[13] On the project's financing, see http://www.tidallagoonpower.com/investment/tidal-lagoon-swansea-bay/. 'Swansea tidal lagoon: 'Substantial' offer from Carwyn Jones', BBC News (10 January 2018) https://www.bbc.co.uk/news/uk-wales-politics-42634021 A recent response to an FOI request withheld the nature of the financial relationship between Tidal Lagoon (Swansea Bay) PLC and Welsh Government on the grounds of it being in the public interest to withhold 'details associated with the private sector alliances'. See https://gov.wales/sites/default/files/publications/2020-01/ATISN%2013595.pdf

[14] 'Ours to Own: From first mover to mass manufacture – Building a new British industry from our natural advantage' http://www.tidallagoonpower.com/wp-content/uploads/2016/09/Ours-to-Own_Tidal-Lagoon-Power_Oct-2016.pdf

[15] https://capefarewell.com/latest/projects/energy-renaissance.html

[16] Andrew James Roberts, *The social amplification of benefit: Risk, identity and renewable energy*, PhD Thesis, Cardiff University, p. 104 http://orca.cf.ac.uk/131506/

[17] See *The social amplification of benefit*, p. 134.

[18] Levitas, 'On dialectical utopianism', *History of the Human Sciences*, 16:1, 137–150, p. 139. Cardiff Bay, ironically where the Welsh Government is housed, would fall under Levitas's definition.

[19] Etienne Balibar, 'After Utopia, Imagination?', in *Political Uses of*

Utopia: New Marxist, Anarchist, and Radical Democratic Perspectives,
eds. S. D. Chrostowska and James Ingram (New York: Columbia
University Press, 2017), p. 163. Originally published as 'Après
l'utopie, l'imagination?', Le Monde (24 November 1997).

[20] David Harvey, A Brief History of Neoliberalism (Oxford: Oxford
University Press, 2007), p. 19.

[21] Russell Jacoby, Picture Imperfect, Utopian Thought for an Anti-
Utopian Age (New York: Columbia University Press, 2005), pp. 11–2.

[22] Levitas, 'On dialectical utopianism', p. 141.

[23] Jan Morris and Twm Morys, A Machynlleth Triad/Triawd
Machynlleth (Newtown: Gwasg Gregynog, 1993). The edition from
which this article will cite is (London: Penguin, 1995). Islwyn Ffowc
Elis, Wythnos yng Nghymru Fydd (Cardiff: Plaid Cymru, 1957).

[24] Machynlleth Triad, p. 80

[25] Robin T. Chapman, Islwyn Ffowc Elis (Cardiff: University of Wales
Press, 2000), p. 46.

[26] Ffowc Elis, quoted in Chapman, p. 46. Chapman, p. 47.

[27] Islwyn Ffowc Elis, Wythnos yng Nghymru Fydd (Cardiff: Plaid
Cymru, 1957). Edition cited: (Llandysul, Gomer, 2007).

[28] Craig Owen Jones, '"Magnifique, n'est-ce pas?": Representations of
Wales and the world in Islwyn Ffowc Elis's Wythnos Yng Nghymru
Fydd', Almanac: Yearbook of Welsh Writing in English, 13 (2008–9),
162–190, pp. 166–7.

[29] Jones, 'Magnifique, n'est-ce pas?', p. 167.

[30] For an English translation of Elis's novel, see
https://futuredotwales.wordpress.com//

[31] Of course, there is room to consider both the inclusion of racism
and the exclusion of climate change as broader political satire.

[32] The dismissal of Labour's pledge for free broadband in the 2019
manifesto as 'broadband communism' is instructive here. '"Broadband
Communism"? Worse Was Said about the Founding of the NHS | Ash
Sarkar', The Guardian (18 November 2019)
http://www.theguardian.com/commentisfree/2019/nov/18/broadban
d-communism-founding-nhs

[33] 'Iconoclastic' is the term used by Jacoby to distinguish it from
blueprint (or pragmatic) utopianism.

Washed Up on Severnside: Life, Work and Capital on the Border of South-East Wales

Gareth Leaman

Let us first acknowledge that the industrial history of the Severn Estuary's urban sprawl provides an indicative snapshot of the entire historical trajectory of capitalist production: the commodification of natural resources for private profit, the exploitation of labour and the crushing of its organised resistance, and a post-industrial ruination when such forms of wealth extraction are no longer expedient. More recently, we can also observe phenomena commensurate with the neoliberal phase of this trajectory: the shrinking of the state and the consequences of the full marketisation of social relations (the casualisation of labour, the gentrification of communities, the privatisation of key services, and so on).

Yet while South Wales may be an exemplar, its circumstances are by no means novel or unique: indeed, these are phenomena to which we can bear witness all over the world. This is not to discard the analytical value of geographical specificities, but rather to place them within their full context: developing an understanding of the dialectic of the global and the local which sustains capital's social reproduction. It is particularly crucial to

351

bear this in mind in the example of Gwent, where the uneven flow of capital between Wales and England plays such a key part in the maintenance of processes of wealth extraction and worker exploitation, and where consequently a lucid analysis of class domination is at perennial risk of misinterpretation as simply a manifestation of national antagonisms.

In recent years, great emphasis has been placed on the apparent economic necessity of increasing the flow of goods and people between South Wales and the west of England. The Western Gateway project, an 'economic partnership' responsible for formalising this initiative, extols the virtues of 'a strong cross-border relationship' and 'high levels of economic integration within and across the area' to '[build] a new future for the British economy'.[1] It is clear from such ambitions that a homogenisation of this region – and indeed, post-Brexit, of the British state more generally – is deemed essential for the project's success, and thus necessitates the eradication of any intra-state political, economic or cultural differences.

The central aim of the Western Gateway project is thus the removal of any barriers that may impede the flow of capital between Gwent and Greater Bristol, opening new markets of housing and employment to ameliorate several overlapping localised crises of capitalism, and effectively subsuming the needs of local economies to that of the whole British state. Giving residents of South Wales greater opportunity to travel across to the south-west of England is intended, in this model, to compensate for limited employment closer to home. Concurrently, enabling Bristolians to take advantage of comparatively cheaper residential properties in Gwent (or 'unlocking housing growth',[2] as the Western Gateway project euphemistically describes it) is posited as a means of deferring the crisis of rising house prices in that city.

As far as capital is concerned, this project has been reasonably successful, with stagnant markets reinvigorated by the potential of expansion and increased competition. The underemployed workforce of South Wales is being 'freed' to commute to the farther reaches of this economic region in pursuit of work opportunities. Meanwhile property developers and landlords can take advantage of the increased housing demand[3] to extract ever-greater profits from tenants[4], coupled with house prices soaring across the region.

Here we are witnessing instruments of the state issuing corrective actions to ensure that capitalist markets continue to function, pointing to the fundamental contradiction at the heart of neoliberal governance: the market's 'freedom' can only be upheld if it is guaranteed through the intervention of the state. Despite neoliberalism being a process by which, as David Harvey puts it, 'state sovereignty over commodity and capital movements is willingly surrendered to the global market',[5] the state nonetheless holds ultimate responsibility for enacting and perpetuating it.

This cycle of deregulation and intervention to meet the needs of capital has long defined the politics and economy of south-east Wales. In recent times, a period of deindustrialisation and 'managed decline' – including a brutal stripping back of the welfare state in the name of the transference of wealth from public to private hands – has given way to an economic stagnation in which there is a finite amount of wealth remaining to extract from increasingly impoverished communities.[6] Consequently, a period of concerted state action is now ensuing as a guarantor of capital accumulation, primarily through facilitating a process of gentrification: 'solving' the problem of impoverished communities by simply importing more affluent residents to displace their current occupants, to the great delight of the private housing sector. To enable this, the state ensures that infrastructure is built to help transport labour away from areas of high unemployment and towards areas with more employers, laws and regulations are changed to stimulate the housing market, and so forth.

In the British state, Westminster are obviously the dominant ideologues, but devolved administrations and local councils are also complicit. The Welsh Labour Government have responded to Tory rule in much the same way as most Labour-run councils: constrained by austerity yes, but internalising that ideology and adopting neoliberal practices to mitigate its worst consequences, typically in the form of encouraging the marketisation of the public sector. Despite its veneer of administrative light-handedness, the diffuse, 'local' arms of the state can only organise themselves within the ideological framework laid out by the central state, all of which combines to serve the ultimate purpose of, as Harvey notes, '[integrating] state decision-making into the dynamics of capital accumulation'.[7]

This is ultimately the sole function of neoliberal governance: to assist the flow of capital and nothing more. Even when ostensibly helping its citizens to live more enriching lives (at least within the severely limited parameters of capitalist realism), it only does so insofar as it is equipping them to be useful labourers, consumers, or a reliable source of rent extraction.

For Gwent, the consequences of this process have been dire: the region's increased 'economic activity' has set in motion a series of interrelated humanitarian crises.

A marked rise in road traffic is leading workers to spend intolerable hours per day on increasingly gridlocked,[8] dangerously polluted roads,[9] or pursuing the inadequate alternative of overcrowded, impossibly overpriced 'public' (in reality mostly privatised) transport. With this comes the perennial threat of environmental catastrophe, with endless short-termist plans to alleviate traffic through the construction of yet more roads, most alarmingly the plans (mercifully scrapped, at least for now) to build a 'relief road' perilously close to the Gwent Levels. The looming housing crisis, while alleviating issues of affordability for residents in the Greater Bristol area,[10] is pushing house prices in the towns of Gwent to unaffordable levels for those who already live there, putting greater numbers at risk of homelessness.[11]

These aren't solely problems of personal economic hardship, or of individual health and well-being. They're also indicative of a systematic failure of the structures that govern us, particularly the total reorganisation of people's lives solely around their ability to sell their labour or pay rent. Our tolerance of this immiseration is facilitated by the warped notions of individualism and freedom endemic to neoliberal ideology, which promotes the purported values of individual freedom while systematically stripping away the social state, the means through which individual citizens can organise on a societal level to ensure *collective* freedom. In the neoliberal state freedom means little more than, as Srnicek and Williams describe it, 'the freedoms to sell our labour power',[12] and thus the 'absence of interference [from the state]' begets a 'woefully emaciated concept of freedom'[13] that 'is entirely compatible with mass poverty, starvation, homelessness, unemployment and inequality'.[14]

We can see along the border of south-east Wales the material consequences of this ideological function: the freedom of the market – the 'opening up' of the Welsh economy to new avenues of capital accumulation – is in fact a state-engineered deregulation of the mechanisms by which its communities can safeguard themselves against destitution. This is what the 'Western Gateway' is giving us: the British government, the devolved Welsh Government, local councils, all are complicit in this granting of the residents of Gwent the freedom to be homeless, the freedom to devote of all their waking hours to precarious, underpaid and unfulfilling jobs, and the freedom to coat their lungs with carbon monoxide in pursuit of this debasement.

This is profoundly devastating for all forms of collective well-being. The alienation of work and the fragmentation of living is straining any means of connection among and between communities. The true depravity here then is the concerted destruction of both residential communitarianism and worker solidarity. As communities become disrupted through gentrification, as rental terms become increasingly unstable and transient, as people spend time further away from home due to lengthened commutes, neighbours transmogrify into strangers, communities into mere clusters of monadic living quarters, and all social cohesion disintegrates.

The impact of deregulation on the workplace is no different. The technological advancements to allow remote working (now the prime mode of white-collar labour post-Covid), the ability to travel further afield for work, the decline of unionisation, and post-Fordist working practices all enable a complete disconnect between people and the product of their labour, and of meaningful relationships between workers.

This all provides little opportunity for consciousness-raising, for building solidarity, for organising against a political status quo that causes such mass suffering and continued economic hardship. In such a predicament, meaningful political activity becomes almost a practical impossibility. This all combines to form a total stultification of life: beyond the abstract goals of capitalist economics, this real human impact – and thus the fundamentally inhumane action of the state – should cause us great alarm.

While here we have universalised much of the human impact of state action upon the communities of south-east Wales, a particular curiosity remains: the presence of an intra-state 'national' border splitting this so-called 'natural economic region'.[15]

In some sense the border divide here is simply representative of the uneven economic development of England and Wales proving beneficial for the British economy, in that the arbitrary (economically, if not culturally) difference between each side of the border has engendered opportunities for exploitation and market expansion at various points throughout the history of British capitalism. Just as in the industrial age transport infrastructure and modes of employment were 'driven through Wales on bearings evidently determined by the shape of the larger economy and trading system',[16] as Raymond Williams describes it, the exhaustion of this conception of Wales' purpose within the British state is now ripe for an exploitation of a different kind.

The resultant deprivation has led to a cheapness of land and underemployment of workers (and thus driving down the wages that workers can command, such is the marketisation of labour), meaning that mere proximity to comparatively richer English border conurbations becomes south-east Wales' main economic asset. In this sense the border is just another relic of a previous model of capitalism that now needs to be deregulated to allow the state to continue aiding market expansion and capital accumulation.

As this process of deregulation is occurring, the border also performs a more invidious function: while the economic division the border has hitherto engendered is proving ripe for a disaster-capitalist reinvigoration of market forces, the supposed cultural differences between the Welsh and English parts of this region serves to sublimate any potential cross-border class consciousness that may arise. While we can observe universal phenomena of class war here, and while it is true that the erasure of vestiges of 'Welshness' is deemed a necessity for maintaining the dominance of the property-owning class, this dialectic often obscures the material reality of capitalist exploitation and engineers a situation in which class antagonism is either obfuscated or mistaken for being solely an attack on a cultural identity. So when, to take one example, the Second Severn Crossing was renamed the 'Prince of Wales Bridge', the subsequent outcry tended to focus merely on this symbolism as an abstract act of bigotry or cultural erasure in itself, rather than its material consequences, namely the lubrication of the flow of capital within the UK and all the ancillary in-humanity contained therein.

This mobilisation of nationalist tension is in many ways intrinsic to neoliberalism's reproduction. As Harvey writes:

> the neoliberal state needs nationalism of a certain sort to survive. Forced to operate as a competitive agent in the world market and seeking to establish the best possible business climate, it mobilizes nationalism in its effort to succeed.[17]

This is as true of *intra*-state nationalisms (where they exist) as *inter*-state, and is the means through which non-national antagonisms are easily co-opted by the reactionary avatars of the state: witness, for example, how

quickly the likes of Alun Cairns have portrayed any mis-
givings about the Western Gateway project as being
'anti-English'.[18]

Where class antagonisms do emerge among coalescing
social groups in border conurbations – there is undoubtedly a tension of wealth disparity in which richer
displaced Bristolians are having a disruptive effect upon
the comparatively poorer residents of the settlements they
move into – this is cynically framed by politicians and the
capitalist class as evidence of a Welsh-versus-English
'xenophobia', rather than a material anxiety typical of
working-middle class tensions in newly gentrifying communities regardless of any cross-border movements of
people. We can thus observe here the stoking of a
'negative solidarity'[19] in which the exploited workers of
south-east Wales are invited to turn their ire on similarly
exploited (albeit to varying degrees) English workers, at
the expense of a coherent dissent against their true class
antagonists: rentiers, landlords, employers, and the state
forces that empower them.

If we deem these conditions to be intolerable, then the
challenge is to conceptualise means of overcoming them.
Fortunately, while the political settlement described here
saturates human behaviour absolutely, there is still
contained within it transgressive possibilities. In the par-
ticularity of 'Severnside' there is the potential to begin
this escape through recognising and subverting the neoliberal state's instrumentalisation of the difference between
England and Wales when it is convenient, and erasure of
it when it's an inconvenience, for it tells us much about

how the working class can organise in the face of continued domination.

First, we can recognise that there is a value in the divide between 'Welshness' and 'Englishness' that *strengthens* transnational class solidarity, in that the assertion of both identities in protest of the border erasure protects both from full assimilation into 'Britishness' – that is, the British capitalist state of which they are constituent parts. An analysis that gives primacy to class relations above 'national interests' aids this, in that it reveals the true purpose of this cross-border agglomeration as being in service of exploitation of Welsh *and English* workers and residents by Welsh and English employers and landlords, rather than simply manifesting Welsh–English national antagonisms in a way that conceals the real beneficiaries of these circumstances.

From this, we can recognise that, given the reflexive Welsh nationalism the issue of the border has inspired as a latent reaction against capital expansion, there must be some value in its assertion and mobilisation. This would suggest that the 'Welshness' being erased here – apparently that which cannot be assimilated into British capital – is in fact a sense of community, or at least its cultural memory, that is proving stubbornly unproductive for the latest state facilitation of market forces. Gwyn Alf Williams attests to this when he writes of this thread of 'Welshness' weaving its way through different compositions of capitalist domination upon the residents of South Wales, starting with the very formation of this polity:

At a human level, these men and women who were being shovelled like small coal over the face of their country were united only by fragile and intangible threads; by the kinship and community patterns of that seasonal-becoming-permanent migration which had become a Welsh way of life, by a diffuse sense of identity, by a new identity born of conflict.[20]

It is interesting to note here that Williams describes this 'intensely Welsh' community as having the quality of *'turning its incomers into* that novel breed, the South Walian'[21] (emphasis mine), which suggests something *re-sembling* a national character yet not formed by one in any essentialist sense, but is rather a distinct structure of feeling forged by the material conditions created by uneven and combined capitalist development in this small part of the world. Dismissing the red herring of national cross-border antagonisms helps us to focus on the ways in which community destruction and workplace atomisation are the true loci of class conflict, and so consequently where solidarities must be defended or re-forged in the ruins of neoliberal destruction.

One possible counter to this – which would serve us well in the borderland communities of Gwent – is a 'red belonging' in which social bonds are formed through a shared sense of class subjugation, rather than modes of solidarity associated with workplaces or housing arrange-ments, as the neoliberal smashing of these forms have rendered them solely the preserve of the reactionary right to define: a solidarity of 'blue belonging'. As Mark Fisher explains, this 'red belonging offers something different to traditional forms of belonging (faith, flag, family...)'[22]:

> As opposed to the essentially spatial imaginary of Blue belonging – which posits a bounded area, with those inside hostile and suspicious towards those who are excluded – Red belonging is temporal and dynamic. It is about belonging to a movement: a movement that abolishes the present state of things, a movement that offers unconditional care without community (it doesn't matter where you come from or who you are, we will care for you anyway).[23]

This reconstitution of forms of solidarity will allow us to fight for a new, post-neoliberal world that fights against the inhumanity of our actually existing conditions. Matt Colquhoun posits lucidly the question this will allow us to ask of ourselves in this task 'to find solidarity without similarity: a unity which is not unified'[24]:

> How do we exist outside of capitalism, defining ourselves within its midst through processes of negation and difference, without scaling up the logics of capitalism's mandatory individualism?[25]

We cannot fight on the terms set by the state: the atomisation of life, the smashing of workplace solidarity, the stoking of nationalistic tendencies – these are all divisive tactics that a newly organised working class need to subvert as neoliberalism inevitably pivots to a more overtly authoritarian form of capitalism.[26]

Any campaign for the improvement of workers' rights to live and work in more humane conditions must demand something truly new, a 'form of existence which cannot be expressed with a capitalist vocabulary',[27] so what superficially appears to be a problem of infrastructure can be solved with a demand for adequate housing, so that the challenges of deindustrialisation can be met with a re-evaluation of how self-organisation of the working class must transcend obsolete forms of employment, and so forth. In so doing, construction can begin of a society that imagines a life beyond that of selling labour to cling on to fractured communities: one that engenders a collective humanity that transgresses neoliberal individuation and reasserts a solidarity forged by class antagonism. From this, we can demand more out of what it means to live, and never stop fighting for it.

---

[1] 'Western Gateway: Propelling a greener, fairer, stronger Britain'
https://western-gateway.co.uk/wp-content/uploads/2020/02/Western-Gateway-ENGLISH-WEB.pdf

[2] Ibid.

[3] Joshua Searle, 'Interest in the Newport and Gwent housing market is growing', *South Wales Argus* (19 August 2020)
https://www.southwalesargus.co.uk/news/18660381.interest-gwent-housing-market-growing/

[4] Sam Ferguson, 'Young Newport family forced out of home by rising city rents', *South Wales Argus* (11 January 2019)
https://www.southwalesargus.co.uk/news/17351013.young-newport-family-forced-home-rising-city-rents/

[5] David Harvey, *A Brief History of Neoliberalism* (Oxford: Oxford University Press, 2007), p. 66.

[6] Saul Cooke-Black, 'Newport is now the "most deprived" area of Wales', *South Wales Argus* (15 October 2020)
https://www.southwalesargus.co.uk/news/18796764.newport-now-most-deprived-area-wales/

[7] Harvey, p. 76.

[8] Cathy Owen, 'The M4 in Wales: The reasons for the congestion and number of crashes', *WalesOnline* (3 November 2019) https://www.walesonline.co.uk/news/wales-news/m4-wales-reasons-congestion-number-17086504

[9] Estel Farell-Roig, 'Terrifying figures show how dangerously polluted Wales roads are even with 50mph speed limits', *WalesOnline* (10 October 2019) https://www.walesonline.co.uk/news/wales-news/air-pollution-levels-roads-wales-17057913

[10] Marcus Hughes, 'The people moving to Wales from Bristol because houses are half the price', *WalesOnline* (20 January 2019) https://www.walesonline.co.uk/news/wales-news/people-moving-wales-bristol-take-15693144

[11] Sam Ferguson, 'Young Newport family forced out of home by rising city rents', *South Wales Argus* (11 January 2019) https://www.southwalesargus.co.uk/news/17351013.young-newport-family-forced-home-rising-city-rents/

[12] Nick Srnicek and Alex Williams, *Inventing the Future: Postcapitalism and a World Without Work* (London: Verso, 2015), p. 79.

[13] Ibid.

[14] Ibid.

[15] 'Cross-border Western Gateway will form new 'powerhouse' in UK economy', *gov.uk* (2019)

https://www.gov.uk/government/news/cross-border-western-gateway-will-form-new-powerhouse-in-uk-economy

[16] Raymond Williams, 'Wales and England' in *Who Speaks For Wales?*, pp. 16–26 (p. 22).

[17] Harvey, p. 85.

[18] 'Row as Alun Cairns calls Plaid Cymru MP anti-English', BBC News (2018) https://www.bbc.co.uk/news/uk-wales-politics-45470990

[19] cf. Alex Williams, 'On negative solidarity and post-fordist plasticity', *Splintering Bone Ashes* (2010) http://splinteringboneashes.blogspot.com/2010/01/negative-solidarity-and-post-fordist.html

[20] Gwyn Alf Williams, *When Was Wales?* (London: Penguin Books, 1985), p. 182.

[21] Gwyn Alf Williams, pp. 186–187.

[22] Fisher, 'Abandon Hope (Summer is Coming)' in *K-Punk*, pp. 573–584, (p. 577).

[23] Ibid., p. 578.

[24] Matt Colquhoun, *Egress: On Mourning, Melancholy and Mark Fisher* (London: Repeater Books, 2020), p. 200.

[25] Ibid.

[26] cf. Harvey, pp. 78–79: 'But all is not well with the neoliberal state, and it is for this reason that it appears to be either a transitional or an unstable political form.'

[27] Colquhoun, p. 199.

For Land or Money – Care and the Welsh Farm

Siwan Clark with Alex Heffron

One of us is a farmer's daughter's daughter who grew up in Cardiff, the other born at the foot of the Swansea Valley and now finds himself on a small dairy farm in Sir Benfro. In truth, rural Wales is not really our *cynefin,* but then neither is the city. We're caught between two lands. When Siwan visits her family's farm she helps with the chores, but is aware she never has to face the relentless grind and countless immediate demands that is the life of a small farmer. Still it's possible for her to sound authentic talking to her city friends, laughing with faux self-deprecation about being a 'Welsh stereotype' when elaborating stories to colleagues at university in England, after spending Easter feeding pet lambs. And though Alex might live and work on a small farm, he too can't escape the sense of not being a 'real farmer'. Yet perhaps this tension is representative of Wales.

Wales is a country that was at the heart of the industrial revolution – fuelled by the land, resources and workers of the Welsh country – but whose reputation revolves around sheep; a country whose language is steeped in the farm and its metaphors but whose population mostly resides in towns and cities; a country characterised by small farms that have been reducing in number and growing in size for decades, particularly since neoliberalisation. Siwan used to laugh at her mother for worrying that her children would be 'two generations away from the land' but as she gets older, she feels her concern grow in her. A paper on Welsh farmers from 2013 reports the attitudes of 'younger farmers (below 55)' with no further explanation given or needed. The Welsh people are increasingly 'two generations away from the farm.'

Caught between Brexit, Covid-19 and climate change, Welsh farming is at a crossroads. Do we turn to increasingly intensive agriculture, such as we have seen with the continued growth of large poultry farms in Powys, a cause of degradation of the river Wye. Do governmental bodies continue to overlook the pollution and slurry running into the river Teifi – what was once a thriving habitat for sewin and salmon and a site of cultural importance with coracle fishing. Or do we take the path of 'de-agriculturalisation', of 'rewilding' lands that have been cultivated for millennia? How else could farming face what Robat Idris calls the 'fierce crosswinds … that are so powerful that they pull the slates off the roof' and threaten to tear the industry down entirely? How can we think about farming in a transformative way that appreciates what is worth preserving but eschews a conservative nostalgia?

Agriculture represents 0.8% Gross Value Added to the Welsh economy, 30% higher than the UK average of 0.6%. In 2018, agriculture, forestry, and fishing represented 3.2% of the workforce jobs in Wales, compared to the UK average of 1.1%, rising to over 12% of jobs in some counties. Of the agricultural land in Wales, 80% is designated by the EU as a Less Favoured Area (with lower production potential) due to the mountainous terrain and wet climate, meaning that much of the land is given over to livestock grazing, particularly sheep.

Frances Richardson outlines how the agrarian change brought about by the industrial revolution took a different course in Wales, particularly in the north-west, compared to England. In the latter, economic modernisation saw a transition from the household economy to a capitalist society of landowners, tenants, and landless wage labourers. In the area of Sir Caernarfon that Richardson studies, there was conversely a growth in subsistence smallholding. This led to a large number of what Marxist agrarian theorists Levien, Watts and Yan call 'semiproletarians' and pluriactive' households reproducing themselves through various combinations of agriculture, waged labour, and self-employment, where women often ran the family's smallholding while men worked in quarries and mines. These patterns of landownership and farm size persist today, with Welsh farms half the size of the UK average. 54% of holdings in Wales are less than 20 hectares (roughly the size of Buckingham Palace gardens).

The rural communities formed around these small to medium farms make up the vast majority of the communities where Welsh is the language of daily life; 43% of agricultural workers speak Welsh, compared with 19% of the general population. They are the site of uprising and militant activism, from the Rebecca Riots to much of Cymdeithas's early direct action, to the arson of Meibion Glyndŵr. They are a site of displacement and injustice, from Tryweryn to Epynt, and of community and re-silience, from the traditional collaboration and sharing of equipment by farmers to the spontaneous networks of mutual aid that sprang up during the Covid-19 pandemic. They are the site of patriarchal norms and patrilineal in-heritance, of familial exploitation, and of insular conservatism. They are a site of stubbornly enduring Welsh culture, from Plygain in Sir Drefaldwyn to Hen Galan in Sir Benfro. They are a site of rich complexity and contradiction.

In recent years, farms and rural communities have hosted an ageing population and economic decline. Between 1991 and 2006, the rural Welsh population aged at almost twice the rate of the Welsh average, itself the country with the oldest population in the United Kingdom. Between 2008 and 2018, while Cardiff's pop-ulation grew by 9.5%, the population of Ceredigion contracted by 2.6%. Much of this population change is driven by migration, with young people from rural areas leaving for education and employment while older people migrate to them for retirement.

While the number of principal (full-time) farmers has remained relatively stable in recent years, the total number of farm workers has declined by more than 16% in the last 20 years. Around 25% of UK farmers live in poverty, exacerbated by the crumbling public services of rural areas and resulting higher cost of living. (The ONS estimates that rural families spend on average £2,700 more a year on everyday goods than their city counter-parts.) Farmers have turned to foodbanks, unable to afford the food that they produce, whilst working themselves – and often their families – to the bone.

Here we should point out that there is class differentiation within farming – farming is not a homogenous social group. Bernstein, building on Lenin's critique of Chayanov, has persuasively argued that farmers in the Global North are petty commodity producers, stratified into three sub-divisions, characterised by their ability to either expand in size, maintain it relatively comfortably, or struggle to reproduce themselves. The larger the farm, the greater the levels of capitalisation and the more exploitation of wage labour. Those at the lower end, generally the smaller farms, are what this essay focuses on.

The persistence of small farmers in the face of capitalist accumulation, has long been a topic of debate for Marxist theorists, from Kautsky to Mao. Tony Cliff has highlighted that Marx's assumption that large-scale capitalist farming would quickly replace small farms, providing the framework for larger, collectivised farms, has not born true. One explanation is self-exploitation, what Teodor Shanin (paraphrasing Chayanov) describes as 'excruciating labor by underfed peasant families damaging their physical and mental selves for a return which is below that of the ordinary wages of labor power' undertaken in order to remain on the land. In Jairaj Banaji's words: 'the progress of big industry does not necessarily entail the disappearance of small units. It ruins them, renders them superfluous from an economic point of view, but these units have enormous reserves of resistance.'

Interpretations of – and attitudes toward – this

tendency to self-exploit in order to remain on the farm vary wildly. To Linda Price, researching family farms in Powys, it is a futile attempt to maintain patriarchal structures, patrilineal inheritance and the legacy of forefathers that costs farmers and farmers' sons their mental health and 'farmers' wives' their life's work and autonomy.

Ryan Galt, in his 2013 research into Community Supported Agriculture (CSA) in California, raises another possibility. CSAs are partnerships between the community and the farm, where members invest a stake in the farm and receive a share of its produce. They are intended to provide affordable, local food to communities whilst providing the farmer with a fair and stable income. In his analysis, Galt finds that the more socially embedded a CSA is, the *more* the farmer engages in self-exploitation, suggesting that E.P. Thompson's moral economy 'cuts both ways' and farmers' dedication to the ideals of CSA leads to their increasing self-exploitation. This is echoed in Ryanne Pilgeram's 2011 study of sustainable farming in the Pacific Northwest: 'The only thing that isn't sustainable ... is the farmer'. She finds that sustainable farming is so labour-intensive and poorly compensated that sustainable farmers tend to be white, to have middle-to-upper-class backgrounds and educational privileges, to rely on lucrative off-farm income, to rely on the super-exploitation of unpaid volunteers and/or to engage in severe self-exploitation. In addition, sustainable farmers' business models are often only viable through cultivating connections with upper-class consumers prepared to pay a premium, something several of the farmers she interviews resent. One farmer tells her that his friend left sustainable farming after 'he got tired of turning chicken shit into rich people'.

These accounts of self-exploitation suggest two conclusions: first, that the problems in farming and food production, as in so much of Welsh society, are linked to other socio-economic problems and cannot be solved in isolation. The main problem is a capitalist food system, built on commodification and exploitation of workers and nature in the rural hinterlands that requires endless expansion in the pursuit of capital accumulation, dominated by monopoly and monopsony powers. A simultaneous cause, effect and false justification for this system – in Wales and worldwide – is a society so unequal that raising prices to fairly compensate producers would plunge even more people into food poverty. 14% of Welsh households suffer food insecurity. This enables those with vested interests to frame low food prices as a matter of social justice which – as Carwyn Graves argues – is a hegemonic idea that must be disrupted if we are to ever have a sustainable and just food system. There are no quick fixes or innovations that can remedy what is a systemic, global dysfunction engineered to serve the interests of capitalists. As Jason Moore puts it:

> The cost of working-class reproduction is strongly conditioned by the price of food. One means of extracting surplus value more effectively is therefore the reduction of the value of food ... through the appropriation of unpaid work/energy.

Second, the concept of 'self-exploitation' and the ambiguous moral and political implications of working for something other than money echoes a central theme in feminist economics: care work. In a lecture titled *For Love and Money: The Distinctive Features of Care Work*, feminist economist Nancy Folbre characterises care work as 'work where concern for the well-being of the care recipient is likely to affect the quality of the service provided'. This kind of work violates the assumptions of neo-classical economics and the neoliberal systems formed in its image in several ways, with direct parallels to farming. Care work challenges hegemonic economic ideas:

- Much care work does not involve a direct market transaction: it is 'off-GDP' and therefore ignored in economic accounting. This parallels the land steward-ship aspect of farming which has been subordinated to maximising yield through intensification.
- Care work is multidimensional and hard to measure, and care is improved if the provider cares about the recipient. Monetary incentives based on measurable outcomes are unlikely to ensure the best quality – they simply incentivise the prioritisation of measurable di-mensions and the performance of characteristics that are measured. Similarly, we increasingly recognise that farmers' work should not simply be to maximise yield at the expense of ecological systems, though this is what they have been incentivised to do for decades since the 'Green Revolution'. The careful stewardship of a farmer who loves the land he farms and wishes

to preserve it for the next generation cannot be replicated through monetary incentives.

- It complicates the notion that work is a 'negative' to minimise. Any person 'rationally' maximising leisure time and consumption would certainly not choose to become either a mother or a small farmer! The idea that people might be motivated by something other than money is a perfect example of something self-evident to any ordinary person but which orthodox economists have only just begun to address in papers with titles such as 'Non-Monetary Incentives and Work as a Source of Meaning'.

- The fact that workers are motivated by something other than money sets them up for exploitation in a capitalist system that will pay workers – or small farmers – the lowest possible amount to ensure compliance and to enable maximal surplus value.

- How and why do people end up in jobs that are systematically underpaid in this way? Folbre explores the role of 'endogenous preferences' in this process. This is economic jargon for the idea that our preferences – the things we value – are shaped by the life we lead and the society that we live in. In contrast, neo-classical economics assumes that preferences are 'exogenous to the model' – fixed and set outside the economic system somewhat magically. In care work, preferences are endogenous, in that beginning care work – perhaps through gendered socialisation – shapes the carer's preferences towards doing more care work, making them what Folbre calls 'prisoners of love'. Farming remains a strongly inherited profession; growing up on a farm shapes a desire to remain there. In *Nowt But a Fleeting Thing*, a documentary on farming poverty, a young man who has returned to Cumbria to farm remarks that, 'I've got roots I can't seem to get away from'.

Parallel to feminist economic analysis of care work, a sociological account of care practice has grown from feminist ethics and has already begun to link good farming with good care. Anna Krzywoszynska conceptualises care in farming as 'the totality of those activities which enable the maintenance, continuation, and repair of the farming "world"', which involves key elements of attentiveness, responsibility, and competency. Emerging concepts include the related ideas of Annemarie Mol's 'tinkering' and John Law's *'choreography* of care', capturing the creative and experimental nature of farming care practices in response to constantly shifting circumstances. The social reproduction of the smallholding depends upon the often unseen, unpaid, gendered care work.

In her account of learning how to work on a vineyard, Krzywoszynska draws on the similarity between Joan Tronto's account of good care and Stuart and Hubert Dreyfus's model of attaining expertise to argue that good care is dependent on having 'a situated and experiential understanding of the world of action'. Local, embodied, experiential knowledge – a 'know-how' borne of learning by doing rather than a 'know-what' of facts – is a key theme in the academic literature on care in farming.

In particular, recent research explores how this local,

experiential knowledge comes into conflict with externally imposed, national or international bureaucratic systems of regulation, inflexible systems rooted in control rather than care. Two research papers investigating the perspective of farmers and vets on biosecurity (disease control) in cattle explore this conflict. In the latter, vets were questioned about different farmers' biosecurity practices. They broadly sorted farmers into two groups, 'true cowmen' and 'commercial farmers', both with their own conception of good farming. Most – though not all – of the vets preferred working with the commercial farmers: they accepted their advice, had enough capital for investment, and operated the farms as a regulated, ordered machine. The 'true cowmen', on the other hand, approached biosecurity through networks of community trust and through intense familiarity with and monitoring of their herds. It is striking to consider the farmers' practices that vets and government regulators consider problematic for biosecurity, such as visiting other farms, attending markets and developing relationships of trust and reciprocity when buying, selling and sharing animals.

While biosecurity is clearly important, 'concerns' comprised all the communal, social parts of farm life – a life that can often be extremely isolated. Neoliberal systems of regulation demand atomisation and individualism: they are fundamentally at odds with the way Welsh farming communities have operated for centuries. Euros Lewis's description of life at Epynt, before the land was seized by the military in 1940, comes to mind:

A real, live, good, creative community is really messy and that's one reason perhaps ... bureaucrats really don't like community.

Through a lens of care, we see that Welsh family farms cannot survive without community and the embodied, local knowledge embedded within it. If these communities are radically disrupted – through trade shocks or externally imposed bureaucracy and further neoliberalisation – it will be a long and maybe impossible task to re-establish them.

How has the Welsh Government negotiated and shaped this rural economy of care? Welsh farming policy encapsulates the contradictions of devolved government: it is one of the policy areas in which the Welsh Government has most autonomy but where the limits of its powers impose biting constraints. Without the power to regulate monopolies, to determine trade policy, or set its own agriculture budget, the Welsh Government is consigned to reforms at the margins which have tended to pursue a neoliberal green-capitalist agenda.

[Here a caveat is in order. In a bold and important departure from Westminster policy, the Welsh Government won a case in the Supreme Court to retain its Agricultural Wages Board – including the power to set higher farm workers' wages and improved holiday allowance – when Cameron's government abolished the board in England.]

This reformist tendency is evident in Welsh policy on farm subsidy. Subsidies play a central yet controversial role in Welsh farming. Currently, the main subsidy is the

Basic Payment Scheme (BPS), paid per hectare of land managed. In 2018–19, the BPS accounted for 84% of Welsh farm income, up from 69% the previous year – without it, most small farms would not survive. In addition to this the *Glastir* scheme provides payments for agri-environment services. However, this was previously limited by the rules of the EU's Common Agricultural Policy (CAP), and now post-Brexit, is limited by Westminster, as Wales' spending on agriculture will likely need to remain in line with the Barnett Formula. Wales will soon introduce its replacement for the BPS, with its new Sustainable Farming Scheme. The fundamental basis of this scheme is known as Payments for Ecosystem Services (PES), which is another neoliberal attempt to value nature and land stewardship. At time of writing, it's still under consultation, but it seems that the scheme will pay farmers for actions such as planting trees, protecting rivers and restoring peat lands, which is an improvement over the previous subsidy regime. However, the white paper produced by the Welsh Government talks about 'competitiveness', 'innovation' and 'efficiency' – in other words, the continuation of neoliberalism. While appearing to be progressive and environmentally-minded, PES schemes, particularly if they are not accompanied by other reforms such as improving land access, subsidy caps or active farmer clauses – can further entrench local and global inequality without meaningful environmental impact. Ultimately, it is not possible to put a price on natural processes – what Marx called 'the free gifts of nature' – and the neoliberal approach fails to grasp this in its pursuit of financialisation.

Artificially inventing a 'market price' for the environment is therefore a fundamentally inadequate response, as capitalism is predicated on the exploitation of ecological systems in the pursuit of value creation. Replacing the BPS – which essentially operates as a (very unequal) basic income to farmers – with a system of PES, without imposing a subsidy cap or an adequate active farmer clause, creates a rentier's paradise, in which large landowners receive significant streams of income from the government. Combined with the UK Government's commitment to 'restoring nature' or rewilding 30% of Britain by 2030, what emerges is a 'green-washed' strategy of rural depopulation, a new process of enclosure, which would have serious implications for Welsh communities and the Welsh language. As Dafydd Morris Jones, long-time critic of rewilding, argues, we should question a view of nature that positions it as something external to human civilisation that we visit from cities, rather than something that humans are, and always have been, a part of. An ecosocialist politics, which sees indigenous peoples as part of the ecosystem, is not compatible with neoliberal rewilding.

Without a radical revolution of the global food economy, most rewilding or conservation efforts (a problematic concept worthy of further discussion) simply amount to the reduction of food production in some areas in order to intensify it elsewhere. In other words, it will further subordinate countries in the Global South via a neo-colonial framework exploited by transnational corporations. The opening of the UK market to lower standard USA products is therefore an integral part of the

Westminster government's plans to roll back domestic agricultural production, simply outsourcing the carbon emissions and environmental degradation that accompanies intensive food production, rather than stopping it, in a bid to appear carbon neutral. Increasing reliance on foreign food imports and global supply chains also threatens our food security, as was made clear by the disruption caused by the Covid-19 pandemic.

The attempt to fight climate change and biodiversity loss through incentivising 'green' behaviour in farmers is a reformist neoliberal 'solution' to a crisis of capitalism caused by its own contradictions; it disrupts small farmers' localised care practices without addressing the structural forces that drive them to intensify production. It is the agricultural equivalent of mandating meticulous lesson-planning protocols without decreasing class sizes, or of introducing new NHS targets without reversing funding cuts. Cloaked in the rhetoric of environmentalism, it is a further step towards a neoliberal Welsh landscape.

Perhaps unwisely, we end this chapter with its shortcomings. First, for reasons of coherence and length, this chapter has centred the 'archetypal' small Welsh family farm. While necessary for my argument, this has involved an erasure that is politically troubling at best. Given the role that the 'pure' and 'simple' farmer has historically played in the ideology of far-right movements, any attempt to essentialise and romanticise rural life must be challenged. Absent from this chapter and worthy of further exploration are issues such as the exploitative capitalist relations between petite-bourgeois farmers and their labourers; the unequal distribution of and access to land; the role of migrant labourers in rural economies and communities; the way that queer farmers and single women disrupt an industry still rooted in the nuclear family; conservative rural respectability and how it can punish those on the margins; the Welsh Kale and their place in Welsh-speaking Wales; the stories of those who have left and are leaving the farm; the experience of people of colour and farmers of colour in Welsh rural life; the inextricable link between agriculture, food production and imperialism old and new. This is a far from exhaustive list but one which we hope challenges a reading of this chapter as the singular story of rural Wales.

Second, we have offered little in the way of practical solutions or policy suggestions. Our aim is to present a new way of thinking about farming and its challenges, rather than to prescribe a simplistic remedy. With this in mind, we want to end the chapter with a quote from Anna Krzywoszynska that could as well describe the practice of activism and political writing as farming and care:

> What characterises care is not a detached analysis of available facts, but a careful experimentation by an involved actor who recognises that not all can be known, but that something has to be done nonetheless.

Interview with Butetown Matters

Elbashir Idris, Shutha Saif
& Nirushan Sudarsan

Shutha Saif, 18, brought up in Butetown, currently in St David's College studying English, Law and Design. As a young female Muslim, she was struck by the lack of role models and was inspired to raise her own voice through activism and various media, and is now an active member of Butetown Matters.

Nirushan Sudarsan, Law and Politics Student at Cardiff University, 21, moved from Sri Lanka to Cardiff as an 8-year-old. A former pupil of Cathays High he now lives in Grangetown, where he has been a member of the Grange Pavilion Youth Forum for 6 years, and is deeply concerned with the inequalities in the 'Southern Arc' of the city and the need to secure greater recognition for those communities within the city's institutions.

Elbashir Idris, MSc Birmingham, 26, was brought up in Butetown to Sudanese parents, and at the time of interview is out in Sudan working on community development projects in the context of the country's political restructuring. His work in community organising there has been heavily influenced by his involvement with Citizens UK since 2013.

Ed: How has your upbringing and formative experiences in Cardiff shaped your outlook, influenced your values and the activities you are currently involved in?

Elbashir: Regarding Butetown and the Southern Arc and the things that go down there it's not exactly the kind of place where you are granted much opportunity, especially in terms of the conventional employment route that people ordinarily have expectations about. When I was younger, obviously, careers as doctors and lawyers were everyone's dreams, but over time they slowly diminished. That was true of me also, and seeing a lot of those around me choosing more menial employment, I decided to try my hand at something different, and had to stick to my guns. It's certainly the case that you come to feel that the odds are stacked against you, and that the obstacles in the race soon become apparent, and that a lot of the kids you grew up with and rode bikes with end up doing things you want to avoid.

Nirushan: Yes, for sure there are difficulties and challenges that we see in the areas that we live in, especially in terms of those opportunities, and sustaining the drive and ambition you need. For sure there are people who have been led to take certain decisions that have affected them in a number of ways. At the same time there's a lot of pride in the area, and we've got to recognise that people are keen to represent their communities and we don't want others telling us that our area is 'bad'. And it isn't; there's a lot of stigma about these neighbourhoods in other parts of the city, and I'm still not sure how they're sustained and there's a challenge in addressing people's perception of what we can achieve. As communities it's fair to say that we regularly feel let down by the authorities and those in power, and it becomes a normal pattern that you start to understand better as you get older. That's to say, the reason is often that we don't have access to the right spaces and until we do, we'll face these problems – and so it's so important to break these barriers of perception that exclude us and give people access so that they can achieve. It's not that people here don't have ambitions it's just there's a dearth of opportunities for people to take advantage of – it's about giving them equal access.

Shutha: When I was listening to Nirushan there talk about pride, I was thinking about how growing up, living all my life in Butetown and going to school, even as young as primary school I was quite conscious from a young age of more attractive areas towards Cardiff Bay or the Wetlands, and I didn't want to be associated with the Docks. If people asked me where I was from and I said Butetown, I would be quick to emphasise that didn't mean the Docks – because I was very conscious of the kind of ideas that people had of the area. But now, growing up, I feel that this is my community, and believe it or not it has a greater sense of community than a lot of areas I've been to in Cardiff – and I feel it's a really tight-knit and passionate community. That's one reason why we have a lot of pride in where we're from and try to give back to the community to create those opportunities that other areas might take for granted. Even now there may be more choices emerging but it's restricted in comparison.

Ed: So at what sort of age did you start to become more po-litically motivated and begin to reflect on the fact that the situation you describe is not an accident, and to what extent is politics an area you feel you can meaningfully engage with?

Shutha: I feel that with my age bracket that a lot of the older generation probably think that we're not politically aware or conscious of what is happening. I feel the opposite; obviously the era of the iPhone, the way in which social media is going, people are a lot more aware of what's going on. If there's news it will get to us, and we'll be the people who are going to spread that and respond in a particular way. We're the people who are going speak out. I'm so happy now that the vote has gone to 16-year-olds because I feel that they are the driving force for the future, and it makes more sense that we get a say. It's maybe not so easy to understand because it's not something that's taught to us from a young age, but definitely being exposed to situations, especially if you're from environments like Butetown and Grangetown – where as you grow up you become aware of greater op-portunities elsewhere – you start to think, why? It definitely makes you more politically conscious. I mean you'll get people coming into schools, the police telling you not to use drugs, don't do this, don't do that – I felt that we always had that being pushed on us even at Mount Stuart – but nobody talking to us about the *right* things to do. I think the lack of that is what leads people to go on and do the opposite.

Nirushan: I really didn't pay attention and only started to sense what was going on around the age of 16, I was just doing what kids do, playing sport, hanging out. But at that age I started having more conversations with community leaders, and they talked a lot at that time – around 2016 – about how the Bay had been redeveloped over a number of years and that they weren't really reflected in those changes. I'd never really thought about it, but then I'd go down the Bay and see no one from Butetown or Grangetown working there, or anybody looking like us – and I started to question it. I mean in theory when areas are redeveloped it's meant to be about people there being given opportunities and capitalising on the changes. And then once I started to understand the experiences, the perceptions, especially those communities of colour and how that looked from the perspective of inequality and how they were being left out, I realised that this was not something that had been missed by accident. It clearly reflects deep structural inequalities that had been perpetuated over the years. And in those conversations wider concerns came up around interactions with the police, with employers, with the council – how these different power holders affect the community – and I started to realise how a lot of it comes back to politics. From then on I started to pay attention and to listen, because if you don't get in the room and if you don't know what's happening you'll be left behind. You just realise there's something wrong and you don't want it to stay that way.

Elbashir: I think I became politically switched on in 2003 and the outbreak of the Iraq War and seeing the first

Tomahawk missiles being fired into Baghdad. I mean I was young at the time but it was definitely memorable. I was thinking to myself as a kid, why the hell is this going on? I was transfixed by the theatrics of war, and as a kid you're seeing this and you start to reflect a little deeper, and of course it turns out that it's politics behind that. You see all this on your screen and increasingly on social media and you wonder how you can help out, and then of course you realise that politics doesn't have to be on a massive, grand scale and you can do things on a very local scale. What happens in local legislation has a massive effect on people's lives. Unfortunately, you foster the mindset – which is very draining – that everything is political. You're angry about it and you want to make a change, and you've got to start in your own community.

Ed: I'm wondering as the younger generation whether the historical episodes that have affected Tiger Bay and the Docks – the clearances in the 60s and the 'development' of the Bay in the 1990s – impact you in terms of the attitudes that are passed on. Do people talk about these events in an explicitly political way, and the domination of communities by private enterprise, and is there still a sense that people can fight and resist despite what's happened?

Nirushan: There are I think a lot of people and a lot of areas who feel they are not listened to, and the same things happen time and again; often someone will tell me something similar happened 10 or 15 years ago ... and it's just history repeating itself. You get that feeling that people feel inevitably let down at every point. I think in particular amongst younger people you get an understanding that these are persistent issues, but not perhaps an appreciation of the factors at play. I mean this is why conversation about power and the role of developers is so important, and that once people realise they're being shut out of decision-making there's a realisation of what is going on. Likewise, there are people who are more tuned in and understand that this has always been the case – and that they will always want to try, to campaign, to turn up and represent their families and their communities. Of course, it's a separate issue how you affect change; it's difficult of course because there are so many factors, so many small decisions happening, and I'm still learning myself. But it needs to happen, because in a few years' time some of the places we live in will become unrecognisable. We need to be more united in our opposition in that respect, and we're definitely not there yet.

Shutha: As teenagers I think we're still really trying to make sense of it all, and that's another reason why political education is so important and why politics should involve the youth. It can actually be quite tormenting to be kept in the dark about these issues and then to come out of education and to be faced with it all. So I'm just finishing college and I'm seeing things going on around me ... bringing it back to the community I look at what's happening with something like the Paddle Steamer and I'm thinking to myself well that's part of the community and somewhere I walk past almost every day of my life.[1] For developers they don't look at the spaces in the same way because it's not their community, and this is one of the reasons different communities in Cardiff need to get to know each other and relate through their strong feelings for what they have. I think it's partly because you don't have that much, and what you do have you want to look after. The passion is definitely there and the desire to make a difference amongst the youth, but I feel we just don't know enough – and that's where education needs to come in.

Elbashir: People have obviously felt disempowered and the usual route of going through elected representatives and raising your qualms has just felt too slow and unresponsive. In recent years I feel that there has been an awareness of a general dissatisfaction to the point where people are asking what they can do themselves instead; for sure there's a sense that we are stronger together and whilst campaigning for me had felt like a more middle-class pursuit, more recently it has seemed to me that a working-class community like Butetown has been more willing to step up. I definitely feel that we have increasing organisational skills and that we have the capability to strategize.

Ed: Ok, so in a way that takes us up neatly to the present situation and the developments that are happening to Cardiff under the leadership of a Labour Council. I'm interested in whether you regard the current politics of the city as representing a repetition of the sort of politics of the past that has failed many areas, and equally whether you see any reasons for optimism.

Nirushan: I think in recent years we've seen developments that have motivated the younger generation to campaign –

people who want a better world free from the problems we
face now. BLM has of course talked about structural racism
and developed conversations around it. Meeting people
like Bash and Shutha has shown to me there are people
who care and that the city they live in is somewhere they
want to be proud of; to say 'this is my city, this is what I
want it to look like'. Also there were problems in the past
that were solved by communities working together, kept
places together, and that spirit carries through and
provides hope. We work on the shoulders of people who
have worked in the past and paved the way for our generation. When protests happen around BLM it gives us an
opportunity to think about where we can put our
resources. In the case of something like the BAME
Taskforce that the Council has set up, whatever I think
about it, it's up to us to ensure that they deliver on its
promise and develops a plan that ensures communities on
this side of Cardiff can achieve what they want to achieve.
You can't put forward huge plans like those for an arena
in Cardiff Bay without engaging and listening to those it
will affect. But what really gives me hope is all the people
I saw in the protests last year and the fact that the
pandemic has shined a light on the deep structural inequalities in our communities. Lots of people we know are
struggling because they've lost their work, people are
dying, and whilst these are the consequences of the
pandemic, they are also a result of the longstanding inequalities that we see. People realise that and this is why
they are out campaigning and why they are angry. And
that's a good thing, because once you realise there's an
issue you can plan, and the more conversations you have,

the more positive it can be and it's about us using that energy in the right ways. The more we can get into the right spaces, the more we can have discussions like this, the more people will become aware and we can affect Cardiff in the way we want it to be in the next 10 years.

Shutha: Yes, I really agree with Nirushan, in particular what he says about lockdown and people becoming more aware, including the protests where you could see the anger and the passion in people. And partly it's because you have the time, away from your busy life, where pre-pandemic you didn't really have time to reflect on the things that are going on so you become more accepting because you have to do this and that. But with a lockdown you're becoming more isolated, you're seeing these things happen and you're more aware; this is happening, that is happening – now I really have to think how am I going to stop that? How am I going to make a difference? How am I going to help the community? If we weren't aware then, we're definitely more aware now and I think it's a good position to be in. People are more aware and educated coming out of lockdown, and hopefully now people will have a more active role in shaping their own future and having a say on what goes on within the community. Also another reason for hope is that whilst I got into my activism and writing spoken word poetry because I didn't really see that in the community from people such as myself – people of colour, Muslim, female – now I feel like there's a lot more and that it happened quite quickly as well, and I love to see it. There's a lot of people like me not just in Butetown but in other parts of the city taking an active role within their communities to try and make a difference

– just being people to look up to really, and the more it happens the more I feel then we'll have more reason to make a change and be part of the difference.

Elbashir: I mean I feel because of the protest and a greater level of activism institutions such as the council are having to take people's views into greater consideration. There is perhaps a realisation that various developments need to benefit from support or acceptance and that if it's not there that will become a problem. But there's a whole lot of work to do; for example, what might actually make a difference is participatory budgeting where the community is involved in the distribution of resources. If that took off and spread that would diminish the control of local authorities, and of course it is doubtful that they want to cede power in that way. And whilst there's a great deal of hope it's very easy to fall into divisive situations especially with hyper-emotional traumas that are experienced. It's very easy to see tensions and even hatred arise where people don't want to sit at the same table as other groups to work towards the social cohesion that we need.

Ed: Thanks for your contributions, it's been great speaking to you. One last brief question I'd like to put to you is how you see all this within the wider context of UK politics. What are your views in this regard: post-Corbyn, do you see it as increasingly difficult if not impossible for the kind of politics we need to develop down in Westminster or do you hold out hope that things can change?

Elbashir: Generally not. I would push for Welsh independence. I can't really see Westminster working towards the sort of integration needed and there is definitely not a great deal of consideration of people of colour, and it has not ever really cared for Wales throughout its history. I think the Welsh people, we could really take care of its future. Obviously the UK is a nation-state that relies heavily on its conventions and going against the grain is really difficult, but as long as people are voicing their concerns it's a live issue. Will Westminster take action and provide more devolution? Unlikely perhaps. But I think the pandemic and the response has shown quite a lot what Wales can do compared to Westminster.

Nirushan: For sure the pandemic has shown the strain of the relationship between the two powers. Naturally it raises new challenges and problems. For me, the issues I am concerned with relate to local authority and the Welsh Government so for me Westminster is not a place I want to focus my attention on. It's not to suggest either that things are much better here; they're not. We can't just put the blame there and say it's all fine here whilst all the problems emanate from Westminster. You have to be real that both of these places have challenges and it's about how they can improve as institutions. I think it's too early to say that we're done with Westminster because we have problems of our own.

Ed: Yes it's interesting you make this point because this is partly what the book addresses. In a way you could rephrase it as the question of what is the point of indepen-

dence if we continue with the same form of politics? We have this idea that Wales does things different but what the book reveals is that we don't do things as differently as we like. If some form of independence is a possibility, then what is the point if we recreate all those issues affecting us now.

Shutha: I agree with a lot of what's just been said. There's a long way to go, but definitely changes are being made and people are taking more of an active and leading role in their communities, in Cardiff in general, and there is hope that things might change at a wider level. There is hope, but it's a long road, and that's why it's all the more important that people take part and get involved in discussions and conversations like these, because that's where the changes will actually begin.

---

[1] The Paddle Steamer is a community café in Butetown, Cardiff. It has been an iconic establishment for many decades, and is an important meeting point for Cardiff's long-established Somali and Yemeni communities, serving halal and culturally-appropriate foods in an alcohol-free environment. Community leaders and solicitors regularly use the café to meet with vulnerable residents to support them with their complex needs, from state benefits advice to immigration and asylum guidance. Cardiff Council's Planning Committee voted in 2021 to demolish the café to make way for social housing, rejecting calls from community campaigners to include a space for a replacement cafe.

Editor biographies

Dan Evans is a former academic who is now a support worker, writer and activist based in Cardiff. He has written for publications such as *Jacobin*, *New Socialist*, *Open Democracy*, *O'r Pedwar Gwynt* and *Planet: The Welsh Internationalist*. His book on Welsh identity in British Wales will be out in early 2022 with University of Wales Press, and he is currently writing a book on the rise of the petite bourgeoisie for Repeater Books. He is the host of the Welsh politics podcast Desolation Radio.

Kieron Smith is a researcher and writer whose work focuses on Welsh culture and society. He has written widely on aspects of the English-language culture of Wales, including the monograph *John Ormond's Organic Mosaic* (UWP 2019) and the collection *New Theoretical Perspectives on Dylan Thomas* (UWP 2020, edited with Rhian Bubear). He lives in Swansea.

Huw Williams is a Senior Lecturer in Political Philosophy at Cardiff University. He is an occasional activist and has published essays, chapters, articles and books on a variety of issues, from the Welsh language to global justice. His latest book is *Ysbryd Morgan* (UWP 2020), a volume on Welsh intellectual history.

Author biographies

Catrin Ashton lives in Bedlinog in the south Wales valleys. She is a Communist.

Georgia Burdett is a therapist and tutor for children with autism. She completed a PhD on cultural representations of disability at Swansea University.

Siwan Clark is a student, writer, singer-songwriter and activist. After working in documentary filmmaking and teaching English, she is currently studying for an MSc in Social Research Methods at UCL with a focus on qualitative research into Welsh hill farming. In 2020, she worked with fellow Undod members Robat Idris and Alex Heffron to organise a day of action to Save Welsh Farming.

Faith Clarke is a journalist and is co-editor of the radical journalism platform, voice.wales, where she specialises in feature writing, focusing mainly on issues of social inequality, racism and discrimination. She has an MA in International Journalism from Cardiff University.

Steffan Evans graduated with a PhD from the Wales Governance Centre, at the School of Law and Politics at Cardiff University in 2018. His thesis looked at the impact of devolution on social housing regulation in Wales and England, exploring how and why the law had diverged between both nations. Since graduating Steffan has worked with TPAS Cymru and is currently working at the Bevan Foundation. His chapter is written in a personal capacity.

Jamie Harris is a lecturer in Literature and Place at Aberystwyth University. His research interests include Welsh Writing in English, devolution, and utopianism. He is currently working on a range of projects to do with electricity generation and literature.

Mike Harrison is a criminology and criminal justice lecturer at the University of Derby. He has a PhD in Criminology from the University of South Wales. Mike's doctoral thesis was entitled 'A Case Study Analysis of How Public Order Policing is Interpreted and Practised in South Wales'. His current research focuses on the interface of devolved and non-devolved powers that influence policing in Wales.

Joe Healy is a PhD student at Cardiff University's School of Modern Languages. He is originally from South London but has lived in Cardiff for several years. His research focuses on the French and Spanish states' responses to various social movements over the period since the 2008 financial crash. His writing deals with nationalism, state power, neoliberalism and social movements in Wales and beyond.

Alex Heffron is a first generation farmer, father, husband and student, in the *Mynyddoedd Preseli* where he helps run a small, collective-ish mixed farm based on principles of agroecology and regenerative agriculture. He writes on issues of agrarian Marxism and organises with Undod for a socialist independent Wales.

Rae Howells is a journalist, academic and poet. She has worked as a journalist for more than 20 years and was a founding director and editor of the hyperlocal news co-operative Port Talbot Magnet. She sits on the National Union of Journalists' Welsh Executive Council and on the advisory board of the Independent Community News Network (ICNN). Her co-authored book, Hyperlocal Journalism (Routledge, 2018), contains chapters on the Welsh media industry and her research into the news black hole in Port Talbot. Her poetry collection, The Language of Bees, will be published by Parthian in 2022. She tweets @raehowells.

Robat Idris is a native of Ynys Môn where he still lives. As as an inhabitant of the Druids' HQ, he was appalled by the prospect of a new nuclear power station at Wylfa, with its many threats to people, environment and culture, and campaigned against it for many years with PAWB (People Against Wylfa B). A retired vet, Rob is currently occupied by the task of being an inconvenient pebble in the shoes of those who drive the juggernaut of destruction in its many forms. He is a member of Cymdeithas y Cymod (Fellowship of Reconciliation), Cymdeithas yr Iaith, and Undod, and promotes community regeneration in Gwynedd and Ynys Môn as a member of SAIL. Role model – Tȟašúŋke Witkó (Crazy Horse).

Calvin Jones holds a PhD in the Economics of Tourism and Major Events. He has been involved in the development of a number of measurement tools for sustainability, including the pilot Environmental Satellite Accounts for Wales and the Tourism Environmental Satellite Account for Wales. His research interests focus on sustainable regional development, energy economics, and AI, automation and future skills. Calvin is currently Deputy Dean (Public Value & External Relations) at Cardiff Business School. He is a failed novelist, rock star and screen writer, but served a successful and rewarding period in Nelson Mandela's security detail. He is a winner of both the Moss Madden Medal in regional science, and the People's Choice Award at the 1996 International Snow Sculpting Championships.

Mabli Siriol Jones is from Grangetown, Cardiff. She has worked in politics and as a campaigner for LGBT rights and reform of the asylum system. She is the current Chair of Cymdeithas yr Iaith.

Rhian E. Jones is a writer, critic and broadcaster from South Wales who now lives and works in London. She writes on history, politics, popular culture and the places where they intersect. She is co-editor of *Red Pepper* and writes for *Tribune* magazine. Her books include *Clampdown: Pop-Cultural Wars on Class and Gender* (zerO, 2013); *Petticoat Heroes: Gender, Culture and Popular Protest* (University of Wales Press, 2015); *Triptych: Three Studies of Manic Street Preachers'* The Holy Bible (Repeater, 2017) and the anthology of women's music writing *Under My Thumb: Songs That Hate Women and the Women Who Love Them*

(Repeater, 2017). Her latest book is *Paint Your Town Red: How Preston Took Back Control and Your Town Can Too* (Repeater, 2021).

Savanna Jones recently completed a masters in public policy and works in the higher education sector in Wales. Her focus has been on widening access to higher education and inclusion. She is a Board Member of the charity Mudiad Meithrin and works with Welsh language organisations in facilitating anti-racist practices and encouraging inclusive spaces for ethnic minority people.

Gareth Leaman is a writer from Newport. His work has appeared in Planet, Poetry Wales, Tribune and elsewhere.

Polly Manning is a writer based in Swansea. Her work focuses upon the experiences of young people in rural and post-industrial South Wales. She is currently working on a collection of short stories.

Sam Parry is a Ph.D. candidate in Political Economy at Cardiff University, where he studies the links between culture, geography and the economy through a Marxist lens to explain the peripherality of some European nations, namely his home of Wales. His work is researching the viability of using dependency and world-systems theory to explain the core-periphery paradigm that exists in Europe.

Dafydd Huw Rees has taught philosophy at Cardiff University since 2015, working with the Coleg Cymraeg Cenedlaethol to develop the subject in the medium of Welsh. He works on ethics, political theory, and philosophy of religion, specializing in the philosophy of Jürgen Habermas. He is currently at work on a project about devolution and political legitimacy.

Angharad Tomos is a writer and campaigner. She has been an activist with Cymdeithas yr Iaith since the mid-70s, and is a former chair of the organisation. She is a children's writer and novelist, and has also written for theatre and TV. She has been a columnist for *Yr Herald* since 1994. She lives in Penygroes, Dyffryn Nantlle.

Dr Frances Williams is a writer and researcher with a background in education and contemporary art. She won a doctoral scholarship to study the relation between the field of Arts in Health and devolution at Manchester Metropolitan University in 2016, completing her thesis in 2019. She currently lectures at Wrecsam Glyndwr University.

PARTHIAN

WALES: ENGLAND'S COLONY?

Martin Johnes

From the very beginnings of Wales, its people have defined themselves against their large neighbour. This book tells the fascinating story of an uneasy and unequal relationship between two nations living side-by-side.

PB / £8.99
978-1-912681-41-9

RHYS DAVIES: A WRITER'S LIFE

Meic Stephens

Rhys Davies (1901-78) was among the most dedicated, prolific and accomplished of Welsh prose writers. This is his first full biography.

'This is a delightful book, which is itself a social history in its own right, and funny.'
– The Spectator

PB / £11.99
978-1-912109-96-8

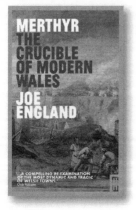

MERTHYR, THE CRUCIBLE OF MODERN WALES

Joe England

Merthyr Tydfil was the town where the future of a country was forged: a thriving, struggling surge of people, industry, democracy and ideas. This book assesses an epic history of Merthyr from 1760 to 1912 through the focus of a fresh and thoroughly convincing perspective.

PB / £18.99
978-1-913640-05-7

TO HEAR THE SKYLARK'S SONG

Huw Lewis

To Hear the Skylark's Song is a memoir about how Aberfan survived and eventually thrived after the terrible disaster of the 21st of October 1966.

'A thoughtful and passionate memoir, moving and respectful.'
– Tessa Hadley

PB / £8.99
978-1-912109-72-2

ROCKING THE BOAT

Angela V. John

This insightful and revealing collection of essays focuses on seven Welsh women who, in a range of imaginative ways, resisted the status quo in Wales, England and beyond during the nineteenth and twentieth centuries.

PB / £11.99
978-1-912681-44-0

TURNING THE TIDE

Angela V. John

This rich biography tells the remarkable tale of Margaret Haig Thomas (1883-1958) who became the second Viscountess Rhondda. She was a Welsh suffragette, held important posts during the First World War and survived the sinking of the *Lusitania*.

PB / £17.99
978-1-909844-72-8

BRENDA CHAMBERLAIN, ARTIST & WRITER

Jill Piercy

The first full-length biography of Brenda Chamberlain chronicles the life of an artist and writer whose work was strongly affected by the places she lived, most famously Bardsey Island and the Greek island of Hydra.

PB / £11.99
978-1-912681-06-8

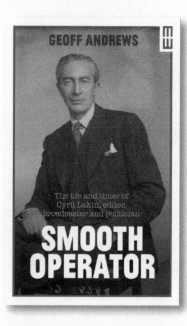

SMOOTH OPERATOR

Geoff Andrews

Cyril Lakin was the epitome of a smooth operator. From a humble background in Barry, Cyril Lakin studied at Oxford, survived the first world war, and went on to become a Fleet Street editor, radio presenter and war-time member of parliament. As literary editor of both the *Daily Telegraph* and the *Sunday Times*, Lakin was at the centre of a vibrant and radical generation of writers, poets and critics.

Geoff Andrews brings a fresh perspective to the life and times of a fascinating man who was involved in the national story at a time of great change for the United Kingdom and Wales.

HB / £20
978-1-913640-18-7

BETWEEN WORLDS: A QUEER BOY FROM THE VALLEYS

Jeffrey Weeks

A man's own story from the Rhondda. Jeffrey Weeks was born in the Rhondda in 1945, of mining stock. As he grew up he increasingly felt an outsider in the intensely community-minded valleys, a feeling intensified as he became aware of his gayness. Escape came through education. He left for London, to university, and to realise his sexuality. He has been described as the 'most significant British intellectual working on sexuality to emerge from the radical sexual movements of the 1970s'.

HB / £20
978-1-912681-88-4